15^{00}
#004

Madame Benoit's
WORLD OF FOOD

Books by Madame Benoit

Madame Benoit's Microwave Cook Book
Madame Benoit Cooks at Home
Madame Benoit's Lamb Cookbook
Encyclopedia of Canadian Cooking
Canadiana Cookbook
Enjoying the Art of Canadian Cooking
My Secrets for Better Cooking
The Best of Jehane Benoit

Madame Benoit's
WORLD OF FOOD

Madame Jehane Benoit

McGraw-Hill Ryerson Limited

Toronto   Montreal   New York   St. Louis   San Francisco
Auckland   Beirut   Bogotá   Düsseldorf   Johannesburg
Lisbon   London   Lucerne   Madrid   Mexico   New Delhi
Panama   Paris   San Juan   São Paulo
Singapore   Sydney   Tokyo

MADAME BENOIT'S WORLD OF FOOD

1 2 3 4 5 6 7 8 9 10 9 8 7 6 5 4 3 2 1 0

Printed and bound in Canada

Canadian Cataloguing in Publication Data

Benoit, Jehane, date
Madame Benoit's world of food

Includes index.

ISBN 0-07-082974-8

1. Cookery, International. I. Title.

TX725. A1B46 1980 641.59   C80-094337-6

Photographs by René Delbuguet

Contents

Introduction

Writing this book was like taking a trip with unusual people to unusual places, where unforgettable food was discovered, eaten and enjoyed. Many a time, acquiring some of these recipes was an amusing experience; for instance, the Jugged Lamb I ate in a small pub in Perth. The chef gave me the recipe written in his grandmother's language, Gaelic. Back home, I first had to find the genius who could translate it for me, then I had to make the Jugged Lamb three times before I found out what Grandmother meant by "large handful," "small whisper" (little salt) and "a bonnet-full of spinach." "She gathered her vegetables in her own garden in an old woolen bonnet," the chef explained to me, in reply to my letter. "When full, it was enough for that day or that recipe!"

Or our Welsh hostess, telling us about the Christmas meal in Wales. "It could be described in four words, 'bastes and bakes and bickers and boozes,'" she explained, as she handed me her recipe. Included in the dessert were shortbreads, about which she wrote, "My only concession to the *strangers*," meaning the Scots! This gives you an idea of the Welsh temperament!

Can one travel without looking for the good places to eat, talking to many of the people involved with them and remembering some of the best meals, even after many years? I do not think so, since this is part of enjoying distinctive customs which characterize the many countries of our planet. I would agree that a potato is a potato whatever the country, but the preparation of it in each country will give it certain pecularities and characteristics native to that part of the world.

Anyone interested in food history will soon realize the background of our daily food is not only based on agriculture but also on social customs and history. The gardeners of the world have, for centuries, aimed at growing better-tasting produce, concerning themselves with the beauty of food, as well as the perfection of its taste. If one thinks about food along these lines, this will create a close relationship with it which, without doubt, will stimulate a good cook's imagination, and is sure to inspire anyone who is indifferent to food. After all, cooking is not a difficult art, providing one looks upon it as a delightful, creative adventure!

I witnessed a perfect example of food creativity, imagination and presentation a few years ago in London, England. I was invited to a luncheon at a very elegant private club on ladies' day. My host was recognized as a distinguished epicure; with our Scotch and water (no ice), his version of Sardines and Cheese was served. The butler entered pushing a cart and, after showing each ingredient to the host, he proceeded to make the canapés.

The small, golden smoked Norwegian sardines were drained on a few layers of absorbent paper. Then each one was laid on a finger of whole-wheat bread, buttered with creamed unsalted butter. After this, a wedge of perfect, well-aged Parmesan cheese was grated over each canapé to completely cover the sardines. They were then taken to the bar's kitchen to be browned in a 350°F. (180°C) oven. During that time, our Scotch was served. When the canapés were done, they were placed on a serving dish with lemon wedges and a small bowl of minced chives. Before taking a canapé, we squeezed a dash of lemon and sprinkled chives on top. It was sheer delight! I will admit, it was a very sophisticated atmosphere, but also a good example of what it is to be creative and elegant, even with simple food. After all, it was only sardines, brown bread and cheese!

I am constantly asked how I can write so many recipes, and how I go about putting them together. It is difficult to answer, since I proceed more by feeling than by rule. If you start by thinking of a rose as a rose and a peach as a peach, but also associate a peach with an almond, you can create a delightful dessert in a jiffy by putting them all together. Peel a peach, set it in a clear crystal wine glass, sprinkle with a few wild rose petals, rolled in very fine sugar, and top it with slivered toasted almonds. If you wish to go further and have the sensation of freshness and acidity, add a few drops of fresh lemon juice; if you want a cool, cool feeling, top it with frozen black coffee, simply by finely grating frozen coffee in a food processor when you are ready to serve, and sprinkling it over the rose petals and the peaches. There you have an easy and provocative dessert. Of course, you need the fresh peaches and the wild roses, but both are available in July!

If I do not like a food, I try to find out why. I remember that many years ago just the thought of caraway seeds annoyed me, until one day, reading a garden book, I saw that caraway was of the parsley family! And I cannot let a week pass by without using parsley. The book also mentioned that it resembled Queen Ann Lace, which happens to be my favorite wild flower. To make me feel still more guilty, I read that the root was edible, rather like a delicate parsnip. There was my challenge, as I always enjoy parsnip. The description ended with the fact that Holland was the best source of caraway seeds, and I had always enjoyed Dutch cheese for breakfast, and still do! So after all this, I decided that caraway seeds had to be part of my food repertoire! The first thing I discovered was the refreshing feeling it gave to heavier food. It was not assertive, but it had a pleasant authority — definitely giving a lift to many a food. So, caraway has become part of my cooking life.

While travelling in Scotland, I was told that the Romans had brought the *carvi,* or caraway, to the Scottish moors, which explains why they still call their caraway cakes "Carvi Cakes." So looking to history, I felt a good flavoring for pound cake would be a fair amount of caraway seeds in deference to the Romans, somewhat less fresh-grated ginger in thanks for all that China brought to our world of food, uniting both flavors with the grated rind of a lemon or a lime. I tried it by simply adding the above to my favorite pound cake recipe. Lo and behold, I had a new recipe that I have enjoyed through the years.

I hope the many pleasurable moments I had in my travels — eating interesting food, most of the time, or discovering a new vegetable or fruit or fish — will amuse you and influence you to create your own variations to everyday food or to my own recipes.

I shall always be extremely grateful to the many people I met through those years of travel as they have made this book possible.

In Friendship,

Jehane Benoit

To all my friends around the world

England

In this introduction to English cuisine, I would like to vouch for the perfection of British cooking. As an example, I think back to a meal in London — I am ashamed to admit I have forgotten the name of the place, but not the food. We started with perfect scallops, steamed over white wine, rolled in minced parsley, flamed with Irish whiskey. This was followed by a rack of Southdown lamb (my favorite type) and fresh *petit pois*, cooked with a bouquet of fresh mint, and, to finish, Stilton, whole walnuts and cool port. To this day, this last combination has remained for me a favorite end to a perfect meal. In all of Canada, I have found only one restaurant (in Toronto) which offers such fare, the Stilton at room temperature, not cold and hard, the Port wine cooled, the walnuts nicely presented in a basket.

Another great quality of English cuisine is breakfast and high tea. The English are the true masters of these traditional meals. And at lunchtime countless pubs across the country have special fare. I have often enjoyed these meals and loved it when the pub waiter was serving in his white shirt, red vest and brown or black derby. So English! Do enjoy a pint of superb English beer at the Waterman's Arm Pub in London — one of the best.

Did you ever watch the Master Carver at Simpson's-in-the-

Strand practicing what I call the "high art" of carving at your table a *large* roast of beef into paper-thin, or thick, slices, as you prefer. All of it is performed with dexterity and flair on his silver-domed trolley.

And what about the world-famous Devonshire cream (thick, "clotted" cream, as the English call it) which is used as table cream. When poured over their luscious *petites fraises* or their large sweet strawberries, "divine" is the word.

And the Dover sole! The first time I ate a true Dover sole was in Devon; it had been simmered gently in Devonshire cream.

The Scottish smoked salmon from the icy rushing rivers, the plum pudding, the hard sauce with lots of brandy — these are but a few examples of English food. All over Britain there are restaurants, pubs and inns that serve excellent true British food. If you wish to experiment when you travel in England, look for an interesting paperback book, *A Taste of England*, by Josy Argy and Wendy Riches, written in collaboration with the English Tourist Board. It tells you where to find traditional English food, and even how to cook it.

"Taste of England" is the English Tourist Board motto displayed in all places which the Board has chosen as offering true English food prepared in the traditional manner. My daughter Monique and her husband, travelling through England last year, tried many of these places and were impressed with the meals. And believe me, you do not have to look very hard to find good English food in England!

Favorite Savories and Starters

When I was twenty-one, years and years ago, I spent a week in London at the Savoy Hotel, on my way back to Canada from France. I had chosen that hotel because, unknown to many people nowadays, it had been opened by the great French chef Escoffier, who left his imprint on the cuisine. At the time, he was at the Carlton Hotel in London, and once a week he gave a lecture on the delicacies of English cuisine. It was by invitation only, but my university pass permitted me to go, and I felt most fortunate to be there. He talked about the savories he had created or made famous at the Savoy.

Bacon Bread Savory

Prepare 12 to 24 hours ahead of time, refrigerate covered and bake when ready to serve.

Bacon Butter:

¹/₂ *lb. (250 g) bacon, diced*	¹/₄ *tsp. (1 mL) savory or sage*
¹/₂ *cup (125 mL) butter*	¹/₄ *cup (60 mL) fresh minced parsley*
2 green onions, chopped fine	

Fry bacon over medium heat until crisp and brown. Cream butter and green onions together until well blended. Add savory or sage and parsley and mix until butter has a green tint. Add bacon and its fat and mix again.

Remove the crust from as many slices of bread as you wish to have. Butter each slice generously with bacon butter and pile them in 2's. Cut in sticks or in 4. Place them on a baking sheet and refrigerate. When ready to serve, preheat oven to 400°F. (200°C) and brown the bacon bread squares 20 to 25 minutes. The top should be brown and crisp, the middle soft and tasty. This same butter is delicious served with baked potatoes. *Yield: 1 cup (250 mL) bacon butter.*

Cheshire Cheese Savory

Escoffier created this one in answer to requests for the ever popular Welsh Rarebit. He was very fond of English apples, especially those of Kent, and of Cheshire cheese, still one of the most famous English cheeses. For years I could buy it at McConnacher's Old English Cheese Shop in Montreal. It is a mild, mellow-flavored cheese that can be red, white or blue in color. Escoffier used to mix the colors to create a special effect. Cheddar can replace the Cheshire, and for the apples I like McIntosh best. I serve it often as an appetizer rather than as a savory.

> 2 tbsp. (30 mL)   1 cup (250 mL) grated
>   unsalted butter   Cheddar cheese
> 2 McIntosh apples   freshly ground pepper
> 1 tsp. (5 mL) fresh
>   lemon juice

Melt butter in a medium-sized, heavy metal saucepan. Peel, core and slice apples. Add to the butter with lemon juice. Simmer over medium heat to soften apples, but do not let them brown. Add grated cheese and pepper and stir just enough to mix everything and to soften the cheese. Cover small rounds of toasted bread with the mixture and place on a baking sheet. Cover and keep in a cool place until ready to serve.

To serve, place under the oven broiler, 3 in. (7.5 cm) away from direct heat. Broil until brown. (Watch closely as they brown quite fast.) *Serves 6.*

Priddy Beef Rolls

I had made many a trip to England before I set foot in Somerset. We were coming back from a romantic trip to Devon, when we decided to follow the road to Somerset County. When we stopped around eight P.M., hungry and tired, we noticed a charming pub named "The Miners Arms" and realized we had reached Priddy as planned. In we went to the "meeting room," as the owner called it, to refresh ourselves. When asked if I wanted "light, strong or dark," I was lost. Playing it safe, I said "light" and received a huge bock of cool beer (I usually drink half a cup at a time). This was served with a plate of black steamed bread, thinly sliced, and the following cold beef rolls which were superb. The chef (whom I met, of course) was a woman, wife of the bartender, and she told me the Priddy Rolls were at their best prepared the day before, to bring out their excellent flavor. They are worth the cost of the meat and the pâté.

> 2 tbsp. (30 mL) soft
>   butter
> 1 tsp. (5 mL) dry
>   mustard
> 1 tsp. (5 mL) salt
> ¼ tsp. (1 mL) pepper
> 2 lb. (1 kg) beef
>   tenderloin
>
> 1 cup (250 mL) liver
>   pâté or foie gras
> finely chopped parsley,
>   and chives or green
>   onions (green part
>   only)

Cream butter with mustard, then add salt and pepper. Spread over the meat. Preheat oven to 400°F. (200°C). Place meat on a rack and roast 25 minutes, uncovered. Let cool 30 minutes on the rack, then wrap tightly in foil paper. Refrigerate overnight.

The next day, slice the cold meat as thin as possible. You will need a good sharp knife or else ask your butcher to slice it on his cutting machine, the same way he would for thin bacon.

Mash pâté until soft, and spread it on each slice of meat. Roll tightly. Dip each end in the finely chopped parsley and chives, which have been mixed together. Secure rolls with toothpicks if necessary. Place in a container or dish, joined sides down. Cover and refrigerate until ready to serve. *Serves 10 to 14 as an appetizer.*

Potted Shrimp

There are many ways of making this well-known English specialty, but the very best I've ever tasted are those at the world-famous Ivy restaurant in Soho, where celebrities vie with the superb food for attention. It consists of shrimp paste mixed with whole shrimp. This is served as an appetizer or, in small quantities, as a savory.

1 cup (250 mL) unsalted butter	1/4 tsp. (1 mL) tarragon or thyme
1 garlic clove, crushed	1/2 tsp. (2 mL) salt
1 lb. (500 g) small cooked shrimp	1/4 tsp. (1 mL) pepper
	1/8 tsp. (0.5 mL) mace

Melt 3/4 (190 mL) of the cup of butter, then add garlic and half of the shrimp. Heat thoroughly, but briefly, over very low heat; do not simmer. Add seasonings, and purée in a blender or food processor for 30 seconds, on and off, or mash with a fork — whichever method is used, the mixture must be creamy.

Heat rest of shrimp in the remaining 1/4 cup (60 mL) of butter and add to puréed mixture. Stir gently until mixture starts to cool — it's quicker if the bowl is set over ice cubes.

Pack mixture into crocks or little dishes and cover with foil or plastic wrap. Refrigerate until ready to serve; it will keep 3 to 4 days. While good served with Melba toast or thinly sliced buttered brown bread, at the Ivy it is spread on thin slices of smoked salmon and sprinkled with pepper. *Yield: 6 small crocks.*

London Delight

One summer, in 1972, during a stroll in London in Germyn Street, I caught sight of a beautiful display of fresh fish and shellfish. The fishmonger saw my interest and came out of his shop and told me about this amazingly good, yet simple, way to cook scallops.

1 lb. (500 g) scallops	chutney
1/2–3/4 lb. (250–375 g) side bacon	

Use fresh scallops, if possible, but if using frozen, thaw and dry them. Place side by side in the bottom of a shallow broiler pan, and put bacon on a grill rack over the scallops. Cook in a 450°F. (230°C) oven until the bacon is crisp and brown — about 5 minutes.

Remove grill and bacon, cook scallops another 4 minutes, then place on a warm platter. Salt and pepper to taste, surround with bacon and serve with a bowl of chutney. Sheer delight with toasted Hovis bread or any good whole-wheat bread. *Serves 2 to 4.*

Brawn

When I was in England in 1963, I decided to go to Devon and Cornwall. In Devon I stayed at the Beacon Hill Hotel. On a beautiful spring day, my friends and I decided to go on a picnic; we felt it was so English. The hotel prepared a basket for us and, in woods fragrant with new violets, I had my first taste of the cold molded meat known as brawn or mold. I was so pleased with the flavor and texture of our Norfolk Brawn that I started to collect brawn recipes from different parts of England. I came back from every trip with a new recipe. I did not taste them all in the same atmosphere of Devon violets, but I could close my eyes and dream.

In the Edwardian era, brawn was the elegant mainstay of English country house breakfasts, some held on the terrace, some served before or after the hunt — Norfolk Brawn, Lancashire Brawn, Oxford Brawn, Ayrshire Mold, to name just a few.

For some reason brawn has acquired an unfortunate image with the years. People tend to think of it as a bunch of scraps in a colorless jelly, and certainly nobody seems to make it. Yet, a well-made brawn or mold can be just as good as any *pâté,* and it's very easy on the food budget.

The work is not involved; the meat goes through a long, slow simmering and never needs to be stirred. That, in fact, is the secret of perfection in these recipes. One or two thin slices of cold molded meat, set on shredded lettuce or garnished with watercress, with a bit of lemon juice squeezed on top, make a lovely cool entrée for a summer meal. Any of the following recipes will keep eight to fifteen days refrigerated.

Oxford Brawn

Molded jellied beef is almost a lost art, yet it is so pleasant and one of the best cold beef dishes. The use of canned consommé (my way) eliminates the long process of making jellied bouillon.

1 cup (250 mL) hot water	¼ cup (60 mL) chopped sour or dill pickles
1½ lb. (750 g) boneless chuck beef	10-oz. (284 mL) can beef consommé
1 envelope unflavored gelatine	pimiento
	parsley heads
⅓ cup (80 mL) chopped celery	½ tsp. (2 mL) salt
1 medium onion, finely chopped	1 tsp. (5 mL) prepared horseradish
	1 tsp. (5 mL) capers

Pour hot water over beef, cover and simmer over low heat until tender. (This is important to the recipe. The meat must cook slowly, without any reduction of the water; it may take 1 to 1½ hours.) Cool, then remove meat and reserve broth. Place meat in a food chopper or processor, using the coarsest blade. Or, chop with a sharp knife—this is the English way and the one I prefer. You should have about 2 cups (500 mL) of ground beef.

Sprinkle gelatine over ¼ cup (60 mL) of the cooled broth. Add celery and onion to remaining broth, simmer 10 minutes, then strain. Reserve broth and add celery, onion and sour or dill pickles to the ground beef. Add enough broth to the undiluted consommé to make 2 cups (500 mL). Heat, add gelatine and stir until dissolved. Pour a thin layer of gelatine mixture into a well-oiled 1-quart (1 L) mold or 9 × 5 in. (22.5 × 12.5 cm) loaf pan and refrigerate until set, 30 to 40 minutes. Decorate set gelatine with strips of red pimiento and heads of parsley.

Add remaining gelatine broth, salt, horseradish and capers to beef mixture and spoon gently over set gelatine. Refrigerate until set and serve unmolded on a platter, with a green salad or sliced tomatoes. *Serves 6 to 8.*

Norfolk Brawn

In Norwich, England, they sometimes call this "Pink and White" or Smoked Pork Cheese. Whatever the name, serve it cold with the Mustard Brawn Sauce for a real treat.

a 3-lb (1.5 kg) smoked cottage roll	*1 tsp. (5 mL) crushed peppercorns*
2 small pig's feet	*1 tsp. (5 mL) sage*
8 cups (2 L) cold water	*Mustard Brawn Sauce*
1 thick slice of lemon, unpeeled	*(see below)*

Put cottage roll, pig's feet and water in a saucepan, bring to a boil, then skim if necessary. Add lemon slice and simmer, covered, over low heat until the meat falls off the bones, which may take 2 to 3 hours.

Cool and strain, reserving the bouillon. Remove the bones, keeping the meat in pieces, then dip each piece lightly into combined pepper and sage (only a sprinkling is needed). Place in an oiled 2-quart (2 L) mold or individual molds.

Boil bones and bouillon again, uncovered, over high heat, until reduced to 3 cups (750 mL). While still hot, strain over meat, cover and refrigerate 8 to 10 hours.

To serve, unmold, garnish with watercress or lettuce and pass the Mustard Brawn Sauce.

Mustard Brawn Sauce:

2 tbsp. (30 mL) brown sugar	*a pinch each of salt, pepper, ground cloves*
3 tbsp. (50 mL) cider or wine vinegar	*4 tbsp. (60 mL) vegetable oil*
1 tsp. (5 mL) strong prepared English mustard	

Beat all the ingredients together for 2 minutes with a rotary beater. Place in a sauceboat.

Joints, Grills and Vintage B and K: Main Course Dishes

Sole Connaught

In London, the Connaught Hotel in Carlos Place is my "three-star" favorite. The drinks are always perfect and the food superb — may it never change. One of their spring specials is sole (fresh Dover, of course) and asparagus.

1 lb. (500 g) fresh	*2 tbsp. (30 mL) lemon*
asparagus	*juice*
salt	*2 green onions, finely*
1/8 tsp. (0.5 mL) pepper	*chopped*
grated peel of 1/2 lemon	*1 tsp. (5 mL) Dijon*
4 fillets of sole	*mustard*
3 tbsp. (50 mL) butter	

Clean asparagus and cut into 2- or 3-inch (5–7.5 cm) lengths. Drop into boiling water and boil rapidly, uncovered, for 5 minutes. Mix salt, pepper and lemon peel. Divide equally over each fillet.

Place some asparagus at one end of each fillet. Roll up and secure with toothpicks or tie with soft string. Place rolls side by side in a generously buttered baking dish.

Melt butter, add remaining ingredients and mix well, then pour over fish. Bake at 400°F.(200°C) for 10 to 15 minutes, basting twice. Serve with thin, buttered, parsleyed noodles. *Serves 4.*

Embassy Beef and Kidney Pie

This recipe was given to me by the chef of the exclusive Embassy Club in London, who referred to it as "Vintage B and K Pie." It is served cold and thinly sliced at lunch, or made into small pies and served hot, as an entrée at night.

1 beef kidney, diced
1 lb. (500 kg) stewing
   beef, diced
1 cup (250 mL) fat from
   kidney, diced
3 onions, chopped
3 cups (750 mL) hot
   water

1 tsp. (5 mL) salt
1/2 tsp. (2 mL) pepper
1 tsp. (5 mL) dry
   mustard
1/2 cup (125 mL) flour,
   browned*
1/2 cup (125 mL) cold
   water

Melt kidney fat until crisp; no other fat should be used. Add kidney and stewing beef gradually, and brown over high heat for 2 minutes after all the meat has been added. Add onions and continue to brown. Pour the hot water and seasonings over the meat and onions and bring to a boil. Cover and cook over low heat for 2 hours, or until the kidney is tender. When cooked, thicken the broth by adding the browned flour blended with the cold water.

Line an earthenware pie dish with Hot Water Pastry (recipe follows) and pour in the creamed beef and kidney. Top with crust and bake for 1 hour at 375°F. (190°C). *Serves 6 to 8.*

Hot Water Pastry:

1/4 cup (60 mL) water
1/2 cup (125 mL) lard
2 cups (500 mL)
   all-purpose flour
1/2 tsp. (2 mL) salt

1/2 tsp. (2 mL) savory
1/4 tsp. (1 mL) sage
1/2 tsp. (2 mL) baking
   powder

Bring water to boil and add lard. Remove from heat and stir until creamy and smooth. Stir together in a bowl with the remaining ingredients. Mix well and shape into a ball, then wrap and refrigerate 1 hour. Roll on lightly floured board and use as indicated. *Yield: enough pastry for 1 pie.*

*To brown flour, simply spread it on a flat pan and heat slowly in a 300°F. oven as if you were making Melba toast. Cook until light brown, stirring occasionally. Pass through a sieve to remove all lumps. (To store, keep it in a glass jar in a cold place.)
   Browned flour can also be purchased in food stores.

English Roast Beef and Browned Potatoes

The English have long enjoyed their food plain, the idea being that their dishes should taste of what they are and be supplemented only by those garnishes that enhance rather than mask the flavor of food.

No one will doubt the fact that England gave mankind its most savored beef steak and roast. Britain is still the home of prime quality beef, even though the Hereford (white-faced, hardy, terracotta steers), the Shorthorn and the Aberdeen Angus (my very favorite), all British breeds, dot the earth's pasturelands. The English have had centuries to decide on just how to cook their meats, what the best cuts are and the best way to prepare and garnish their traditional meat dishes.

Years ago in a Sussex pub, I was taught by André, an English chef with a French name, the following method to cook a "joint" of my favorite Aberdeen Angus beef. In England, a roast is a "joint." They recommend for "unattended" cooking the medium method of roasting — it also gives a lighter finish. A perfect way to cook any good roast.

> a 3-5-lb. (2-4 kg) beef   flour, salt, pepper
> roast of your choice   6-10 potatoes
> beef suet, size of an egg

Wipe meat with a cloth dipped in cider or wine vinegar or Scotch. Chop the suet finely. Rub the roast all over with flour, then place skin-side down on a trivet and set in a dripping pan. Salt and pepper to taste. Cover top with chopped suet. Let stand 20 minutes before placing in a preheated 400°F. (200°C) oven.

Peel potatoes and cut in halves lengthwise. Place in a saucepan and pour rapidly boiling water on top. Boil 5 minutes over high heat. Drain, reserving the water. Add a teabag to it and use for the gravy. Place potatoes cut-side down under trivet holding the roast.

After the roast has been in the oven 30 minutes, lower heat:

> 375°F. (190°C) for a 3-lb. (1.4 kg) roast; roast another 15 minutes.
> 325°F. (160°C) for a 4-lb. (1.8 kg) roast; roast another 22 minutes.
> For a 5-lb. (2.27 kg) roast — same as 4-lb. roast.

OR

Place roast in center of oven preheated to 375°F. (190°C) and roast:

beef on bone — 15 minutes per lb.
beef without bone — 20 minutes per lb.

Whatever temperature is used, let roast stand in warm place for 15 minutes before serving. Make gravy with the reserved tea-flavored potato water.

Before carving, roll the browned potatoes in a generous amount of finely chopped parsley or chives and make sure that meat and potato platters and plates are very hot.

Simpson's-in-the-Strand Yorkshire Pudding

How impressed I was when, at nineteen years old, I had my first roast of beef with an enormous square of Yorkshire Pudding at Simpson's-in-the-Strand. It is still there, and just as famous. If they are known for their superb roasts of beef they are as well known for their Yorkshire Pudding. A simple recipe, but different from any others I know.

6 tbsp. (90 mL) all-purpose flour	2 cups (500 mL) milk, room temperature
a good pinch of salt	1 tsp. (5 mL) olive or vegetable oil
2 large eggs, room temperature	beef drippings

Place flour and salt in a good-sized bowl, and make a well in the center. Break eggs into the well, then gradually add the milk, beating constantly with a wire whisk until thick and creamy. Add olive or vegetable oil and *beat patiently for 10 minutes* (yes, it is long, but a must to reach the perfection of Simpson's-in-the-Strand. *Cover and let it stand 1 hour.*

When ready to cook, beat again for 2 minutes. Pour into the hot drippings of the pan in which you have cooked your roast. (It will sizzle when you pour it in.) Bake 20 minutes in a 400°F. (200°C) oven. *Serves 6.*

Spiced Beef

Very English and also Scottish; very good hot or cold. This is a traditional dish for Plough Monday, the Monday after Epiphany (or Twelfth Night, as the English call it). The preparation is spread over nine days; the result is worth the time and work involved.

Through the years so many have requested this recipe that it is a pleasure to present it here. This recipe was given to me by my old and faithful Scottish butcher who served me for twenty-three years—his meat was always flawless. He taught me many things, including his own recipe for spiced beef.

a 5-lb. (2.5 kg) lean
  brisket round
1 tbsp. (15 mL) crushed
  juniper berries**
1 tsp. (5 mL) each
  ground mace and
  pepper
1/2 nutmeg, grated
a good pinch of cayenne
  pepper
1/2 cup (125 mL) brown
  sugar

1/3 cup (80 mL) coarse
  salt
2 cups (500 mL) beef
  consommé
1 small onion
2 medium carrots
2 bay leaves
1 tsp. (5 mL) thyme
1 stalk celery, with
  leaves
3/4 oz. (21 g) saltpeter*

Rub meat all over with a bit of table salt. Place in a dish and keep in a cool place or refrigerate overnight. Next day run meat quickly under cold running water and wipe dry.

Mix juniper berries and spices with sugar and rub well into the meat. Return to cool place or refrigerate for 3 days, turning it once. On the 4th day, rub in coarse salt and pour back over the meat any sugar mixture that may have dripped off—it will be sort of syrupy by this time. Return meat to cool place or refrigerator again and leave there 1 day for each pound (500 g) of meat, turning it once a day.

To cook, rinse well and tie if necessary. Place meat in a large pan and pour consommé on top. Bring to a boil, add remaining ingredients, then cover and simmer over low heat 3 to 4 hours,

*Saltpeter is optional. It gives the meat a redder color, but it also makes it drier and coarser in texture.
**See note, p.138.

or until tender. Add 2 cups (500 mL) of hot water after 2 hours of cooking and turn meat every hour. Serve hot, thinly sliced, with boiled potatoes and carrots.

To serve cold, put meat in a deep dish, pour cooking broth over, cover and refrigerate 24 hours. Slice paper-thin and serve with pickled beets and potato salad.

Chicken Livers Devon

In many parts of England, Mothering Sunday (the fourth Sunday in Lent) is still observed. On returning from Wales we passed through Devonshire, and the first night we stopped at the Beacon Hill Hotel. They were celebrating Mothering Sunday with the traditional supper, an entrée of Chicken Livers Devon, spit-roasted Leg of Lamb with fresh mint sauce, Suet Pudding, Seakale and, of course, the Mothering Cake, which is a sort of fruit cake.

The Chicken Livers Devon were so good that we decided to make a short TV demonstration about them the next day. Since that day in 1961 I have never stopped making them—unusual and delicious.

1 lb. (500 g) chicken livers	*2 tbsp. (30 mL) brandy*
3 tbsp. (50 mL) flour	*1 large onion, finely chopped*
1 tsp. (5 mL) paprika	*4 medium apples, cored and sliced*
¹/₂ tsp. (2 mL) each salt and pepper	*2 tbsp. (30 mL) brown sugar*
¹/₃ cup (80 mL) butter or margarine	

Clean chicken livers and cut in half. Blend flour, paprika, salt and pepper and toss livers in mixture until well coated. Sauté in 4 tbsp. (60 mL) of the butter over high heat 3 to 4 minutes, or until brown, stirring constantly. Pour brandy on top, stir and remove livers to a hot plate.

Add onion (but no fat) to same pan and stir over medium heat until golden. Add to liver.

Melt remaining butter in pan; add apples and sugar and stir over medium heat until apples start to soften, about 5 minutes. Add the liver and onions, toss together a few seconds and taste for seasoning. *Serves 4 to 5.*

Mirabelle Chicken Foie Gras

When I am in London at least one meal at the sophisticated, elegant Mirabelle is a must. This recipe is a favorite luncheon entrée. Along with it comes a side dish of thickly sliced tomatoes, flavored with a few spoonfuls of brandy mixed with curry powder and a pinch of sugar.

1 whole chicken breast, split	1/2 cup (125 mL) heavy cream
3 tbsp. (50 mL) butter	1/2 cup (125 mL)
1 tsp. (5 mL) salt	chopped parsley or
freshly ground pepper	chives
1/2 cup (125 mL) French pâté de foie gras	

Bone and skin breasts and cut each in half to make 4 pieces. Melt butter until nutty brown in color and sauté chicken over medium heat 20 minutes, or until tender, turning 3 to 4 times. Salt and pepper, remove from pan and set side by side on a meat platter.

Add pâté and cream to butter in pan, and heat while stirring with a wooden spoon or wisk. When very hot (do not boil), pour over chicken and cool.

Cover platter with foil and refrigerate until needed. Then roll each sauce-laden piece in fresh parsley or chives and serve. *Serves 2 (large portions) or 4 (small).*

Wartime Sausage Grill

A month after the end of World War II I went to France, by request, to do some work. I was on the first civilian ship to leave Canada — destination England. It was quite an adventure. I stayed two weeks in London before going on to France. With the kind help of dear friends, now both departed, I was able to get a room at the very elegant Dorchester Hotel. At that time lack of food and food rationing made things difficult even for the best of hotels. On the first morning they suggested their special sausage grill for breakfast. It was served piping hot on their lovely silver-domed platter. Lifting the cover, I discovered two small, dry NAFI sausages with canned sweet potatoes and half a slice of Canadian bacon; nevertheless, it was so popular that it is still offered on their breakfast buffet, but with fresh cooked sweet potatoes and the best pork sausages.

1 lb. (500 g) link pork
   sausages
1 can sliced sweet
   potatoes, well drained
2 apples, unpeeled,
   cored and sliced into
   ¹/₄-in. (.5 cm) pieces
2 tbsp. (30 mL) melted
   margarine

¹/₂ tsp. (2 mL) salt
1 tbsp. (15 mL) brown
   sugar
6-8 mushroom caps
   (optional)
4 bacon slices, cut in
   half
salt and pepper

Place sausages in a bowl, pour boiling water on top, then let stand for 2 minutes. Drain well and place on the oiled rack of a broiling pan. Set sweet potato slices and apples around the sausages. Brush everything with some of the melted margarine, then sprinkle with salt and brown sugar.

Broil 4 to 5 in. (10 to 12.5 cm) from direct heat, until the sausages are browned on one side. Turn everything and brush with the remaining margarine. Add mushrooms and bacon, oiling tops of mushrooms with fat in the pan. Salt and pepper lightly, then broil until sausages are browned on other side.

To serve in "Dorchester style," place each sausage link on a finger-length strip of toasted bread, lightly buttered and sprinkled with a bit of curry powder. Surround with the sweet potatoes, topped with the bacon, and place mushroom caps and apple slices alternately around the edges of the plate. All of it, of course, served on a silver tray with a dome cover. *Serves 6*.

Old Compton Street Tomato Romance

I believe that nothing brings back the flavor of a certain day of a trip like remembering the special taste or look of a dish. When I'm feeling nostalgic, I close my eyes and remember with a smile some of the "good moments." This tomato salad, which I have never seen anywhere else, was served at a small, dark food shop with a dining corner of two tables and four chairs. The exciting aroma that greeted me as I approached the shop made me enter. There I had the justifiably famous (unknown to me until then) Tomato Salata of Señor Ortega. The whole place reeked of spices, pepper, etc., right there in the middle of London. He made the salad to order and gave me a choice of fresh basil or rosemary (just received from Italy he said!) and purple or white garlic crushed with coarse salt — all prepared in front of me. We should have more Señor Ortegas in this world!

4 medium-sized	1 tsp. (5 mL) wine vinegar
tomatoes, unpeeled	1 tbsp. (15 mL) chopped
3 tbsp. (50 mL) brandy	fresh basil OR 1/2 tsp.
1/4 tsp. (1 mL) pepper	(2 mL) rosemary
a pinch of sugar	1/2 tsp. (2 mL) coarse salt
1 tbsp. (15 mL) olive oil	1 garlic clove, peeled

Slice tomatoes and place in a salad bowl. Pour brandy on top. Sprinkle with pepper and sugar. Cover and let stand 1 hour. (Señor Ortega had this part of the salad ready.)

Mix oil, vinegar, basil or rosemary and pour over the tomatoes when ready to serve. Crush garlic with coarse salt in a pestle and mortar, or with the back of a large wooden spoon. Sprinkle over tomatoes and serve. *Serves 4.*

Port Wine Jelly

A must in England with roast goose or turkey. Try it instead of cranberries.

1/2 cup (125 mL) sugar	1 envelope unflavored
1 cup (250 mL) water	gelatine
grated peel and juice of	1 cup (250 mL) port
1 lemon	wine

Bring sugar, water and lemon peel to a boil for 5 minutes, stirring until sugar is dissolved. Meanwhile, soak gelatine mixture in lemon juice.

Stir boiling-hot syrup into gelatine mixture and stir until gelatine is melted. Let cool 20 minutes, then add wine. Pour into 3 jelly glasses or a well-oiled mold, and refrigerate until set. Cover with foil until ready to serve. *Yield: 2 cups (500 mL).*

Teatime Treats and Other Sweets

In the fifties I was invited by BOAC on a special trip to London to learn all about English baking. I certainly did not learn everything, but for a start I was taken to Richard Hand of London, famous for Chelsea buns, and there I learned a great deal. First, I was interested in the beautiful names—Banbury Tarts, Cornish Splits, Market Drayton Gingerbread, Bath Buns, Parkins, Chelsea Buns and so many more. I was also given a two-minute lesson in food history:

"We take English country buns and cakes for granted, when their history and tradition would literally fill a book. Gingerbread, for instance, was long known in Europe before it became an English favorite in the fifteenth century. But the English added to its lore — it was called 'Fairing' because the small spice cakes garnished with angelica, violets or almonds were bought at fairs to be given as gifts. In London they were known as Parliamentary Gingerbread, or 'Parleys' for short, as they were part of teatime at Parliament. Hampshire was known for its 'Gingerbread Husbands.' Bath had Gingerbread Valentines, while Shropshire's Market Drayton is considered the home of the original English Gingerbread; Devon's Widecombe Fair Gingerbread served with hot spiced ale vies with Drayton for first place."

In England there are dozens of small breads with quaint names: sowens, farles and baps, Cornish splits, East Kent huffkins, manchets and shigs, for example. Of all these, English muffins, crumpets and Sally Lunn have been and still are the most popular and are known around the world. They are easily made with just a few ingredients, available in our supermarkets. English muffins are made with yeast and do not resemble the North American type of muffin, which is made with baking powder.

Breads, like people, have certain characteristics; English crumpets are served at teatime, the Sally Lunn is a favorite with salads and so on.

During the early 1900s, bread-making gradually moved from the kitchen into the bakery; today there seems to be a strong move back to the kitchen. I fully understand this, as the satisfaction of producing a fine loaf or a perfect muffin cannot be exaggerated.

Richard Hand's Chelsea Buns

The Richard Hand Company in London is known as the oldest original maker of Chelsea Buns. Four generations of one family have managed the business, which is still situated in the now renowned Pimlico Road. It is worth a visit there on your next trip. The owner gave me this recipe with permission to use it on my cooking show at CBC. We received hundreds of letters asking for the recipe.

4 cups (1 L) all-purpose
   flour
1/2 tsp. (2 mL) salt
3 tbsp. (50 mL) sugar
3 tbsp. (50 mL) butter
2 tbsp. (30 mL) warm
   water
1 envelope dry
   granulated yeast
1 1/2 cups (375 mL) milk
4 eggs
3 tbsp. (50 mL) butter

3 tbsp. (50 mL) sugar
1/4 tsp. (1 mL) cloves
1/2 tsp. (2 mL) allspice
1 tbsp. (15 mL)
   cinnamon
1/2 tsp. (2 mL) coriander
   (optional)
4 tbsp. (60 mL) currants
egg wash: 1 egg beaten
   with 1 tbsp. (15 mL)
   cold water

Stir the first 4 ingredients together with your fingers or a fork to make a mealy mixture. In another bowl, stir 1 tsp. (5 mL) of sugar into the warm water, add yeast and let stand 10 minutes. Scald milk and let cool until tepid.

Beat the 4 eggs and stir with milk and yeast. Gradually add flour, just enough to make a smooth, soft dough. Knead 5 minutes, cover and let rise in a warm place until double in bulk.

Punch down dough and knead 3 to 5 minutes. Roll into a square for large buns; for small ones divide dough in half, roll each half into a square and use half of the following quantities for each piece.

Cream butter with sugar and spread over dough. Fold dough in half and roll again into a square. Mix spices, sprinkle over dough, then sprinkle currants over. Roll tightly like a jelly roll and cut into 1¹/₂-inch (3.75 cm) slices.

Lay slices side by side on a greased baking sheet and let stand 30 minutes. Brush with beaten egg wash, then sprinkle generously with sugar. Bake in a 375°F. (190°C) oven 20 to 30 minutes, or until top is brown. Remove from pan and let cool on a rack. *Yield: 12 large or 24 small buns.*

Cornish Splits

These are sometimes called "Thunder and Lightening" when they're filled with molasses and rich cream. Serve them warm, split open and filled with jam and sour cream, if thick, rich Cornish cream isn't available.

1 tsp. (5 mL) sugar	*1 cup (250 mL) milk*
2 tbsp. (30 mL) hot	*3 tbsp. (50 mL) butter*
water	*3–4 cups (750 mL-1 L)*
1 envelope granulated	*all-purpose flour*
dry yeast	*1 tsp. (5 mL) salt*

Stir sugar into hot water, add yeast and let stand 10 minutes. Scald milk with butter and let cool until tepid. Sift 3 cups (750 mL) of the flour with the salt.

Stir yeast and milk together, then gradually add sifted flour, beating well. Slowly add more flour until you have a soft dough. Knead 5 minutes, or until smooth, cover and let rise in a warm place until double in bulk.

Punch down, knead gently and roll out ¹/₂ in. (1.25 cm) thick. Cut into biscuit-like rounds, set on a greased baking sheet, cover and let stand 30 minutes.

Bake in a 400°F. (200°C) oven 15 to 20 minutes, then split, garnish and serve while still hot. *Yield: 12 to 16 biscuits.*

Maria Floris Chelsea Buns

In 1968 I had the great pleasure of meeting Maria Floris. A Hungarian by birth, she came to England and soon owned and managed a most successful pastry shop. I always admired her zest for life, her professional standards and devotion to her work. She made superb Chelsea Buns. This is her recipe, quite different from Richard Hand's buns as they have no spices and are more delicate in texture. They are an Easter favorite in London and Floris displays them on silver trays surrounded by spring flowers.

¹/₄ cup (60 mL) milk	¹/₂ tsp. (2 mL) salt
¹/₂ cup (125 mL) margarine	¹/₂ cup (125 mL) sugar
1 envelope active dry yeast	1 egg, slightly beaten
	juice and grated rind of 1 lemon
¹/₄ cup (60 mL) warm water	1 cup (250 mL) sifted icing sugar
1 tsp. (5 mL) sugar	2 tsp. (10 mL) fresh lemon juice
2–3 cups (500–750 mL) all-purpose flour	2 tsp. (10 mL) water

Scald milk, remove it from heat, then add margarine and let cool. Mix yeast, water and 1 tsp. (5 mL) sugar in a small bowl and let stand for 10 minutes.

Stir 2 cups (500mL) of the flour with salt and the ¹/₂ cup (125 mL) sugar into a large bowl. Add cooled milk, well-stirred yeast mixture, egg and the juice and grated rind of 1 lemon. Beat thoroughly and add enough of the remaining flour to make a soft dough.

Turn onto a floured board and knead about 10 minutes, until smooth and elastic. Place in a greased bowl, cover and let rise in a warm place until doubled, about 1¹/₂ hours.

Stir dough down, punch off pieces and shape into round buns about 1¹/₂ in. (3.75 cm) in diameter. Set 2 in. (5 cm) apart on a greased baking sheet and let rise about 30 minutes, until doubled. Then bake in a preheated 400°F. (200°C) oven 10 to 12 minutes, or until lightly browned; immediately set on a cake rack to cool.

Mix remaining ingredients to make a lemon glaze and drizzle about 1 tbsp. (15 mL) of this over each bun. Serve while still slightly warm. *Yield: 1¹/₂ dozen buns.*

Bath Buns

On a visit to the famous biscuit-makers, Fortt's of Bath, who pride themselves on having produced the original Bath buns, I was offered some for "tea" that were hot, fresh and fragrant from the big ovens. The tea was a rare Chinese, the buns were served in a beautiful, hot earthenware bowl with cool, thick Devonshire cream instead of butter. Could one forget such a perfect tea?

1 tsp. (5 mL) sugar	3 eggs, beaten
2 tbsp. (30 mL) hot water	3-4 cups (750 mL-1 L) all-purpose flour
1 envelope dry granulated yeast	¹/₂ tsp. (2 mL) salt
1 cup (250 mL) milk	1 tbsp. (15 mL) each candied lemon and
¹/₂ cup (125 mL) soft butter or margarine	orange peel
4 tbsp. (60 mL) sugar	1 egg beaten with 2 tbsp. (30 mL) water

Stir sugar into hot water, add yeast and let stand 10 minutes. Scald milk and let cool until tepid. Cream butter with sugar, then mix in beaten eggs. Sift 3 cups (750 mL) of the flour with the salt.

Stir yeast with warm milk and add to egg mixture with candied peel. Gradually add sifted flour, then slowly add more flour until you have a soft dough. Knead until satiny and smooth, then cover and let rise in a warm place until double in bulk.

Shape dough into buns and place on a greased baking sheet. Glaze with egg wash and sprinkle tops with coarse sugar or 2 small pieces of candied peel on each. Cover and let rise 30 to 40 minutes in a warm place. Bake in a 375°F. (190°C) oven 20 to 25 minutes and let cool on a rack. *Yield: 12 to 14 buns.*

English Muffins

An English muffin should always be torn apart for toasting. At home it is difficult to make muffins that look like the commercial type, all the same size and shape. These may be irregular here and there, but how good they are! When in London enjoy them at Fortnum & Mason at teatime.

1 envelope active dry	1 tbsp. (15 mL) sugar
yeast	1 tsp. (5 mL) salt
¹/₂ cup (125 mL) hot	¹/₂ cup (125 mL) non-fat
water	dry milk
1 tsp. (5 mL) sugar	4–5¹/₂ cups (1 L–1.4 L)
1 cup (250 mL) hot tap	all-purpose flour
water	1 egg
3 tbsp. (50 mL) butter,	cornmeal
room temperature	

In a cup stir together the first 3 ingredients. Let stand 10 minutes. Mix the next 5 ingredients with 3 cups (750 mL) of the flour in a large mixing bowl until well blended; then add the yeast mixture. Beat at medium speed in an electric mixer for 2 minutes (3 minutes by hand). Then beat in the egg and mix well.

Begin to add the remaining flour ¹/₄ cup (60 mL) at a time, until the dough is a rough mass that falls away from the sides of the bowl. Reserve at least ¹/₂ cup (125 mL) of the flour for the board or work surface. Turn dough onto this flour and knead by hand for 5 to 8 minutes. (If your mixer has a dough hook beat 6 minutes.)

Then turn dough into an oiled bowl. Cover with plastic wrap or a tea towel and let rise in a warm place until double in size, about 1 hour.

Then punch down and knead in bowl for 30 seconds; let it rest for 10 minutes. Sprinkle the work surface with cornmeal — a few spoonfuls should suffice. Turn dough on it and roll out until ¹/₄ in. (0.625) thick. If dough resists the rolling pin and pulls back, let it rest 2 minutes, then resume rolling. Finally, cut into 3-in. (8 cm) rounds. Sprinkle rounds on both sides with more cornmeal and place on table next to each other. Cover with towel and let them rest and rise until they are about ¹/₂ in. (1.25) thick, about 15 to 20 minutes.

To cook: Heat a heavy griddle, pancake pan or large cast-iron frying pan. (The pan is ready when a piece of newspaper placed in the middle turns brown.) With a spatula, gently place muffins on the griddle, leaving space between each. Cook 2 minutes on each side, turning with spatula. Reduce heat to quite low, and cook an additional 5 to 6 minutes on each side. If they scorch, lower the heat. With an electric stove, it is a good idea to remove the pan from the heat for 1 minute, after cooking for 2 minutes on each side. Calculate the cooking time as if the pan were still on the heat.

Cool on a metal cake rack. To toast, pull apart with the tines of a fork or with your fingers. Muffins will keep 3 to 4 months in the freezer. *Yield: 24 muffins.*

Old-Fashioned English Crumpets

This recipe was given to me by a very amusing farm woman, Mrs. Coggan, in Berkshire. She urged me not to forget that the difference is in the boiled potato and that a lifetime was not enough to learn how to make a perfect crumpet. I am still trying but I think mine are pretty good!

1 potato, peeled	*1 tsp. (5 mL) salt*
2 cups (500 mL) water	*2 cups (500 mL)*
1 envelope active dry	*all-purpose flour*
yeast	

Slice potato and boil until soft. Drain, mash and let cool until lukewarm. Add yeast and let stand until bubbly (about 30 minutes); stir in salt and flour. Beat the batter at least 4 minutes and let it rise in a warm place (about 30 minutes). Beat 3 minutes and let rise again. Repeat this 2 more times — this creates the porous texture of the crumpets.

To cook, grease about twenty 3½-in. (9 cm) crumpet rings (use small cans that have been opened at both ends and cleaned thoroughly or buy small flan rins at any kitchenware shop — they are costly but last a long time). Place rings on a greased griddle or large cast-iron frying pan. Pour batter into rings to a depth of about ⅓ in. (1 cm). Cook over medium-low heat about 20 minutes, or until crumpets are filled with little holes and somewhat dry on top. Do not turn—they will cook through and should remain flat underneath and a bit rounded on top. *Yield: 18 to 20 crumpets.*

Crumpets

In the summer of 1959 I was travelling through the English countryside with a CBC crew to film country life. My research, of course, centered on food. We had tea one day at a charming English inn in Surrey. The crumpets were made at the fireplace on a stone griddle supported by carved stone rings. They were served with whipped butter and a pot of homemade *confiture de cassis* (black currant jam), and the inn owner, who made them, gave me the recipe. Without the stone and the unbleached English flour they are not as perfect, but surely the best I could ever produce.

1 tsp. (5 mL) sugar	¹/₂ cup (125 mL) bran
¹/₄ cup (60 mL) warm	flakes
water	¹/₄ cup (60 mL) wheat
1 envelope active dry	germ
yeast	¹/₂ tsp. (2 mL) each salt
2¹/₂ cups (625 mL)	and soda
lukewarm milk	1 cup (250 mL)
3 cups (750 mL)	lukewarm water
all-purpose flour	

Dissolve sugar in warm water, add yeast. Stir well and let rest 10 minutes. Stir and add to lukewarm milk.

Stir together in a large bowl the flour and the yeast mixture. Add bran flakes and wheat germ and beat until thoroughly mixed. Cover and let rise in a warm place until bubbly. Beat it well, cover and let rise again until bubbly. Repeat process a third time (this is the secret of a light and airy crumpet).

Stir together salt, soda and lukewarm water. Add to sponge mixture and beat well. Set aside, covered, in a warm place for 20 to 25 minutes.

Grease crumpet loops or rings (canning jar rings are good to use). Place on a *medium*-hot griddle or, if you don't have a griddle, in a cast-iron frying pan. Pour enough batter to cover bottom of ring completely, but only enough to fill it halfway up. Cook over medium heat until top is set and full of bubbly holes — this should take about 10 minutes. Remove rings, turn crumpets over and cook second side lightly.

Note: The heat of the griddle or frying pan is most important, so that the crumpet will brown nicely on each side yet still remain light. Test one or two when you make them for the first time.

Market Drayton Gingerbread

Whether cut into biscuits or imprinted with a molded design, these are best gilded with icing. They say "gilded" instead of iced because in the old days the gingerbreads were baked in a slab, the top covered with cloves and the head dipped in gold and patterned to form a *fleur-de-lis*. This went on until the nineteenth century. Even today, at Christmas, you can see them in the Drayton Market in Devon and all over England, covered with a thin sheet of gold, which is edible. I am sure this sheet is a custom that comes from Persia and other Asiatic countries and it is still used in many ways in Morocco.

2 cups (500 mL) sifted all-purpose flour	½ cup (125 mL) soft butter or margarine
2 tsp. (10 mL) ground ginger	1 tsp. (5 mL) soda
	1 tbsp. (15 mL) milk
1 cup (250 mL) dark brown sugar	1 egg
	2 tbsp. (30 mL) honey

Mix flour, ginger and brown sugar in a bowl and cut in butter or margarine until mealy. Dissolve soda in milk, then whisk in egg and honey. Add to flour mixture and blend with hands that have been dipped in flour (the dough will be stiff).

Roll, then cut into ½-in. thick (1.25 cm) circles. Bake in a 350°F. (180°C) oven 18 to 20 minutes. Let cool slightly on baking sheet, then remove and cool on a cake rack. *Yield: 18 to 24 biscuits.*

Grassmere Apple Cake

The Lake District is renowned not only for its beautiful scenery, but also for Westmorland Gingerbread and beautiful Grassmere cakes; the ginger cakes are flavored with a combination of orange and lemon rinds plus a good amount of grated fresh ginger root. Try this seasoning with your own favorite recipe.

4 cups (1 L) all-purpose flour	*6-9 apples*
1/2 tsp. (2 mL) salt	*3/4 cup (190) mL) sugar*
1 tsp. (5 mL) baking powder	*1/2 tsp. (2 mL) each ground cardamon and cinnamon OR 1 tsp (5 mL) cinnamon*
1/2 cup (125 mL) sugar	
3/4 lb. (375 mL) butter or margarine	*1 cup (250 mL) icing sugar, sifted*
2 eggs, beaten	*juice of 1/2 lemon*

Grease a 9 × 13 in. pan (22.5 × 32.5 cm). Sift flour twice with salt and baking powder. Add the 1/2 cup (125 mL) sugar and butter or margarine and cut in with 2 knives or a pastry blender until it has a mealy texture. Add beaten eggs and blend in with your fingers. Divide dough in half and pat one half into the bottom of pan. Grate unpeeled apples and spread over dough in pan.

Mix the 3/4 cup (190 mL) of sugar with the chosen spice. Sprinkle over apples, and gently pat on remaining dough. (Do not pack as tightly as the bottom dough or the texture will be too heavy.)

Bake in a 325°F. (160°C) oven for 55 minutes. Set the pan on a cake rack to cool, then spread top with icing sugar mixed with enough lemon juice to give it spreading consistency. To serve, cut into squares. *Serves 10 to 15.*

Connaught Hotel Royal Mince Tarts

Eat twelve mince tarts between Christmas and New Year's day if you want twelve lucky months to follow, as the saying goes. Unless you're counting calories, it's not a painful feat to eat them, equally good hot or cold.

At teatime, the Connaught serves them as miniatures — just one delightful bite in each.

uncooked pastry of your
choice
4 tbsp. (60 mL) melted
butter
¹/₃ cup (80 mL) sugar
4 egg yolks

grated peel and juice of
1 lemon
2 cups (500 mL)
prepared mincemeat
4 egg whites
¹/₃ cup (80 mL) sugar

Roll out the pastry dough very thin and cut into 12 circles, each large enough to line a 2-in. (5 cm) muffin tin.

Blend next 4 ingredients thoroughly, and when light and creamy add mincemeat. Fill tarts ³/₄ full, but do not cover. Bake in a 350°F. (180°C) oven 25 to 30 minutes.

To make a meringue, beat egg whites until stiff, adding sugar gradually and beating hard at each addition. When tarts are done, remove from oven and top each with some meringue. Return to oven 5 to 10 minutes, or until meringue is golden brown.

Do not use meringue if you wish to keep the tarts (6 to 8 days). Wrap individually and keep in a cool place. *Yield: 12 tarts.*

Treacle Tart

This Norfolk specialty is true to the original recipe when made with golden syrup and English black treacle. This version has no breadcrumbs, and it freezes very well.

pie dough of your choice
1 cup (250 mL)
imported golden
syrup*
2 tbsp. (30 mL) treacle*

2 tbsp. (30 mL) butter
grated rind of ¹/₂ lemon
2 eggs, well beaten with
3 tbsp. (50 mL) cream

Line an 8-in. (20 cm) pie plate with pie dough, bake and let cool.

Warm syrup, then add treacle. Remove from heat, add butter and lemon rind and stir until butter is melted. Thoroughly stir in the egg and cream mixture. Pour into the cooled crust and cook in a 350°F. (180°C) oven until custard is set, about 15 to 20 minutes. Let cool, then top with whipped cream or chopped walnuts. *Serves 4 to 6.*

*The golden syrup and treacle can be replaced by 1¹/₄ cups (320 mL) of molasses for a slightly different flavour.

Yorkshire Christmas Cake

The stout in the cake gives it special color and flavor. It can be replaced by milk or any beer, but· then it is no longer a "Yorkshireman's Delight."

4 cups (1 L) flour
1/4 tsp. (1 mL) each
    nutmeg and salt
1/2 tsp. (2 mL) each
    cinnamon and cloves
1 cup (250 mL) soft
    butter
2 cups (500 mL) brown
    sugar
1 cup (250 mL) currants
1 cup (250 mL) Sultana
    raisins

1/2 cup (125 mL)
    candied mixed peel
1/2 cup (125 mL)
    chopped walnuts or
    almonds
4 eggs, well beaten
1 tsp. (5 mL) baking
    soda
1/2 cup (125 mL) whole
    candied cherries
1 cup (250 mL) stout

Sift together 3 times flour, nutmeg, salt, cinnamon and cloves. Reserve 1/2 cup (125 mL).

Cream butter and brown sugar until light and very creamy. Add the flour mixture gradually, beating well after each addition.

Place in a bowl currants, raisins, mixed peel, almonds or walnuts; stir with the reserved flour. Add to flour mixture gradually, beating at each addition.

Add to the beaten egg the soda mixed with 1 tsp. (5 mL) of milk. Stir and pour over fruit mixture. Add the cherries and stir until blended. Add the stout and stir again.

Pour batter in 1 large or 2 or 3 smaller pans of your choice, well rubbed with shortening (do not use butter).

Bake in a preheated 250°F. (120°C) oven — 1 hour for each pound of cake batter is the rule. Check with a cake tester. Cool thoroughly in pan, then set on wire cake rack before unmolding.

To prepare and serve this cake in true Yorkshire fashion, wrap the cooled cake in a cloth dampened in stout. Twelve to 24 hours before serving, cut cake in 4 layers with a long sharp knife. Spread suet-free mincemeat on each layer. Rebuild the cake and top with a thick layer of almond paste. Do this only if you are serving the cake at one sitting or in 2 to 3 days.

Devonshire Molded Rhubarb

For some reason all my favorite rhubarb recipes are from England. This one I first tasted while sitting with friends in their enchanting rose garden in Essex. The pink jelly, set on crystal that sparkled in the sun, was surrounded with beautiful tiny roses.

4 cups (1 L) rhubarb, cut in ¹/₂ -in. (1.25 cm) pieces	*¹/₂ cup (125 mL) sugar*
1 envelope unflavored gelatine	*grated peel of 1 orange*

Simmer rhubarb in a covered saucepan with 3 tbsps. (50 mL) of water for 8 to 10 minutes, or until tender. Strain, reserving the juice, then blend remaining ingredients and add to juice. Stir over low heat until sugar is dissolved, then add to rhubarb and stir well. Pour into a well-oiled 1-quart (1 L) mold and refrigerate until set. If you wish, serve this with a bowl of Rosemary Sugar (recipe follows). *Serves 4.*

Rosemary Sugar:

2 cups (500 mL) sugar	*4 tbsp. (60 mL) dried rosemary*

In a mortar bowl, mix sugar and rosemary together with a wooden spoon until rosemary is crushed and blended in well.

Place in a glass jar and cover tightly for 24 hours, shaking it 2 or 3 times during this time. The faint flavor of rosemary is delightful with any rhubarb dish.

Pre-Victorian Rhubarb Pastry

Mrs. Emily Birkett, the owner of a charming English pub in Cumberland, specializes in reviving authentic recipes from Old English cuisine. She graciously offered me these, beautifully written in script. We had lunch at her pub and she served a superb hare pâté, with little breads baked on a hot stone in the fireplace and brought to our table on a wooden bread board with a big jar of mixed pickles.

pastry for a 2-crust pie
¹/₂ cup (125 mL) oatmeal
1 tbsp. (15 mL) treacle or molasses
6-8 rhubarb stalks, cut in 2-in. (5 cm) pieces
¹/₂ cup (125 mL) muscat or seedless raisins
¹/₂ cup (125 mL) sugar
grated peel of 1 lime or lemon
cream or milk

Line a buttered 8-in. (20 cm) pie plate with pastry, sprinkle with oatmeal and pour treacle or molasses over. Mix rhubarb, raisins, sugar and peel and pour over oatmeal.

Cover with pastry, slit top and brush with cream or milk. Bake in a 400°F. (200°C) oven 30 to 40 minutes, or until crust is golden brown. *Serves 6.*

Superb Connaught Plum Pudding

A recipe given to me by the pastry chef at the Connaught Hotel in London, where we had a memorable Christmas dinner in the sixties. It has a lot of fruits, but no flour, which makes it light and perfect. It was flamed with great dash with the best of whiskeys. The hot pudding was set on a large silver tray in a ring of fresh holly, topped with a high-domed cover. The big silver dome was lifted and one little match set off a superb spectacle. Do try to flame it with whiskey.

1/2 cup (125 mL) grated
   unpeeled apples
1/2 cup (125 mL)
   chopped beef suet
1/4 cup (60 mL) chopped
   walnuts
2 tbsp. (30 mL) diced
   candied orange peel
2 tbsp. (30 mL) diced
   candied lemon peel
2/3 cup (160 mL) diced
   candied citron peel
1 1/2 cups (375 mL)
   seedless raisins
1 cup (250 mL) currants
1 tbsp. (15 mL)
   cinnamon

1 1/2 tsp. (7 mL) ginger
1/4 tsp. (1 mL) nutmeg
1/2 tsp. (2 mL) allspice
1/4 tsp. (1 mL) salt
1 cup (250 mL) sugar
1/3 cup (80 mL) apricot
   jam
2 cups (500 mL) fine
   dry breadcrumbs
4 eggs
2 tbsp. (30 mL) milk
1/3 cup (80 mL) brandy
   or rum
1/3 cup (80 mL) white
   wine or orange juice

In a large bowl combine all the ingredients, except the last 4, and mix thoroughly. Beat eggs, then add to them the remaining ingredients. Add to the fruit mixture and mix thoroughly with your hands — a spoon cannot blend this thick mass properly.

Oil and sugar a 1-quart (1 L) mold or two 1-pint (500 mL) molds. Fill 2/3 full, cover tightly and steam—the quart (1 L) for 5 1/2 hours, the pints (500 mL) for 4 hours. *Serves 8 to 10.*

Wales

I shall never forget the crazy, carefree, delightful experience we had in Cardiff in the hilly heart of Wales. We travelled many miles in a small bus to get to our "Wales Home Feast," at the home of our very amusing hostess. During a live TV show, when we discussed the Christmas customs in Wales, she remarked that it could all be described in four words: "bastes and bakes and bickers and boozes." She worked with me again, "live on the Tube," and made her delicious Leek Soup, quite different in approach to the French vichyssoise. We roasted a nice fat goose that was stuffed — you guessed it — with leeks, lots of leeks, because, as you may know, it is *the* "thing" in Wales. Her dessert was a superb sorbet, the likes of which I had never tasted before, and shortbreads, her only concession to what she called the "Strangers" (Scots). I thank her for the cheerful, pleasant memories.

The beauty of Wales itself, especially the countryside, is worth a trip of its own to do it justice.

A Wales Home Feast

Welsh Leek Soup

4 medium to large leeks
2 tbsp. (30 mL) butter
2 large onions, chopped
4 medium potatoes,
    peeled and diced
3 cups (750 mL) hot
    water
2 tsp. (10 mL) salt
pepper

1 cup (250 mL) heavy
    cream
2 cups (500 mL) hot
    milk
1 tbsp. (15 mL) butter
1 tsp. (5 mL) dry
    sherry, for each plate
    of soup

Wash white part of the leeks and about 2 in. (5 cm) of the green. Slice thinly.

Melt butter in a large saucepan, add chopped onions and stir over medium heat until they are a golden color here and there. Add leeks and cook for 10 minutes more, stirring often. Add potatoes, hot water, salt and pepper. Cover and simmer until potatoes are tender, about 25 minutes.

When ready to serve, add the remaining ingredients, except the sherry. Stir until boiling.

Pour 1 tsp. (5 mL) of sherry into each soup bowl and fill with boiling-hot soup. Serve with a basket of homemade Welsh Cacen-Gri (Griddle Scones) or hot buttered crackers (the large, old-fashioned type). *Serves 6.*

"Very Sociable" Welsh Roasted Goose

In the Welsh language, "very sociable" means the very best, because one who is not liked or admired is called "unsociable." It seems to be important enough to apply even to a "well-roasted goose."

a 6-8 lb. (3-4 kg) young
goose
1 lemon, cut in half
6 leeks, washed and
chopped (green and
white parts)
2 tbsp. (30 mL) fresh or
dried sage

1 tbsp. (15 mL) salt
1/2 tsp. (2 mL) pepper
2 cups (500 mL) dry
bread cubes
1/4 tsp. (1 mL) nutmeg
1 cup (250 mL) chicken
bouillon
4 tbsp. (60 mL) brandy

Place leeks in a saucepan and pour boiling water on top to cover. Boil, uncovered, for 5 minutes. Drain and reserve 1 cup (250 mL) of this water to make the gravy (if you have no chicken bouillon available).

Rub goose inside and out with the lemon halves. Mix together well-drained leeks, sage, salt, pepper, bread cubes and nutmeg. Stir until well mixed. Stuff the goose with this mixture. Truss and prick the skin with the point of a knife in several places to let the fat run out while it is cooking.

Place on a rack in a roasting pan. Do not cover. Bake in a preheated 400°F. (200°C) oven for 20 minutes, then lower heat to 350°F. (180°C) and continue roasting 20 to 25 minutes per pound (0.5 kg) in all. When the goose is ready, place on a warm platter, cover with foil and let stand about 20 to 30 minutes before carving.

To make the gravy, first remove the fat with a large spoon. (It is easy with goose as the fat remains on top of the brown juices. Many people prize the fat to cook with or to spread on toast.) Leave a little fat on the juice and add the chicken bouillon or the reserved leek water and the brandy. Stir over medium heat, scraping the bottom and sides of the pan. Strain into a hot sauceboat and serve. *Serves 8.*

1750 Superb Welsh Rarebit

An unusual old recipe. Serve after a concert or play with red wine or after the game with a bock of beer or for a light lunch with a green salad.

1 tsp. (5 mL) soft butter	*3 tbsp. (50 mL) dry red*
¹/₂ tsp. (2 mL) French or	*wine or port*
German mustard	*¹/₂ lb. (250 mL) strong*
4 slices crusty French	*Cheddar cheese*
bread	

Cream together butter and mustard. Butter bread with this mixture. Place a slice of bread in each of 4 ramekins or oven-proof cups. Pour an equal quantity of wine or port over each slice of bread. Slice cheese paper-thin and lay as many slices as desired over the bread. Place in a preheated 375°F. (190°C) oven until cheese is melted and slightly brown here and there, about 10 to 15 minutes.

Serve with salted nuts and a glass of port or light claret wine. *Serves 4.*

Gin and Grapefruit Sherbet

This can be made eight to ten days ahead of time, if it is kept well covered and frozen. Remove from freezer fifteen minutes before serving. Serve in champagne coupes with a small elegant decanter of gin on the table — each person can use more gin if so inclined!

As our hostess remarked, the Welsh have a formidable reputation as drinkers.

4 large grapefruit	*³/₄ cup (190 mL) dry gin*
³/₄ cup (190 mL) sugar	*grated rind of 1 lemon*

Peel grapefruit, removing all membranes and white part of the skin, and cut into sections. Place in a sieve set over a bowl, press the fruit gently, then let stand for 1 hour.

Measure the juice, adding enough water to make 1¹/₂ cups (375 mL) of liquid. Place in a saucepan, add sugar and boil 5 minutes, stirring until sugar is dissolved. When it has formed a syrup, pour into a blender and let it cool, then add the reserved grapefruit segments, the gin and the lemon rind. Blend until it turns into a thick liquid. Pour into a mold. Cover and freeze. *Serves 6.*

Staple Fare

Welsh Leek Pie

This is a superb recipe which can come as a pleasant change to the often-served quiche. It is not very well known in this country, but in Wales it is family fare. Try it at your next buffet supper, served hot with sliced cold chicken or turkey.

6 leeks
¹/₂ cup (125 mL)
chicken stock
juice and grated rind of
¹/₂ lemon
2 tbsp. (30 mL) butter
4 eggs
¹/₄ cup (60 mL) heavy
cream

2 cups (500 mL)
small-curd cottage
cheese
salt and pepper
3 tbsp. (50 mL) fine dry
breadcrumbs
pastry for single-crust
8-in. (20 cm) pie

Clean leeks and cut both the white and green parts into 1-in. (2.5 cm) pieces. Bring chicken stock to a boil along with lemon juice, lemon rind and butter. Add the leeks and cook, uncovered, over medium heat for 12 to 15 minutes. (Reserve the cooking stock.)

Beat together eggs, cream and cheese until well blended and creamy. Add ¹/₂ cup (125 mL) of the leek stock while stirring. Then add the whole mixture to the cooked leeks and remaining stock. Simmer for a few moments, stirring until the mixture thickens to the consistency of a light cream sauce. Do not let it boil. Add salt and pepper to taste.

Grease a pie plate and dust it with fine breadcrumbs. Line with pastry and flute the edges. Pour in the leek mixture. Bake in a preheated 375°F. (190°C) oven for about 40 minutes, or until the top is golden brown and the custard is set. *Serves 4 to 6.*

Cacen-Gri (Welsh Griddle Scones)

(Pronounce these *kah-see-gree.*)

These are much like our hot baking powder biscuits, but much lighter and sweeter, and should definitely be served with unsalted butter.

On our TV show in Wales, we cooked them on a hot griddle set on a wood stove. The griddle was heating over low heat while we prepared the scones.

¹/₃ cup (80 mL) cold butter	1 tsp. (5 mL) cream of tartar
2 cups (500 mL) all-purpose flour	a good pinch of salt
¹/₂ cup (125 mL) wheat germ	4 tbsp. (60 mL) currants
1 tsp. (5 mL) baking soda	2 tbsp. (30 mL) sugar
	1 cup (250 mL) buttermilk or sour milk

Rub the butter, using the tips of the fingers, with flour and wheat germ, until grainy. Add baking soda, cream of tartar, salt, currants and sugar. Mix thoroughly with a spoon for at least 2 minutes. Add the buttermilk or sour milk to make a light biscuit dough that can be rolled.

Cut into rounds 3 in. (8 cm) across and roll on a lightly floured board. Set on hot griddle (use a heavy cast-iron frying pan when no griddle is available).

Cook about 4 to 5 minutes on both sides, turning them only once. They should be well browned on both sides. *Yield: 10 to 12 scones.*

Note: They can be baked in a preheated 400°F. (200°C) oven but they lose crispness and flavor.

Scotland

Scotland has long been famous for its baking, and the Scots insist that nowhere in the British Isles will you find better bread.

In 1954 I spent a week in Edinburgh and took a two-day course on Scottish bread at Mrs. Macpherson's School. She advertised that she taught only pure Scottish Clan baking and that she was a specialist on "solid fuel cookers." I remember asking myself what these could be and, as a matter of fact, that was the inducement to participate in her classes. A solid fuel cooker turned out to be a gas stove, of which she was very proud. Another amusing expression of "Mac's," as she called herself, was "fire the Baps" (or whatever was baking), which meant cook them in the fuel oven. Then you could watch them turn gold through a big square window in the door.

I learned a lot in just two days and ate enough morning rolls to gain a few pounds, I'm sure.

Cock-a-Leekie Soup

I have eaten "Cock-A-Leekie," "Cockie-Leekie" and "Cock-A-Leeky," which seems to have as many names as ways to make it. Basically it is a chicken and leek soup; sometimes it has prunes and/or beef bones, sometimes not. The one I enjoyed most was served at a pleasant family hotel in Selkirk. We were on our way to Edinburgh on a fine, nippy cold January day when a strong wind was blowing from the North Sea. The steaming hot Cock-A-Leekie was most welcomed. After dinner I asked the chef if he would give me the recipe and the next day, after much thought, he said that as I was Canadian he would. For years I have made it the "Selkirk way" and the pleasure of its flavor never dwindles. The prunes, soaked in whiskey, were a specialty of the house and are worth every bit of extra work and cost involved.

4–6 leeks	*1 bay leaf*
3 bacon slices	*1/8 tsp. (0.5 mL) thyme*
a 5-lb. (2.5 kg) roasting	*1 tbsp. (15 mL) salt*
* chicken*	*1/2 tsp. (2 mL) freshly*
10 cups (2.5 L) water	* ground pepper*
1/2 cup (125 mL)	*1/2 cup (125 mL)*
* chopped celery leaves*	* prunes, cooked, pitted*
1/4 cup (60 mL) chopped	* and chopped*
* parsley stems*	*1/4 cup (60 mL) whiskey*

Clean leeks and cut the white and tender green parts in 1-in. (3 cm) pieces. Set aside.

Place chicken with its giblets in a soup kettle. Add the water, celery leaves, parsley, bay leaf, thyme, salt and pepper. Cover and bring to a rolling boil over high heat. Reduce heat and simmer (without boiling) until chicken is very tender, about 1 to 2½ hours.

Skim the fat from the top and strain the soup. Chop the chicken meat and giblets coarsely and return to the strained broth. Add the leeks and simmer again, covered, 30 minutes, or until the leeks are tender.

Soak prunes in whiskey while the chicken is cooking and add to soup when ready to serve. Taste for seasoning and serve with a basket of hot biscuits. *Serves 5 to 8.*

Fish, Lamb and Fowl

St. Andrew's Grilled Finnan

I never knew what true Finnan haddies were before I ate Cullen Skink at a friend's farm in Scotland, listening to the fierce winds of the North Sea blowing through the big black fir trees. I learned that Finnan (or Findan) haddocks were named after a small village near Aberdeen. In the old days, they were sprinkled with salt water and smoked, then dried over seaweed.

Our Scottish ancestors brought the delicacy to our shores, and as a child I remember my mother serving "Scots Fish" for breakfast. During World War II, I ate a poached Finnan in Halifax that rivals my remembrance of the Scottish type.

Basically, Finnan haddocks can be grilled, steamed, poached or made into a loaf, and have an affinity to butter, milk and potatoes. They are a budget item which please even those who care little for fish. In Scotland, the St. Andrew type is heavily smoked and usually served grilled. Topped with a poached egg, it is a treat to be enjoyed.

1 lb. (500 g) Finnan haddie, divided into 4 portions *1 cup (250 mL) hot milk* *3 tbsp. (50 mL) unsalted butter or margarine*	*4 poached eggs (optional)* *¼ cup (60 mL) minced parsley*

Place the fish in a dish and pour the hot, but not boiling, milk on top. Cover and let stand 4 hours (this will tenderize the fish and prevent the drying effect of direct heat during the grilling period). Remove from the milk and wipe as dry as possible with absorbent paper towels.

Cream butter and spread 2 tbsp. (30 mL) of it on one side of the fish. Place on a grill, buttered side up, and set 4 in. (10 cm) from the source of heat. Broil 4 minutes, then turn, spread with remaining butter and broil 2 minutes.

Poach the eggs while the fish is cooking. To serve, place the fish on hot plates, top each piece with a poached egg and sprinkle with the parsley. Add 3 to 4 tbsp. (50 to 60 mL) of the milk used for soaking to the melted butter in the bottom of the grill pan. Warm over direct heat and pour over the fish. *Serves 4.*

Crisped Golden Whiting

Whiting is, of course, a specialty of the English Channel and the Baltic Sea. It has a fine texture and is flaky, with a delicate flavor.

At home I use the silver hake which comes from New England, and I have also made it often with Canadian fillet of sole. Follow the directions closely in this recipe and you will be more than pleased with the result, regardless of the type of fish used. Try it also with whole trout.

4 fillets of sole or other fish	2 tbsp. (30 mL) flour
1 tsp. (5 mL) vegetable oil	1 tsp. (5 mL) paprika
salt and pepper	bacon fat
1 egg white, lightly beaten	

Brush fish on both sides with oil. Salt and pepper, then dip in egg white. Mix flour and paprika. Sprinkle on one side of the fish.

Heat bacon fat in a cast-iron frying pan. Add the fish, floured side down. Sprinkle the second side with the remaining flour and fry until crisp and golden, turning only once. Do not overcook; 4 to 6 minutes is usually enough. *Serves 4.*

Jugged Lamb

I enjoyed this Jugged Lamb in a small pub in Perth, on a rainy, misty noon. The chef told me he had received this recipe from his grandmother. He wrote it for me in Gaelic, so needless to say I had someone in Canada translate it.

3 tbsp. (50 mL) butter
2 onions, quartered
3 lb. (1.5 kg) neck or
  shank of lamb
4 tomatoes, peeled and
  chopped
1 stick celery, diced
salt and pepper
1½ tbsp. (25 mL) flour
1¼ cups (310 mL)
  consommé

2 tbsp. (30 mL) fresh
  lemon juice
2 tbsp. (30 mL) red
  currant jelly
1 tbsp. (15 mL) chopped
  parsley
⅓ cup (80 mL) dry port
  wine

Preheat oven to 350°F. (180°C). Melt 1 tbsp. (15 mL) of the butter in a frying pan; lightly brown the onions over medium heat. Add lamb and sear with onions. Place tomatoes and celery in a buttered casserole dish. Add meat and onions. Season to taste.

Melt the remaining butter in same frying pan; when browned add flour and stir until well blended, then add consommé. Stir until creamy, add lemon juice and pour over meat. Cover and bake 2 hours. Ten minutes before serving, add red currant jelly, parsely and port wine. Stir well. Serve very hot in a casserole, with parsleyed rice and green peas. *Serves 6.*

Lamb and Bacon Pie

Unusual and interesting enough to be party fare. A pie without pastry, the crust is the meat topped with a tasty mixture that cooks into a creamy custard.

4 eggs
½ cup (125 mL) table
  cream or milk
1½ cups (375 mL)
  small bread cubes
1 lb. (500 g) ground
  lamb
grated rind and juice of
  ½ lemon
1 small onion, finely
  chopped
1 tsp. (5 mL) salt
½ tsp. (2 mL) ground
  ginger

¼ tsp. (1 mL) thyme
5-6 bacon strips
1 cup (250 mL) sharp
  Cheddar cheese,
  grated
½ cup (125 mL) diced
  celery
2 cups (500 mL) milk
½ tsp. (2 mL) each salt
  and celery salt
¼ tsp. (1 mL) garlic
  powder

Beat 1 egg with the ½ cup (125 mL) of cream or milk, add bread cubes and let stand 5 minutes. Add ground lamb, lemon rind and juice and next 4 ingredients. Mix well, then use mixture to line bottom and sides of a 9- or 10-in. (22.5 or 25 cm) pie plate.

Fry bacon until crisp, crumble and sprinkle over meat. Then mix cheese with celery and sprinkle over bacon. Beat 3 remaining eggs with the 2 cups (500 mL) of milk, add the ½ tsp. (2 mL) salt, celery salt and garlic powder and pour gently into meat shell.

Bake in a 400°F. (200°C) oven for 15 minutes, reduce heat to 350°F. (180°C) and bake 30 minutes, or until top custard is set. Serve hot or cold, cut into small wedges. *Serves 6.*

Poor Man's Goose

Many Canadians will recognize their scalloped potatoes; what makes it a Poor Man's Goose are the slices of pork, the fresh lemon juice and the surprising fact that it must be served with hot applesauce.

When I was a guest of the Dundee Marmelade factory, in the early sixties, we had Poor Man's Goose, Dundee cake and black tea with marmelade, instead of sugar, for lunch. They were surprised that I had never eaten the "goose," as they said, so they presented me with the following recipe. Please try it and do not omit the hot unsweetened applesauce.

1 lb. (500 g) thick pork chops	*1 tsp. (5 mL) sage, fresh if available*
1 bay leaf	*1 cup (250 mL) consommé*
1 celery leaf	
6 - 8 medium-sized potatoes	*1 tbsp. (15 mL) fresh lemon juice*

Remove bones from chops. Place chops in a saucepan with bay leaf, a piece of celery leaf, salt, pepper, the bones and 1¹/₂ cups (375 mL) water. Bring to the boil, then simmer 40 minutes. Strain and measure the consommé — you should have 1 cup (250mL).

Scrub the potatoes — do not peel — boil 15 minutes. Drain, cool, peel and cut into slices.

Place a layer of potatoes in the bottom of a buttered pie dish (in Scotland they use a green oval stoneware dish about 4 in. (10 cm) deep and 8 in. (20 cm) long) and top with a layer of pork chops. Season with salt, pepper and sage. Continue to alternate layers of potatoes and meat until all is used, finishing off with a layer of potatoes.

Add the lemon juice to the strained consommé and pour over the potatoes. Cover with foil paper or a lid. Bake in a preheated 350°F. (180°C) oven for 30 minutes. Uncover and cook another 10 minutes to brown the top. Serve with the following apple-sauce. *Serves 6.*

Applesauce:

4 - 6 apples
¹/₄ cup (60 mL) water
1 tsp. (5 mL) sugar

1 tsp. (5 mL) fresh
   lemon juice
2 tbsp. (30 mL) butter

Peel and chop apples; place in a saucepan with the water. Cook over medium heat until soft enough to beat into a purée (I now purée mine in a food processor). Add the remaining ingredients, beat well and serve. I often omit the sugar completely when I have sweet apples. *Yield: 1¹/₂ cups (375 mL).*

Scot's Way with Turkey

Do not let the funny combination of prunes, walnuts and honey disturb you since you also use a "wee nip of good Scotch" to put it all together for Christmas dinner.

an 8–10-lb. (4–5 kg)
  young turkey
12 large or 18
  medium-sized prunes
¹/₄ cup (60 mL) whiskey
2 cups (500 mL) strong,
  hot black tea
1 medium onion,
  chopped fine
1 lb. (500 g) minced
  pork

1 egg
1 blade of mace, broken
  into small pieces
salt and pepper
12 - 18 walnuts, shelled
¹/₂ cup (125 mL)
  heather honey (or any
  other type)

Wash turkey inside and out with a cloth generously soaked in whiskey. Cover and refrigerate overnight. Place prunes in a glass jar, pour the whiskey and hot tea on top. Cover and keep overnight on kitchen counter to plump up prunes and facilitate removing the stones.

The next day, place in a bowl onion, pork, egg and mace. Stir until well mixed. Salt and pepper. Remove stones from prunes, replacing each with a walnut. Dip each prune in honey (place honey in a bowl of hot water to soften it) and add to stuffing.

Pack this mixture into the turkey, tie the legs and wrap the whole turkey in a double thickness of heavy-duty foil. (In Scotland, they wrap it in a heavy linen soaked in whiskey, however, it is then much more difficult to handle and the results are similar.) Before closing foil, pour the ¹/₄ cup (60 mL) whiskey over the turkey.

Place the roasting pan in a preheated 350°F. (180°C) oven. Roast 1¹/₂ hours, then open top of package. Check on cooking and baste the turkey with the beautifully perfumed juices in the bottom. Pour over any remaining honey. Do not reclose the foil. It may take another 20 to 30 minutes to brown the top and to finish cooking.

Make a plain gravy using a giblet bouillon as liquid, or make a giblet gravy. *Serves 8 to 10.*

Teatime Variations

Aberdeen Baps

These I learned to make at Mrs. Macpherson's School. I have
changed the measurements slightly because of the difference
in our yeast, flour, etc., but this does not affect the taste and
texture of the recipe.

1 envelope active dry yeast	*1 tsp. (5 mL) salt*
1 tsp. (5 mL) sugar	*2 tbsp. (30 mL) bacon fat, lard or margarine*
3 tbsp. (50 mL) tepid water	*1/2 cup (125 mL) hot milk*
4 cups (1 L) all-purpose flour*	*1/2 cup (125 mL) tepid water*

Stir yeast and sugar together in small bowl. Add the 3 tbsp.
(50 mL) of tepid water. Let stand 10 minutes until creamy and
rising.

Meanwhile, place 3 cups (750 mL) of the flour, salt and fat (at
Macpherson's we used lard) in a large bowl and cut in the fat
until mealy. Mix together the milk and 1/2 cup (125 mL) tepid
water. Stir the yeast, add to the liquid and pour into the flour.
Mix to form a soft dough, adding some of the remaining flour if
necessary. Cover and let rise in a warm place until double in
bulk — it takes about 1 hour to rise.

Spread any remaining flour on the table. Punch down the
dough, and turn onto floured table. Knead lightly, then divide
into small squarish or round pieces, shaping them with your
hands. Dip tops of the pieces in flour. Shake and place on a
greased baking sheet. Cover again and let stand until double in
size, about 20 minutes. Bake in a preheated 400°F. (200°C)
oven 15 to 20 minutes, or until light golden brown. Serve hot.
Yield: 12 to 16, depending on size.

---

*I often add 1/4 cup (60 mL) of wheat germ or bran to the flour, which makes it
more like the English type of flour.

Strone Favorite Scones

Another one of Macpherson's recipes, they were rolled to the size of a pancake and cooked on a hot griddle. At first they are a little tricky to make, but after a few you will get the hang of it. If you prefer, they can also be dropped on the hot griddle from a spoon. Serve them with beaten butter, heather honey (or another type) or homemade strawberry jam.

*3 cups (750 mL)
    buttermilk
¹/₂ cup (125 mL) light
    cream
1 tsp. (5 mL) baking
    soda*

*¹/₂ tsp. (2 mL) baking
    powder
2 tbsp. (30 mL) sugar
1 tsp. (5 mL) salt
2 - 4 cups (500 mL -
    1 L) flour*

Place buttermilk and cream in a large bowl. Mix together soda, baking powder, sugar and salt. Add to milk, then add as much flour as you need to make a dough that is just a little thicker than pancake dough. Mix thoroughly.

Heat griddle pan or grease a baking sheet. Sprinkle table generously with flour. Spoon out some of the batter, shape into a pancake with floured hands and pat flour around the edges. Lift from underside with a spatula and quickly place it on a hot griddle. Brown it on first side, then turn and brown other side. (I can make 5 to 6 at a time.) They can also be baked on a baking sheet in a preheated 400°F. (200°C) oven for about 15 minutes, or until golden brown. Serve hot. *Yield: 6 to 8 large scones or 10 to 12 small ones.*

Midlothian Oatcakes

At Macpherson's they were made thin or thick or in 6-inch (15 cm) rounds, and cut into triangles once cooked. Although the recipe was the same, the oatcakes taste different depending on the treatment.

The secret of these super oatcakes is the very large quantity of butter—*only* butter should be used—and the quality of the oatmeal — never use the quick-cooking type; look for old-fashioned oatmeal.

I cook mine in the oven as I find the griddle heat too uneven on an electric stove, and I have equal success. I hope Macpherson never reads this!

1 cup (250 mL) oatmeal	1 tsp. (5 mL) baking
1/2 cup (125 mL) flour	powder
1/2 tsp. (2 mL) salt	1/2 cup (125 mL) butter
1 tsp. (5 mL) sugar	1/3 cup (80 mL) cold
	water

Place oatmeal in a bowl. Add flour, salt, sugar and baking powder. Stir well until thoroughly blended. Cut in the butter until fine, then add the cold water and mix to a stiff dough.

Turn on a board lightly sprinkled with oatmeal. Knead lightly for a few seconds, then roll out until 1/4 in. (0.625 cm) thick. Use a little flour if dough has a tendency to stick, but use as little as possible. Cut into the desired shape. Place on an ungreased baking sheet. Bake in a preheated 350°F. (180°C) oven 20 minutes, or until light brown in color. As they cool they darken a bit. *Yield: 20 to 25.*

Edinburgh Shortbread

I have tasted many a shortbread in Scotland and I have made many types in Canada. My favorite remains the Edinburgh Shortbread. Any three-star chef in Scotland will tell you that the success of a good shortbread depends on unsalted butter of prime quality, and lots of it; the second point is that the cooked shortbread should be pale beige — overcooking them destroys the delicate flavor of the butter.

When I was taught how to make them they were beaten by hand — at least an hour of work. Now I use my electric mixer and have equal results as far as quality is concerned.

2 cups (500 mL) butter, room temperature	*2 cups (500 mL) cornstarch*
2 cups (500 mL) fruit sugar	*1 cup (250 mL) rice flour*
3 cups (750 mL)	

Place the butter in an electric mixer and beat at high speed until almost white and very creamy, about 10 minutes. Add the icing sugar and beat again at high speed for another 5 minutes.

Sift together twice the flour, cornstarch and rice flour. At the lowest speed of your mixer gradually add the flour mixture, scraping the bowl with a spatula and beating just long enough to well incorporate the flour.

Turn onto a pastry board and knead very gently with the tips of the fingers until smooth. Form into a ball. Wrap airtight and refrigerate 12 to 24 hours.

Cut the ball of dough in 4. Roll each one out ¼ in. (0.625 cm) thick. Cut into any shape you wish or simply as neat squares. Place ½ in. (1.25 cm) apart on an unbuttered cookie sheet. Pierce each shortbread with a fork, inserting it deep enough to touch the cookie sheet. This is not easy to do — you can also leave them plain.

Bake in a preheated 350°F. (180°C) oven 18 to 20 minutes, or until barely colored. Cool on a wire rack. *Yield: approximately 24 to 40, depending on their size.*

Athol Brose

I received this recipe a few years ago as a gift from a Vancouver friend. For generations it has been his family's traditional Christmas drink in Scotland and in Canada. Well worth the expense.

¹/₂ cup (125 mL) liquid honey	4 cups (1 L) Scotch whiskey
4 cups (1 L) tepid water	1¹/₂ cups (375 mL)
¹/₂ lb. (250 g) fine Scottish-type oatmeal	Drambuie
	4 cups (1 L) light cream

Thoroughly mix honey, water and oatmeal in a jug. Cover with a cloth and set aside on kitchen counter for 36 hours to allow fermentation.

Carefully skim off into another jar the liquid on top of the oatmeal. Add to it the Scotch and Drambuie. Mix well and let rest for a few hours.

When ready to serve, add cream — it's best at room temperature, but if you want a cold drink use very cold cream or serve over ice cubes. *Serves 18 to 22.*

Ireland

Although I have travelled through most of England, parts of
Scotland and Wales, the only place I ever went to in Ireland was
Shannon Airport where we had to stop for ten hours because of
bad weather. Yet, I am aware of many traditional foods, sayings and ways of the Irish because of a nanny who took care of
us when I was in my preteens. Her name was Mary Feeney; she
spoke part Irish Gaelic, part English and hardly any French,
which caused much confusion amongst us children, but she was
fun and could tell stories in her funny language like no one
else. Mary was more interested in the kitchen than in the
children, but we gladly followed her there because she could
produce "pretty good fare," as she called it, which we always
sampled eagerly. I remember her sandwiches because before
she came to us we had never tasted such a food, and though my
parents would not eat them we thought they were super. She
used to say, "Nothing to it; put a slice of bread or cheese
between two slices of bread." We knew what she meant and we
knew it could never be three slices of bread. As we ate her
sandwiches with gusto she would always say, "Children, there
is luck in sharing."

Another one of her amusing sayings when we would not
listen or argued amongst ourselves, as children will, would be,

"Children, save your breath to cool your porridge," which was, by the way, our daily breakfast.

One of her pleasures was to have cup of strong black tea, and I do mean strong, in front of the fireplace, while she told us some of her favorite stories. She always sat with her back to the fire and when we asked her why she answered, "Remember, children, that in my country, homes are heated only by open fireplaces, so your heart is warm but your behind is cold and mine has never warmed up."

She often argued with my mother because we only served one kind of potatoes at the evening meal, while in Ireland they would always have two kinds—roast and mashed or boiled and riced, etc.

She talked and talked of the super vegetables she used to eat in Ireland which she insisted we did not have in Canada. She referred to one in particular as "sprouting broccoli," and to her the broccoli we had in the autumn was nothing compared to the Irish "sprouting." One day my mother bought some Brussels sprouts and she was in ecstasy, for here were her sprouting broccoli.

What I owe Mary Feeney for, more than anything else, is the little black book of recipes she wrote for me before her return to Ireland. My mother gave it to me when I was fifteen. Because of Mary Feeney I know a "goodly few" (as she used to say) of "true" Irish dishes, and with time I have taught myself to make them almost as well as she did.

I cannot end these remembrances without saying a word about the excellence of the Shannon Airport restaurant. Their specialty is fish and they really know how to cook it. At lunch we had a very generous plate of beautiful Aran Island scallops, rolled in very thin slices of plaice, lightly broiled and flambéed with Irish whiskey and served very simply with a basket of hot thin oatcakes, nothing else. Good Irish tea and beautiful fruits for dessert.

For dinner, we started with paper-thin slices of their world-famous smoked trout and salmon, topped with a few capers. Then, a clear, strong lamb's consommé served with a decanter of very dry sherry. This was followed by roasted Cock of the North, surrounded by prunes wrapped in bacon, and three dishes of potatoes to choose from or to sample all. For "sweet" we chose "Murphy's Dream," which was a dream of finely diced fresh fruits—I remember pears, peaches, orange sections, and there may have been others, most generously laced with their wonder liqueur, "Irish Mist." A large portion of this mixture covered the bottom of very elegant, round, cut-glass bowls (they may have been Waterford glass), a round ball of fresh raspberry sherbet and one of orange sherbet were placed over the fruit and topped with vanilla ice cream, beaten until creamy with *more* Irish Mist. With our black, not Irish, coffee, we each had a small dish of preserved ginger, cut into small squares, which we stirred in the coffee, one at a time. When the ginger was hot, we ate it, then took a sip of coffee. To me this is much more subtle and exciting than Irish coffee. What a joy to write of all this for you; it is like enjoying the meal all over again.

A "Goodly Few" Main Dishes

Mary Feeney's Partridge

In her little book, Mary wrote that the very best partridges in the world were from the Bog of Allen where she was born and "reared," as she put it. She warned me that only "decent" partridge should be eaten — to this day I never quite understood what that meant.

I believe that the early Irish settlers who came to Québec showed the French-Québec women how to make *perdrix aux chou,* an autumn delight somewhat different than Mary F's recipe, but very similar in flavor.

2 medium carrots, thinly sliced	¹/₂ lb. (250 g) pork sausages
2 medium onions, thinly sliced	2 bay leaves
2 tbsp. (30 mL) bacon fat or butter	¹/₂ tsp. (2 mL) thyme
2 plump partridges, cleaned and tied	1 tsp. (5 mL) salt
1 medium compact cabbage	¹/₂ tsp. (2 mL) pepper
¹/₂ cup (125 mL) diced bacon	³/₄ cup (190 mL) consommé
	2 tbsp. (30 mL) butter
	2 tbsp. (30 mL) flour
	³/₄ cup (190 mL) red wine

Heat the bacon fat or butter in a cast-iron frying pan. Brown partridges on all sides over medium heat. Remove from pan. Add carrots and onions to remaining fat in the pan and brown lightly.

Cut cabbage in 4 to 6 wedges; remove most of the hard core. Place in a saucepan with the bacon, pour boiling water on top— enough to cover. Boil, uncovered, for 5 minutes. Drain.

Fry the sausages until light brown in the fat used for carrots and partridges. Place half the cabbage in a casserole, add sausages and bacon on top, set partridges over this and surround with onions and carrots. Add bay leaves, thyme, salt, pepper and consommé. Top with remaining cabbage.

Place a round of buttered brown paper over the casserole, large enough to fall over the edges. Cover. Bake 2 hours in a 300°F. (150°C) oven.

To serve, set partridges and vegetables on a hot platter. Mix together butter and flour and add to juices in the casserole. Pour in red wine (instead of red wine I use ¹/₂ cup (125 mL) Irish whiskey). Stir until creamy. The sauce is usually hot enough to cook the flour; if not, put back in oven for 10 minutes. Stir and pour over the partridges and cabbage. *Serves 6*.

Roasted Cock with Prunes

Although her recipe card referred to this dish as "Roasted Cock," Mary actually used a lovely capon. The recipe is unusual and full of cuisine finesse.

*A 4–6 lb. (2–3 kg)
  roasting chicken
4 tbsp. (60 mL) flour
juice of 1 lemon
¼ cup (60 mL) butter
4 - 6 bacon slices
½ cup (125 mL) Irish
  whiskey
1 garlic clove, crushed
  and unpeeled*

*1 tsp. (5 mL) salt
¼ tsp. (1 mL) pepper
½ tsp. (2 mL) allspice
12 - 16 soft pitted
  prunes
3 tbsp. (50 mL) heavy
  cream*

Cut chicken into individual portions. Rub each piece all over with lemon juice. Sprinkle here and there with flour. Melt butter in a large frying pan, fry bacon, then add the chicken and brown over medium heat.

When all the pieces are browned, pour Irish whiskey over, light a match to them, and move the pan around — the flame will die quickly.

Add crushed clove of garlic, salt, pepper and allspice. Cover pan and simmer over low heat until chicken is tender; it should take about 40 to 50 minutes and will form its own gravy.

While the chicken is cooking, remove stones from prunes, wrap half a slice of bacon around each one, set on a grill and roast until bacon is crisp and brown.

To serve, place chicken on a warm platter. Add cream to gravy in the pan, scrape pan and pour sauce over chicken. Surround with prunes. *Serves 6.*

Corned Beef with Mustard Horseradish Sauce

In a rush for lunch? Do as they do in Ireland—buy your corned beef on the run, warm it up and serve with this hot sauce . . . a luncheon delight.

1 tbsp. (15 mL)
  cornstarch
2 tsp. (10 mL) sugar
1 tsp. (5 mL) dry
  mustard
¹/₂ tsp. (2 mL) salt
1 cup (250 mL) water
1 tbsp. (15 mL) butter

¹/₄ cup (60 mL) cider
  vinegar
¹/₄ cup (60 mL) drained
  prepared horseradish
  or 3 tbsp. (50 mL)
  freshly grated
  horseradish
2 egg yolks, beaten

Mix dry ingredients in the top of a double boiler, add water and simmer over direct medium heat for 5 minutes. Stir with a whisk for the first minute, or until it thickens.

Remove from heat and blend in butter, vinegar and horseradish. Whisk in beaten egg yolks, then stir over hot water until creamy. Let simmer over the water for 10 minutes. *Yield:* 1¹/₃ *cups (330 mL).*

Puffed-Up Cauliflower

"Puffed-up" is the Irish term for soufflé and it usually implies a light mixture with a golden texture. This well-balanced recipe is actually a creamed cauliflower.

1 head of cauliflower
2 tbsp. (30 mL) butter
2 tbsp. (30 mL)
  all-purpose flour
1¹/₂ cups (375 mL) milk
¹/₂ cup (125 mL) cream

¹/₂ cup (125 mL) grated
  medium Cheddar cheese
¹/₂ tsp. (2 mL) dry mustard
1 tsp. (5 mL) salt
¹/₄ tsp. (1 mL) pepper
2 eggs, separated

Clean and divide the cauliflower into flowerets. Cover with boiling water, then boil, uncovered, over high heat for about 10 to 15 minutes, or until tender. Drain well.

Make a white sauce with butter, flour, milk and cream. When it is smooth and creamy, set aside 2 tbsp. (30 mL) of the cheese, and add the rest to the sauce along with dry mustard, salt and pepper. Remove from heat and stir until well blended.

Add the egg yolks to the sauce, one at a time, beating hard at each addition. Beat the egg whites until stiff and fold them gently into the sauce. Place the cauliflower in a shallow baking dish and pour sauce on top. Sprinkle with the remaining cheese and bake 25 to 30 minutes in a preheated 350°F. (180°C) oven. Serve as soon as it is ready. *Serves 6.*

Whiskey Pie

When Mary baked this pie for the "grown ups," we children had little penny-sized tarts. She said they made children "fluffy," whatever that was. My advice is not to make it penny-size, since it is a very tasty and unusual pie.

1 cup (250 mL) milk
2-in. (5 cm) strip lemon
* peel*
½ cup (125 mL) fine
* breadcrumbs*
2 egg yolks
4 tbsp. (60 mL) melted
* butter*
2 tbsp. (30 mL) sugar

3 tbsp. (50 mL) Irish
* whiskey*
pastry to line bottom of
* 8-in. (20 cm) pie plate*
3 tbsp. (50 mL) black
* currant jam*
3 egg whites
3 tbsp. (50 mL) sugar

Heat the milk with lemon peel and simmer 5 minutes. Remove peel and pour hot milk over breadcrumbs.

Beat the egg yolks until light colored and add to breadcrumbs. Mix, then add melted butter, sugar and whiskey. Stir until well mixed.

Line pie plate with pastry. Spread black currant jam in the bottom and pour crumb mixture on top. Bake in a preheated 350°F. (180°C) oven 35 to 40 minutes, or until golden brown.

Beat egg whites, add 1 tbsp. (15 mL) of the sugar, beat 2 minutes, add the remaining 2 tbsp. (30 mL) of sugar and beat until it reaches the stiff meringue texture. Heap attractively on cooked pie. Return to oven until meringue is browned. Serve cold. *Serves 6.*

Irish Sweet Orange

Although this is a very simple dessert, it's just right after a rich meal. Serve well chilled.

2 oranges, peeled
3 tbsp. (50 mL) orange
* marmalade*

2-4 tbsp. (30-60 mL)
* Irish whiskey*

Cut oranges crosswise into thin slices and set on a serving dish.

Heat marmalade over very low heat, then add whiskey. Stir well and pour over oranges. Refrigerate covered for 6 to 8 hours. *Serves 3.*

Scandinavia

No longer is our knowledge of Scandinavian food confined to Norwegian sardines and Danish bacon or butter. Each part of Scandinavia has its own identity. Travelling through Denmark and Norway I quickly realized the vast differences between each.

I have never been to Finland although it was, for many years, the country I most wanted to see. I just loved their "tailored" taste, their designs, their understanding of wool and their sense of quality, and I was lucky enough to have as a very good friend an elegant, intelligent Finnish woman, Marta. In her own amusing way with words she often says, "I canna cook," which is not true at all. I agree she cooks only when she really feels like it (a few women here and there can do that), but when she does, all of it is delectable and beautifully presented —presentation being a very important part of Finnish cuisine. She has an old Finnish cookbook full of traditional recipes and in summertime we sit together and she translates them for me. Then I adjust and test them. I have found real treasures, such as Spinach Pancakes, Liver Pudding and the way to smoke a leg of mutton. I say a heartfelt "thanks" to my friend Marta for having brought Finland's food and customs to my door, and to Lempi, who worked with me.

The outstanding feature in Scandinavian cooking is, according to most, the *smörgasbord*. In Denmark, it is a great showpiece, as well as a festive pleasure, but it is only a small part of good Scandinavian cooking. As a tourist you encounter the "cold table" almost everywhere, often as a first course. For my part I find this a hindrance to the enjoyment of the main dish, so I have often bypassed the famous *smörgasbord*.

I prefer the cold table of Sweden and Norway — perfect butter, unusual, thinly sliced cheese, herring in a light mushroom or tomato sauce and excellent bread. The ever-present *aquavit* or *akvavit* is served ice cold, but beware—all types are treacherous. The sweetest and smoothest I've ever tasted was in Norway; it was a beautiful golden color, contrary to the usual white, and was served in a block of ice.

In general, I would say that the Norwegians, who are fishermen and sailors, are hard to surpass in their treatment of fish and game dishes. Denmark is nearest to the rest of Europe and therefore more influenced by it. For example, most Danish dishes are served with a sauce, much like the French. However, the Danes use a great deal of whipped cream and fresh grated horseradish, while the French prefer thick rich cream, not whipped, and add tang to their sauces with brandy and such.

The Scandinavian Flavor

Herring: Found all over Scandinavia, fresh, salted, pickled and raw. Fresh herring are at their best when caught from the very cold waters of Norway and Finland during spring.

Salmon: Smoked, it is known as *gravlax*. In Denmark, fresh salmon steak was smoked right at our table in a special smoker that resembled an elegant black box. Since I own one, I can repeat that gourmet experience with our fine Canadian salmon.

Pork: The favorite meat of Scandinavia, Danish ham and bacon being proof of the quality.

Potato: A Scandinavian specialty. Different types are used for fried, mashed or boiled. Steamed or boiled new potatoes are rolled in minced parsley or fresh dill and served with perfect unsalted butter.

Other Vegetables: Cabbage is the most popular and is prepared in unusual ways. Celeriac, or celery root, and Jerusalem artichokes are used often, both of which are not common in North America, yet we have the weather and soil to grow them.

Seasonings: Dill, mostly fresh, but also dried, ground ginger, fresh chives, allspice, capers and mustards are the basic flavorings.

Cloudberries: A wild fruit resembling our strawberries, but more tasty and delicate in flavor. We often find them in America as a preserve. In Finland they make a liqueur from them, but it is difficult to buy here.
Cloudberries can be found in northern Québec, but they don't travel well. They have a high Vitamin C content, so they keep for months without sugar or any other preserving agent.

Lingonberries: Another wild fruit with lots of Vitamin C, they are like our cranberries, but smaller and more delicate in flavor. In North America, they can be purchased fresh in specialty shops, or in many other shops as jam.

Crispbread: There are many types all over Scandinavia. My preference goes to the dry round Finnish or Swedish type, with a hole in the middle, with or without caraway seeds. Non-fattening, crunchy and tasty, excellent with cheese.

Danish Food: Cold Table to Brandy Coffee

Smørboller Soup

Smørboller means a small dumpling cooked in a beef or chicken broth. All over Europe we find small dumplings in soup but the best I ever tasted were the Danish ones. Maybe it was the romantic surroundings of the Rose Garden Restaurant with its masses of roses and beautiful green plants, all of which gave us the feeling of sitting in a garden. In each plate there was a rose petal floating around the tiny *smørboller*. It gave me a happy feeling to think it might have fallen from a rose onto my plate.

*1 cup (250 mL) butter,
room temperature
3 cups (750 mL)
all-purpose flour
1 tsp. (5 mL) salt
2 tbsp. (30 mL) ice
water*

*a small bowl of fresh
dill, chopped
a small bowl of fresh
chives, chopped
4–6 cups (1 L–1.5 L)
consommé*

Cream butter until very light and fluffy. Sift 1 cup (250 mL) of the flour with the salt. Add to the butter gradually, while stirring, then add the second cup (250 mL) of flour in the same manner, then add the ice water and just enough flour to be able to shape the dough into small balls the size of a whole walnut.

Bring consommé to the boil, roll each ball in flour and place them one by one in the boiling consommé. When all have been added, cover and simmer over low heat for 10 to 12 minutes. Serve with the bowls of dill and chives. *Serves 4 to 6.*

Pink Sauerkraut Salad

The pink, of course, is from the beet. If you like sauerkraut you will enjoy this salad. I first ate it at Oskar Davidson's in Copenhagen. I am told that Per Davidson's daughter, Ida, who owns the Scandia Restaurant in Hollywood, considers this salad one of her most successful.

4 medium potatoes
1 large beet, boiled
³/4 cup (190 mL)
 sauerkraut
1 medium-sized dill
 pickle, diced
1 small onion, minced

4 tbsp. (60 mL)
 vegetable oil
2 tbsp. (30 mL) cider or
 wine vinegar
1 tsp. (5 mL) sugar
salt and pepper
¹/4 cup (60 mL) fresh
 dill or chives, minced

Steam potatoes until tender, then cool and peel. Peel and dice
the beet. Stir together in a bowl the vegetables, oil, vinegar,
sugar, salt and pepper. Add the tepid diced potatoes, beet, dill
pickle and onion. Stir gently until the mixture is well coated
with the dressing. Place in a mound in a clean bowl. Top with
dill or chives. Do not refrigerate. It can stand 2 to 3 hours before
it is served. *Serves 4.*

Oskar Davidson's Pickled Beets

Davidson's of Copenhagen, famous around the world for
Danish *smörrebröd*, is a most impressive place for lunch. What
interested me most was the large variety of pickles — the
pickled beets were unusual and very good, served in a long,
narrow white porcelain platter on a thick bed of fresh dill.

2 cups (500 mL) cider
 vinegar
1 cup (250 mL) water
1 tsp. (5 mL) whole
 allspice
¹/2 cup (125 mL) beet
 juice*

1 cup (250 mL) sugar
¹/2 tsp. (2 mL) salt
6 cups (1.5 L) cooked
 beets, diced
2 large red or yellow
 onions, sliced

Boil together 4 minutes vinegar, water, beet juice, whole
allspice, sugar and salt. Add diced cooked beets and sliced
onions. Lower the heat and simmer 8 minutes. Remove from
heat and pour into sterilized jars. Refrigerate.

*Use beet juice from canned beets or from any type of pickled beets. If neither
is available replace by an equal quantity of water. The beet juice gives a
deeper red color to the finished product.

Cold Table Vegetable Salad

Wherever I went in Denmark, I saw unusual and very tasty combinations of vegetable salads. In Canada we rarely use raw or cooked beets in a salad, yet they give a rosy tone to the mixture and are attractive set in a ring of watercress or lettuce leaves or generously sprinkled with finely minced parsley. Celery root (also known as celeriac or celery knob) is available in late autumn and winter. It looks like a white turnip with a rugged surface and has a mild flavor of celery. Celeriac can be peeled, shredded and eaten raw.

1 large or 2 small celeriac, peeled and diced	*juice and grated rind of ¹/₂ orange*
2 cooked beets	*¹/₄ cup (60 mL) mayonnaise*
2 apples, peeled and diced	*salt and pepper*

As soon as the celeriac is peeled and diced, pour boiling water on top. Boil 5 minutes, drain and rinse under cold running water.

Peel and dice beets. Peel and dice apples and place in orange juice immediately. There should be equal quantities of each vegetable.

Gently stir everything together with the grated orange rind, which has been mixed with the mayonnaise. Salt and pepper to taste. (I like to use a rubber spatula to blend the salad.) Line a glass bowl with crisp green lettuce leaves and pile the salad in the middle. In the summertime I sprinkle the top with fresh minced chives. Cover and refrigerate until ready to serve. *Serves 6.*

Fruited Pork Tenderloin

A beautiful dish, prepared in such a manner that one tenderloin will give four good portions with a delicious sauce. At the
Hotel d'Angleterre, where I first tasted it, it was served with
small golden steamed potatoes, rolled in lots of fresh parsley —
it needed no more than that.

1 pork tenderloin	*3 tbsp. (50 mL) butter*
1 tsp. (5 mL) salt	*3 tbsp. (50 mL) sour*
¹/₂ tsp. (2 mL) pepper	*cream*
¹/₂ tsp. (2 mL) savory or	*3 tbsp. (50 mL) heavy*
sage	*cream*
8–10 prunes	*2 tbsp. (30 mL) red or*
1 cup (250 mL) coffee	*white wine*
2 apples, peeled, cored,	
and thinly sliced	

Split tenderloin in 2 lengthwise, place each half between wax
paper and pound it as thin as possible. (This is not difficult
to do since it is a very tender cut of meat.)

Mix salt, pepper, savory or sage. Rub equal amounts on each
pounded tenderloin. Simmer prunes in coffee for 10 minutes.
Let cool, then remove pits. Spread each tenderloin equally with
slices of apples and pitted prunes which have been cut in half.
Roll up each tenderloin as compactly as you can and tie with 3
to 5 strings, a few inches apart. (Before browning each roll it
can be cut into 2 or 3 pieces.)

Melt butter in a large cast-iron frying pan. Carefully brown
each roll, turning it gently. Add cream, sour cream and wine.
Stir and baste each roll. Reduce heat to very low and cover.
Simmer 25 to 30 minutes.

Remove rolls to a hot platter. Stir sauce thoroughly, then
simmer over low heat until reduced by half and thickened. Stir
well, put rolls back in sauce and baste a few times. Cover and
let stand without additional cooking until ready to serve. If the
meat and sauce have cooled, reheat over very low heat just
enough to warm, but do not let it boil. *Serves 4 to 6*.

Danish Ham Casserole

Ham in Denmark is superb. I will never forget my Danish breakfast with freshly baked black or white bread, unsalted butter beaten like whipped cream, a platterful of thinly sliced Danish ham, paper-thin slices of Danish Samsø or Holsterner cheese and big jars of currant jelly or strawberry jam.

The following casserole, with its brandy tomato sauce, should be made with raw ham. It is served surrounded by small whole mushrooms that have been quickly fried in butter.

2 cups (500 mL)	*2 tbsp. (30 mL) celery*
macaroni	*leaves, chopped fine*
1 bay leaf	*1 cup (250 mL) grated*
2 tbsp. (30 mL) butter	*Swiss-type cheese*
1 cup (250 mL) diced	*4 eggs, lightly beaten*
uncooked ham	*2 cups (500 mL) milk*
6 green onions, diced	*1 tsp. (5 mL) salt*
(use green parts also)	*¹/₂ tsp. (2 mL) pepper*

Cook the macaroni with the bay leaf in salted boiling water until barely soft. Drain and rinse under cold running water. Drain again in colander.

Melt butter in frying pan, add the ham and stir over medium heat 3 to 4 minutes. Add the green onions and celery leaves. Stir together for 1 minute. Pour in a bowl, add the cheese and drained macaroni. Stir gently to mix. Pour into a buttered loaf pan. Stir together eggs, milk, salt and pepper. Pour over the macaroni. Bake, uncovered, in a preheated 350°F. (180°C) oven 40 to 45 minutes, or until custard is set and top is browned. Serve with Brandy Tomato Sauce (recipe follows). *Serves 6.*

Brandy Tomato Sauce:

3 tbsp. (50 mL) butter	*1 garlic clove, unpeeled*
3 tbsp. (50 mL) chili	*and cut in half*
sauce or ketchup	*1 tbsp. (15 mL) port or*
2 tbsp. (30 mL) brandy	*Madeira wine*

Melt butter, then add chili sauce or ketchup, brandy and garlic. Simmer 5 minutes, then remove garlic. Add port or Madeira. Pour into sauceboat.

Spiced Dripping

The first time I encountered this was on the cold table at Davidson's. When they explained to me how it was made, I doubted I would enjoy it, but soon changed my mind. It is used on bread, instead of butter, and topped with pâté or smoked meat.

¹/₂ *lb. (250 g) pure lard*	*1 bay leaf*
6 bacon slices	¹/₂ *tsp. (2 mL) thyme*
1 medium onion, sliced	*10 peppercorns*

Place lard, bacon and onion in a heavy metal saucepan. Stir over medium heat until fat is melted. Cook slowly until onion starts to brown here and there, then add remaining ingredients and simmer over low heat for 15 minutes. Let it cool slightly, then strain into an earthenware jar. Cover and refrigerate.

Potkäse

Another cold table favorite. What is interesting is the fact that it is made with any odds and ends of cheese — the more it ages, the better it is. Serve it with thinly sliced black bread, olives and pickles.

Grate finely any amount and mixture of dry cheese and moisten with enough dry port wine to make it soft. Cover and let it ripen 24 hours, at room temperature. Stir, add a bit of rum, salt and pepper to taste and a few dill seeds. Stir well. Pack into a crockery jar and pour just a little port on top. Cover and refrigerate. Take out of the refrigerator an hour or so before serving.

Blackbread

This bread is called *surbrød* in Denmark. I ate it and loved it everywhere, finding many differences in flavor. I was told this had to do with the type of beer and rye flour used. It is easy to make and keeps well. Try it generously spread with unsalted butter and topped with quality cold cuts or a slice of ham.

1 envelope active dry yeast	*3¹/₂ cups (875 mL) rye flour*
1 cup (250 mL) lukewarm water	*1 cup (250 mL) all-purpose flour*
¹/₂ tsp. (2 mL) sugar	*1 tsp. (5 mL) salt*
1 cup (250 mL) Danish beer, room temperature	*1 tbsp. (15 mL) dill seeds*
	¹/₄ tsp. (1 mL) caraway seeds

Mix yeast, water and sugar. Let stand 10 minutes or until foamy. Stir well, pour into a large bowl, add the beer and 2 cups (500 mL) of the rye flour. Stir until thoroughly mixed. Cover tightly with transparent wrap and leave in a warm spot in the kitchen for 8 to 12 hours. This is called a sponge — it will first rise and then fall, which is what gives this bread its sour taste.

When ready to mix, stir sponge, add remaining rye flour, half the all-purpose flour, salt, dill and caraway seeds. Work together until everything is well blended, adding more all-purpose flour if the dough is too sticky. An electric mixer with a dough hook can be used. Cover and let rise in a warm place about 1 hour, or until double in bulk. Sprinkle table with flour, punch dough down, turn onto table and knead until smooth—2 to 5 minutes are usually sufficient.

Divide the dough in half. Shape each half and place in two 9 × 5 in. (22.5 × 12.5 cm) buttered loaf pans. Cover with a towel. Let rise again in a warm place until double in bulk.

Preheat oven to 375°F.(190°C) and bake loaves until brown and crusty, about 50 to 60 minutes. Unmold and cool on a cake rack. Keep wrapped in linen cloth, as they do in Denmark. *Yield: 2 loaves.*

Rose Geranium Cupcakes

Mr. Wernberg, head *pâtissier* at the Hotel d'Angleterre in Copenhagen, is the best there is in Scandinavia. I met him when I visited the Danish Catering Trade School. He offered me these cupcakes with a superb brandied coffee and gave me the recipe for both.

For many years I have grown rose geranium in my garden in the summertime and in a big pot in the house in wintertime. My maternal grandmother taught me how to use them in cooking so it was with surprise and delight that I tasted Mr. Wernberg's cupcakes.

¹/₄ *cup (60 mL) soft* *butter*	²/₃ *cup (160 mL)* *all-purpose flour*
¹/₂ *cup (125 mL) fine* *granulated sugar*	¹/₄ *tsp. (1 mL) salt*
1 *tsp. (5 mL) fresh* *lemon juice*	¹/₈ *tsp. (0.5 mL) baking* *soda*
2 *egg yolks*	2 *egg whites*
	fresh rose geranium *leaves*

Cream together butter and sugar. Add lemon juice and beat with an electric mixer for 5 minutes.

Beat egg yolks until thick and pale yellow, then add to butter mixture and beat at medium speed 2 to 4 minutes. (The beating is important because there is no liquid except lemon juice in these cupcakes.)

Sift together flour, salt and baking soda. Add by spoonfuls to the creamed mixture, beating throughly after each addition.

Beat the egg whites until stiff, then fold gently into the batter.

Butter some 2-in. (5 cm) cupcake molds. Sprinkle the insides with a bit of sugar. Place a rose geranium leaf in each. Spoon batter gently on top — do not fill more than ²/₃ full.

Bake in a preheated 350°F. (180°C) oven 18 to 20 minutes, or until cakes shrink slightly in their molds. Cool on cake rack for 5 minutes. Unmold carefully. Serve leaf side up. (The leaf browns here and there and develops a crispy texture, while generously giving all its beautiful perfume to the cakes.) *Yield: 12 to 14 cupcakes.*

Danish Almond Paste Shortbread

The head chef of Scandinavian Airlines gave me this delicious recipe on a recent trip to Denmark. Quite different from the Scottish type of shortbread; the touch of almond paste is superb.

1 lb. (500 g) unsalted
butter, room
temperature
1³/₄ cups (450 mL) fine
granulated sugar
2 eggs, beaten
4 cups (1 L) all-purpose
flour

¹/₄ tsp. (1 mL) baking
soda
¹/₂ tsp. (2 mL) salt
1 cup (250 mL) finely
chopped almonds
1 tsp. (5 mL) almond
extract
³/₄ cup (190 mL)
almond paste

Cream butter and sugar to the consistency of whipped cream. Add eggs and beat again for a few minutes. Sift flour with soda and salt, gradually add to the creamed mixture, then mix until smooth (easy to do with an electric mixer).

Add chopped almonds, almond extract and paste and blend well. Line a 15 × 10 in. (37.5 × 25 cm) pan with waxed paper. Pat mixture into pan, cover with waxed paper and chill overnight.

The next day, invert contents onto a board and cut dough into strips 2¹/₂ × ¹/₂ in. (6.25 × 1.25 cm). Place on an ungreased baking sheet and bake in 375°F. (190°C) oven 20 to 30 minutes, or until golden. Remove from baking sheet and let cool on wire racks. *Yield: 3 to 4 dozen.*

Liqueur Butter Cookies

These delicious intriguing cookies are golden in color and rich in flavor.

²/₃ cup (160 mL) butter
¹/₃ cup (80 mL) fine
granulated sugar
2 tbsp. (30 mL) Herring
liqueur or brandy
¹/₄ tsp. (1 mL) salt

1¹/₂ cups (375 mL)
all-purpose flour
2 tbsp. (30 mL) sugar
1 tsp. (5 mL) freshly
grated nutmeg

Cream butter until soft and fluffy, then mix in the ⅓ cup (80 mL) sugar, 1 tsp. (5 mL) at a time. Stir in brandy.

Mix salt with flour and add gradually to butter mixture, stirring well after each addition. When well blended, shape into a round ball, cover and refrigerate 30 minutes.

Roll dough out until thin and cut into 1-in. (2.5 cm) strips. Combine the 2 tbsp. (30 mL) of sugar with nutmeg and sprinkle over each cookie. Place on a lightly greased cookie sheet and bake in a 400°F. (200°C) oven 8 to 10 minutes, or until light brown. *Yield: about 36 cookies*.

Copenhagen Brandy Coffee

I was surprised to find so many eggs in Chef Wernberg's superb recipe. It is served cold but *without ice*, and should be refrigerated three to four hours. Try it at your next summer dinner on the terrace.

> 6 eggs
> ½ cup (125 mL) sugar
> 4 cups strong black
>   coffee*
>
> 1 cup (250 mL) fine
>   brandy

Beat eggs with a whisk or electric mixer until a pale lemon color and fluffy. Add sugar, a spoonful at a time, while beating, until mixture is thick and pale beige. The more you beat, the lighter it gets. Stir in slowly the cooled black coffee (like adding oil in a mayonnaise), then do the same with the brandy. Pour into an elegant cut-glass jug. Cover and refrigerate 1 to 4 hours. *Serves 8*.

*Chef Wernberg used freshly ground black Arabian.

Swedish Food: Yellow Pea Soup to Swedish Mumms

The "Steak and Lobster" seen on so many menus across Sweden was really the inspiration and gastronomic pleasure of a popular king of Sweden, Oscar II, and brought to America by the famous "Oscar of the Waldorf," whose real name was Oscar Tschirky. Veal "médaillons," or filets, are pounded and quickly browned in unsalted butter, topped with steamed lobster and served with Sauce Charron, a hollandaise flavored with tarragon, to which is added half its quantity of *tomates concassées.* A superb dish. A steak can be served in the same manner.

When I was four years old my father gave me the great cookbook by Oscar of the Waldorf, with a picture of Oscar which my father had pasted on the first page. I never knew where he got the picture from. Today I find this amusing, as father may have had a premonition of what my life's association with food would be. One has to admit that it was, to say the least, a funny birthday gift to give a four-year-old.

Oscar created the great reputation of the Waldorf in New York in the early 1900s. When he wrote his book in 1908, he was already recognized as outstanding, although barely in his thirties.

The first chapter is entitled "Seasons," with eight pages describing the best seasons for all foods. It is an education in itself to read these pages as they make us realize how little choice we have today in what we think of as our land of plenty. They also emphasize how important it is to serve food at the peak of its quality. Ironically enough, that is what the great French chefs of today are doing — going to the market themselves and choosing only the freshly grown and gathered, which proves once more that nothing is new under our sun. In my long years of life, I have seen so many things from yesteryears being hailed as the discovery of the moment.

Yellow Pea Soup

This soup could surprise many Canadians, especially if they are from Québec. It is prepared with the same type of peas we use, called *äkeröter* in Sweden. This soup is served with *plätter* pancakes once a week during the winter in most Swedish families.

1 lb. (500 g) dried yellow peas	*2 onions, sliced*
	2 leeks, sliced
6 cups (1.5 L) cold water	*¹/₂ tsp. (2 mL) marjoram*
1 lb. (500 g) boned shoulder of pork	*1 tsp. (5 mL) dry ginger*
	a jar of Scandinavian
3 tbsp. (50 mL) coarse salt	*mustard*

Clean the peas and place in a bowl. Cover with cold water and soak overnight.

Spread coarse salt in a platter. Roll the meat in it until completely covered with salt. Wrap in cotton or cheesecloth and refrigerate overnight.

The next day, drain the water from the peas, measure and add enough water to make up the 6 cups (1.5 L). Bring to boil, then add the soaked peas. Rinse the meat quickly and add to the soup. Add the remaining ingredients except the mustard. Bring quickly to a rolling boil. Remove pea shells floating on top, if any, with a perforated spoon. Cover and simmer over low heat until peas and meat are tender.

Remove pork to a hot plate and cut into slices. Grate some lemon rind and sprinkle over the meat. Serve with the soup and mustard. *Serves 8.*

Swedish Kalops

An old-fashioned way of stewing that is easy and tasty. I remember my grandmother cooking a stew similar to this. Serve with boiled potatoes, pickled beets and cranberries (in Sweden they use lingonberries).

2–3 lb. (1–1.5 kg) stewing beef, in one piece	2 large onions, sliced
	15–20 peppercorns
2 tbsp. (30 mL) flour	2 bay leaves
1 tsp. (5 mL) salt	4 whole allspice
1/2 tsp. (2 mL) pepper	1 cup (250 mL) beer or red wine
2 tbsp. (30 mL) bacon fat or vegetable oil	1/2 cup (125 mL) water

Cut the meat into thick slices. Pound with a meat mallet—just enough to break the fibers of the meat, but do not make it paper-thin like a scallop.

Mix flour, salt and pepper together on a piece of wax paper. Roll the meat in it. Melt the bacon fat in a heavy metal pan with a good cover. Brown each piece of meat on both sides, then set aside. Add the onions and stir over high heat until brown here and there.

Wrap the peppercorns, bay leaves and allspice in a square of cheesecloth. Add to onions. Stir, add beer or red wine and water and bring to a full rolling boil. Place the meat in the liquid, lower the heat, cover and simmer slowly until meat is tender when tested with a fork and the liquid is reduced and a bit creamy. *Serves 6*.

Mash and Onions

Although I have never seen this dish anywhere else, in Sweden it is considered an everyday type of family fare.

4 medium onions, peeled and sliced	1/2 lb. (250 g) each ground pork and veal
2 tbsp. (30 mL) bacon fat or margarine	1 tsp. (5 mL) salt
	1/2 tsp. (2 mL) pepper
1/4 cup (60 mL) fine dry breadcrumbs	1 tsp. (5 mL) sage or savory
6 tbsp. (90 mL) each cream and water	1/3 cup (80 mL) consommé of your choice

Melt the fat, add the onions and fry over medium heat until golden brown.

Place breadcrumbs, cream and water, ground pork and veal in a bowl. Mix and blend thoroughly, add salt, pepper, sage or savory. Stir again until well mixed.

Place half the fried onions in a casserole dish, then a layer of the ground meat mixture and spread the rest of the onions on top of the meat. Pour consommé over all. Pierce holes all over with a fork to permit the consommé to seep through the meat and onions. Bake in a preheated oven at 375°F. (190°C) about 35 to 40 minutes. Serve with mashed potatoes. When cold it will slice like a meatloaf. *Serves 4.*

Swedish Eggs over Eggs

Just as I always enjoy a dessert of fruits over fruits, I find that eggs over eggs are an equal epicurean pleasure, and it seems the Swedes think as I do. The sauce here is light and most pleasant.

6 hard-boiled eggs	1/4 cup (60 mL) parsley
1/4 cup (60 mL) butter	or fresh dill, minced
1 large onion, thinly	1 tsp. (5 mL) salt
sliced	1/4 tsp. (1 mL) pepper
1/4 tsp. (1 mL) sugar	1/2 cup (125 mL) light
2 tbsp. (30 mL) fine dry	cream
breadcrumbs	

Quarter 4 of the eggs and place in a casserole. Chop the remaining 2 eggs finely and reserve for the sauce. Melt butter in a frying pan, add onion and cook until soft and light golden in color. Stir in breadcrumbs and the reserved chopped eggs, mix together and stir in the parsley or dill, salt and pepper.

Remove from heat and add cream. Stir until well blended and pour over the eggs in the casserole. To warm up (if necessary), place in a 400°F. (200°C) oven for 5 minutes. *Serves 4.*

Swedish "Plätter Pan" Pancakes

The *plätter* pan is a large shallow frying pan with 2½-inch (6.25 cm) depressions that let you cook six pancakes at once. The Swedes use it to cook this dish, and it is available here in many kitchenware shops. These attractive pancakes are served as entrées or as dessert at teatime.

3 egg yolks	*½ cup (125 mL)*
2 tbsp. (30 mL) sugar	* all-purpose flour*
⅛ tsp. (0.5 mL) salt	*1 cup (250 mL) milk*
3 tbsp. (50 mL) melted	*¾ cup (190 mL) light cream*
* butter*	*3 egg whites*

Beat egg yolks with sugar, salt and melted butter until light and well mixed. Add flour alternately with milk and light cream, beating well at each addition (if possible, use a wire whisk). Cover and refrigerate 1 hour.

Beat egg whites until stiff and fold into chilled batter when ready to cook (this is a thin batter). Melt a little butter in each depression if you use a *plätter pan* or cook them in a hot pan as you would ordinary pancakes. Sprinkle with sugar and serve with cranberries or lingonberries. *Yield: 24 small pancakes.*

Tomates Concassées

Despite its name, this sauce isn't French, but a specialty of Sweden. Use it on fresh trout, salmon or rice or to garnish an omelet. Add to a white sauce or mayonnaise, etc.

6–8 tomatoes	*1 tbsp. (15 mL) finely*
1 small onion, finely	* chopped parsley*
* chopped*	*¼ tsp. (1 mL) each*
2 tbsp. (30 mL) salad	* tarragon and fresh*
* oil*	* dill or dill seeds*
1 garlic clove, crushed	*½ tsp. (2 mL) sugar or honey*

Pour boiling water over the tomatoes in a bowl, let stand 3 minutes, peel and cut in half. Discard juice and seeds and chop tomatoes coarsely.

Fry onion in oil until golden brown here and there. Mix in the tomatoes and remaining ingredients. Cover and simmer over low heat 20 to 25 minutes (don't boil or overcook — it's the slow simmering that's important). Season to taste. *Yield: 2 cups (500 mL).*

Buckwheat Bread

The Swedes like to serve this with butter, thin slices of cheese
— Esrom type — and cold beer.

1 envelope active dry yeast	1 cup (250 mL) hot water
1 cup (250 mL) hot water	1 tsp. (5 mL) anise or caraway seeds
1 tsp. (5 mL) sugar	1/2 tsp. (2 mL) dill seeds
1 1/2 cups (375 mL) crushed buckwheat groats*	3 cups (750 mL) whole-wheat flour
	2 cups (500 mL) all-purpose flour

Stir together yeast, hot water and sugar. Let stand 10 minutes,
or until foamy.

Place in a bowl buckwheat groats that have been either
crushed in a mortar or passed in a food processor for 30 to 50
seconds. Pour hot water on top and stir well. Add anise or
caraway and dill seeds. Stir in half the whole-wheat flour, mix
well, then add the remaining whole-wheat flour. Add 1 cup
(250 mL) of the all-purpose flour. Mix well.

Sprinkle the working board with flour, turn dough on it and
knead vigorously for 5 minutes, or until dough is smooth and
does not stick — sprinkle more flour on board if necessary.

Place dough in a bowl, cover with a cloth and let rise in a
warm place until double in bulk, about 1 hour.

Punch down the dough, divide in half, cover with a cloth and
let it stand 10 minutes. Shape each piece into 1 round loaf or 2
small loaves. Place the round loaf on a greased baking sheet or
the small loaves in two 8 × 4 in. (20 × 10 cm) greased loaf
pans. Cover and let rise until double in bulk.

Bake in a preheated 375°F. (190°C) oven 40 to 45 minutes, or
until crusty and pale gold. Remove from pan only when completely cooled, placing pans on a cooling rack. Keep wrapped in
a cloth. *Yield: 1 round loaf or 2 small loaves.*

*Buckwheat groats are readily available even in chain stores, under the
name *kasha*.

Blueberry Sweet Bread

It's quite unique to find this type of sweet bread made with blueberries, yet my Finnish friend Marta told me that a similar type is made in Finland, using lingonberries or cloudberries instead of blueberries.

I love it warm with blueberry sauce or ice cream melting on top.

1 envelope active dry yeast
1 cup (250 mL) lukewarm milk
1 tsp. (5 mL) sugar
3 tbsp. (50 mL) melted butter
1/2 tsp. (2 mL) salt
1 tsp. (5 mL) ground cardamom

1/2 tsp. (2 mL) ground ginger
2 cups (500 mL) rye flour, sifted twice
2 cups (500 mL) all-purpose flour
4 cups (1 L) fresh blueberries
1 cup (250 mL) sugar

Stir together yeast, warm milk and the 1 tsp. (5 mL) of sugar. Let stand 10 minutes. Stir well and add melted butter, salt, cardamom and ginger. Mix well and add the rye flour. Beat until creamy. Add 1 cup (250 mL) of the all-purpose flour. Mix until you have a soft dough. Turn onto a floured board, knead until smooth, adding more all-purpose flour as needed.

Place in a well-buttered bowl, cover with a towel and let rise until double in bulk, about 1 hour.

Punch down and knead a good 7 to 8 minutes, sprinkling with a bit of flour if dough tends to be sticky.

Butter a 9 × 13 × 2 in. (22.5 × 32.5 × 5 cm) pan. Roll dough to fit the pan. Pull dough all around the pan to make a sort of dish for the blueberries. Pour the berries on top of the dough, spreading them out evenly. Cover and let rise 40 to 45 minutes.

Sprinkle the berries with the 1 cup (250 mL) of sugar. Bake in a preheated 375°F. (190°C) oven 30 to 40 minutes, or until the crust around the pan is a nice golden color. Place pan on a cooling rack. Cut into squares to serve. *Serves 8 to 10.*

Oscar Strawberry Pudding

Strawberry jam covered with fresh strawberries and topped with a light custard—this is a pie without a crust. Very Oscar!

1 cup (250 mL)	*3 eggs*
strawberry jam	*¹/₂ cup (125 mL) sugar*
2 cups (500 mL) French	*2 cups (500 mL) warm*
bread, toasted,	*light cream*
buttered, diced	*¹/₄ tsp. (1 mL) freshly*
2 cups (500 mL) fresh	*grated nutmeg*
whole strawberries	

Butter an elegant 9-in. (22.5 cm) pie plate. Spread bottom with strawberry jam. Top with the French bread. Cover with fresh berries.

Beat eggs, add sugar and beat until light, then add warm cream. Mix thoroughly. Pour over fruit. Bake 30 minutes in a preheated 350°F. (180°C) oven. Cool and serve. *Serves 6.*

Oscar Oranges over Bananas

This was created by Oscar when every one in the U.S.A. was singing "Chiquita Banana." He was willing to help the industry as long as it could be done with flair!

4–6 bananas, peeled	*3 tbsp. (50 mL) fine*
and sliced	*granulated sugar*
grated rind of 1 orange	*juice of 1 orange*
	¹/₄ cup (60 mL) rum

Place bananas in a glass dish. Rub grated orange rind into sugar. Sprinkle over bananas and stir together gently. Mix orange juice and rum. Pour over bananas. Cover and let stand 3 hours before serving, either at room temperature or chilled.

Oscar Champagne Peaches

At the Waldorf this was prepared at our table, and in the thirties was considered sheer elegance. I remember how impressed I was as a sixteen-year-old when the bubbly champagne was poured over the peaches.

2 cups (500 mL) diced watermelon	*¹/₃ cup (80 mL) fine granulated sugar*
2 cups (500 mL) diced cantaloupe	*¹/₄ cup (60 mL) brandy or orange liqueur*
4–5 peaches, peeled and mashed	*1–2 cups (250-500 mL) chilled champagne*

Mix together watermelon and cantaloupe. Add sugar and brandy or orange liqueur to the mashed peaches. Spread over diced melons. Cover and refrigerate.

When ready to serve, pour the chilled champagne over the fruits. Do not mix; simply serve. *Serves 6.*

Swedish Mumms

My friend Marta taught me how to make this traditional Swedish beer punch, and punch it has!

1 pint (500 mL) porter (English type)	*1 pint (500 mL) soda water or mineral water*
1 pint (500 mL) ale	*¹/₂ cup (125 mL) dry gin or dry Madeira*

Refrigerate all ingredients until just before serving, then pour them into a serving container — use a tall stoneware jug or a wooden container if you wish to be authentic — and stir. *Yield: 1¹/₄ quarts (1.16 L).*

Norwegian Food: Green Suppe to Vanilla Boller

Green Suppe

It was freezing cold the first night I arrived in Oslo, even colder than in Canada. As I entered the hotel dining room, a fragrant, appetizing smell greeted me and I asked the maître d' what it was. If you think parsley soup could be dull, as I did, try *Green Suppe* and quickly change your mind. I call it the Norwegian vichysoisse.

2 potatoes, peeled and diced
2 medium-sized onions, peeled and diced
1 tbsp. (15 mL) butter
1 cup (250 mL) water
2 cups (500 mL) fresh parsley, stems removed

2 cups (500 mL) chicken consommé
grated rind of ½ lemon
salt and pepper
1 cup (250 mL) milk
1 cup (250 mL) light cream
8-12 green shrimps

Simmer together in a saucepan potatoes, onions, butter and water for about 15 minutes, or until the potatoes are soft but not overcooked.

Pour into a food processor or blender. Add the parsley and half the consommé. Process 1 minute or blend 3 minutes.

Pour back into saucepan and add remaining consommé and lemon rind. Bring to a boil, then add salt, pepper, milk and cream. Simmer until hot.

Remove shells from shrimps and cut each one in 3 with a sharp knife. Add to soup and simmer until shrimps are pink. Do not let it boil. *Serves 4.*

Fresh Fillets of Herring with Three Sauces

I do not like herring, fresh, salted or otherwise. One night in Bergen I was invited to dinner and the first course was three delicate small fillets of raw herring with three different sauces, each one served in a small bowl. On the table there was a bottle of gold aquavit set in a block of ice. A glass was poured for each guest and I was told I had to take one of the herring then a gulp of aquavit—imagine my dismay! My host and the other guests, all Norwegians, could hardly wait for the delight. I gathered up my courage, dabbed a little sauce on one of the fillets and swallowed both herring and aquavit. Surprise! I realized I had never had perfect raw herring before, to say nothing of the aquavit which was superb. If ever you are in the same situation beware of the cool golden Norwegian aquavit—too many gulps make you see life through a rainbow.

> *12 small raw herring*
> *fillets*

You will need a good fishmonger to prepare the fillets. Keep them refrigerated until ready to serve. In specialty shops you can sometimes find canned fillets of herring without sauce — they are quite good but not to be compared to the fresh.

Pink Sauce:

3 tbsp. (50 mL) soft
*   unsalted butter*
1 tbsp. (15 mL) tomato
*   paste*
¹/₄ tsp. (1 mL) each
*   sugar and salt*

White Sauce:

¹/₄ cup (60 mL) sour
*   cream*
2 tbsp. (30 mL)
*   prepared horseradish,*
*   well drained*
¹/₄ tsp. (1 mL) salt

Green Butter:

1 tbsp. (15 mL) soft
*   unsalted butter*
2 tbsp. (30 mL) finely
*   chopped fresh dill*
1 tsp. (5 mL) fresh
*   lemon juice.*

Do not hesitate to plump the prunes into the Cock-a-Leekie soup and serve with a glass of Scotch for a taste treat.

When your garden is full of fresh herbs, you can make as many
kinds of butters as you wish, then freeze them to add a taste of
summertime to winter meals.

To prepare the sauces: Simply beat the ingredients required for each sauce in separate bowls. Keep at room temperature until ready to serve. The contrast of the cool herring fillets and the tepid sauces is most important.

Each guest uses one sauce at a time on each fillet. *Serves 4.*

Butter-Poached Fish Fillets

Easy and quick to make. I strongly recommend using fresh sole or haddock or cod fillets—any choice is equally good. I also like the simplicity of the sauce—just dill or parsley and fresh lemon juice in quantities to suit your taste.

2 lb. (1 kg) fish fillets of *salt and pepper*
your choice *grated rind of 1 lemon*
¹/₃ cup (80 mL) butter

Soak fish for ¹/₂ to 2 hours in very cold water to completely cover it and add 3 tbsp. (50 mL) of salt. This treatment with the cold salted water prevents the fish from drying out during the cooking period. Remove the fish from the water and dry thoroughly with paper towel.

Melt butter in a shallow baking dish and place the fillets in it. Cover with buttered paper or foil. Bake in a preheated 400°F. (200°C) oven for 10 minutes. If the fillets are thick turn over with a spatula after 5 minutes.

To serve, remove fish with a slotted spoon and place on a hot platter. A few spoonfuls of melted butter, lots of dill and the juice of half a lemon are a good combination for a sauce, which is served separately. *Serves 4.*

Cold Salmon Superb

In Norway they wrap the salmon in parchment paper. Foil gives the same results and is more readily available. I first ate it while flying from Denmark to Norway on SAS Airlines. It was served with the Twisted Cucumber Salad and hot steamed potatoes — the salmon delectable and the contrast most pleasant.

2 lb. (1 kg) salmon,	*¹/₃ cup (80 mL) vodka*
center cut	*or dry vermouth or*
¹/₃ cup (80 mL) melted	*fresh lemon juice*
butter	*salt and pepper*

Place salmon on a piece of heavy-duty aluminium foil, pour melted butter on top, lift the foil all around to form a dish, add vodka or dry vermouth or lemon juice and salt and pepper. Fold and seal edges of the foil with a double fold so that no juices can escape and place on a dripping pan. Bake 40 minutes in a preheated 350°F. (180°C) oven.

When cooked, remove from oven but do not open the foil. Let cool, then keep at least 12 hours in the refrigerator. The juice, when cold, will form a most delicious jelly. Serve on a bed of fresh dill or parsley and garnish with thin slices of unpeeled lemon and cucumbers. *Serves 4 to 6.*

Norwegian Meatballs

Meatballs are to Scandinavia what hamburgers are to us, but they resemble our hamburgers only by the fact that they are made with ground meat.

Each Scandinavian country makes them a different way; the Norwegians use Gjetost cheese, something I thought I could never eat. The night I discovered what a flavor this cheese gave to the meatballs, I realized that any food can be good if used properly. Gjetost looks like a block of soft maple cream, but there ends the resemblance. It is available in cheese specialty shops. (I sometimes use medium Cheddar to replace it.)

Meatballs:

*1 lb. (500 g) ground
beef
1 lb. (500 g) ground
pork
1¹/₂ tsp. (7 mL) salt
¹/₂ tsp. (2 mL) pepper
2 eggs, lightly beaten*

*1 cup (250 mL) milk
¹/₂ cup (125 mL)
whole-wheat flour or
wheat germ
2 tbsp. (30 mL) capers
(optional)*

Place all ingredients, except capers, in a large bowl and beat at medium speed until compact and creamy, or mix vigorously by hand. (Mixing is perhaps the most important step for all Scandinavian meatballs.) Add the capers and stir to mix.

Place a bowl of water next to the meat and shape meat into 1-in. (2.5 cm) diameter meatballs, rinsing hands frequently so that the mixture doesn't stick to them.

Heat 2 to 3 tbsp. (30 to 50 mL) of vegetable oil in a large cast-iron frying pan. Add the meatballs without crowding them too much. Let them brown, shaking the pan gently every few minutes so that they turn in the pan and brown evenly — this takes about 10 minutes. Remove meatballs from pan as they become sufficiently browned. Set aside until ready to serve or add to the sauce.

Clean the frying pan with absorbent paper (do not wash) and use it to make the sauce (recipe follows).

Sauce:

*2 tbsp. (30 mL) butter
2 tbsp. (30 mL) flour
³/₄ cup (190 mL) light
cream
¹/₂ cup (125 mL)
chicken bouillon*

*¹/₂ cup (125 mL)
shredded Gjetost
¹/₂ cup (125 mL) sour
cream
2 tbsp. (30 mL) fresh
dill or parsley*

Melt butter in frying pan, add flour, blend well, add cream and chicken bouillon. Cook over medium heat and stir until creamy. Remove pan from the heat and add cheese. Stir until cheese is melted and add meatballs. Simmer over low heat until hot. When ready to serve add the sour cream, dill or parsley. *Serves 6 to 8.*

Cold "Citron" Chicken

The first time I enjoyed this was in Oslo—it was the main dish of a beautifully set cold table. The table itself was made from that pale natural-colored wood you see everywhere in Norway, and there were no mats or cloth of any kind, just a huge black bowl, filled with masses of yellow daffodils. Some of the plates and platters were heavy earthenware in a shade of deep yellow, others a beautiful green, and small white bowls for the sauces. The napkins repeated the plate colors.

This chicken has become one of my favorite summer dishes.

a 3-lb. (1.5 kg) chicken	*2 tbsp. (30 mL) dry*
1 tsp. (5 mL) coarse salt	*sherry*
15 peppercorns	*½ tsp. (2 mL) salt*
6-8 celery leaves, tied	*¼ tsp. (1 mL) pepper*
together	*2 tbsp. (30 mL) fine*
8-10 stems of parsley,	*chips of lemon rind*
tied together	*2 cups (500 mL)*
6 cups (1.5 L) cold	*shredded lettuce*
water	*1 lb. (.5 kg) cooked*
3 egg yolks	*shrimp or lobster*
1 cup (250 mL) light	*meat*
cream	

Place in a saucepan chicken, coarse salt, peppercorns, celery leaves and parsley stems. Pour cold water on top. Bring to a fast rolling boil, lower the heat and simmer, covered, until chicken is tender, about 1 hour. Cool in its stock.

When the chicken is cold, remove skin and bones and cut the meat into neat pieces. Set on an attractive serving dish.

Beat the egg yolks with the cream and sherry, simmer over low heat, stirring with a whisk, until creamy. Do not let it boil or it will curdle—gentle heat and lots of stirring are important. Season sauce with salt and pepper, and spread, while hot, over the chicken. If you have a zester knife use it to make the thin lemon shreds or use a sharp knife. Sprinkle over hot sauce. Cool. Cover and refrigerate until ready to serve.

To serve, cover the dish with shredded lettuce and place cooked shrimp or lobster meat on it. *Serves 4 to 6.*

Twisted Cucumber in Sour Cream

1 or 2 cucumbers	*ice cubes*
salt and pepper	*sour cream*

Cut ends off cucumbers and make ridges by pulling the prongs of a fork lengthwise all the way around. Then slice as thinly as possible. Place in a dish, add salt and pepper and top with ice cubes. Let stand 1 to 4 hours, refrigerated.

Drain the water by twisting the cucumbers in a cloth. Place cucumbers in a bowl, cover and keep refrigerated until ready to serve, then mix with just enough sour cream to cover. Stir with a fork and sprinkle with pepper. Place in an attractive glass dish. *Serves 4 to 6.*

Fried Parsnips Bergen

Bergen is an important fishing port in Norway. My host took me to a small restaurant full of fishermen who bring in some of their catch when they go there. The specialty of the house was the Butter-Poached Fish, served with fried parsnips—horrors! I thought — until I tasted them, and ever since I have cooked parsnips this way. Of course there were bowls of chopped dill and toasted dill seed, simply browned in butter — try it.

6 parsnips of equal size	*¹/₄ tsp. (1 mL) pepper*
3 tbsp. (50 mL) flour	*3 tbsp. (50 mL) butter*
¹/₂ tsp. (2 mL) salt	

Wash the parsnips with a brush, but do not peel them—that is the secret of a perfect parsnip. (I had to travel to Bergen to learn that.) Place them in a saucepan and pour boiling water on top to cover them completely. Bring back to a fast rolling boil, cover, lower the heat and boil until barely soft. Depending on the size of the parsnips, the time will vary. I have found that 10 minutes is usually needed, but always beware of overcooking them.

Drain, cool, peel and cut into 2-in. (5 cm) pieces. Mix flour, salt and pepper, roll each piece of parsnip in this, then fry in melted butter until golden brown here and there. *Serves 4.*

Applestuvad Potatoes

As a vegetable served with meat, potatoes are steamed or boiled and usually rolled in dill or parsley. As *stuvad*, meaning stewed, they are used as the main dish of a meal. I tasted them first on a beautiful day while travelling on a boat through Norway's *fjords*, which are very dramatic. They reminded me of certain places in the Rockies. The potatoes are served topped with thinly sliced sausages or smoked fish or thick slices of fried bacon.

5-6 potatoes, peeled and
  diced
1¼ cups (310 mL) milk
½ tsp. (2 mL) salt

¼ tsp. (1 mL) pepper
2 apples, peeled, cored
  and diced

Place potatoes in an enamelled cast-iron pan. Pour 1 cup (250 mL) of the milk on top and add salt and pepper. Cook uncovered over medium-low heat until the potatoes are almost done and milk is absorbed. Add apples, stir well and add remaining ¼ cup (60 mL) of milk. Keep cooking until milk is again absorbed and apples are tender. Pour into a warm serving dish and top with pan-fried sausages or thinly sliced smoked sausages or paper-thin slices of smoked fish or thick slices of fried bacon. Serve with it, of course, a bowl of minced fresh dill and parsley, mixed together in equal quantities, and a bowl of whipped butter. *Serves 4.*

Karintkake

This is Norwegian Christmas cake, the only fruit being currants. The flavor of the aquavit is very special, but if it is not available brandy can be used in the same proportions.

1 cup (250 mL) dried	*1 tsp. (5 mL) ground*
currants	*cardamom*
1 cup (250 mL)	*3 tsp. (15 mL) baking*
unsalted butter	*powder*
2 cups (500 mL) fine	*¹/₄ cup (60 mL) aquavit*
granulated sugar	*or brandy*
6 egg yolks	*¹/₂ cup (125 mL) milk*
3 cups (750 mL)	*6 egg whites, beaten stiff*
all-purpose flour	*2 zwieback or 2 tbsp.*
¹/₄ tsp. (1 mL) salt	*(30 mL) fine dry*
¹/₂ tsp. (2 mL) mace	*breadcrumbs*

Cover the currants with cold water and let them soak 1 hour. Drain well. Place butter, sugar and egg yolks in an electric mixer bowl and beat at medium speed for 15 minutes, cleaning sides twice with a rubber spatula. The mixture should look like whipped cream. Add the currants and beat just long enough to blend.

Sift together flour, salt, mace, cardamon and baking powder.

Stir together aquavit or brandy and milk.

Add flour and liquid alternately to the creamed mixture and beat just enough to mix.

Fold in the beaten egg whites. Crush 2 *zwieback* or measure 2 tbsp. (30 mL) fine dry breadcrumbs.

Butter generously a 10–in. (25 cm) Bundt pan. Sprinkle crumbs all over the mold and shake off excess. Pour in the batter. Bake in a preheated 350°F. (180°C) oven 50 to 60 minutes, or until done. Cool 10 minutes on a cake rack, then unmold. Let it cool for 2 hours. Soak a cheesecloth in aquavit or brandy and use it to wrap the cake. Keep in a cool place at least 3 to 5 days before using.

Vanilla Boller

One of the most dramatic moments I've ever experienced was watching the Northern Lights at 4 A.M. in Bodo, the best place in the world to witness such a sight. I can best describe it as a giant play of color and movement, filled with weird music. It was grandiose and overpowering.

When we returned to the hotel in the very early morning we were served fragrant cups of perfect hot cocoa and big fat vanilla *boller* hot from the oven. The next day I met the pastry chef and asked him for the recipe which he graciously offered by saying: "Mix a yeast dough with milk and egg. Fill with a vanilla cream, bake and serve." I thanked him warmly and tried them the first week I was back home. After four trials I had excellent results and have been enjoying them ever since.

Pastry:

1 envelope active dry yeast	2 cups (500 mL) milk 1 egg
1/4 cup (60 mL) lukewarm water	1 tsp. (5 mL) salt 4–4 1/2 cups (1–1.2 L)
3 tbsp. (50 mL) sugar	all-purpose flour
2 tbsp. (30 mL) butter	

Stir sugar into lukewarm water. Sprinkle yeast on top. Stir and let rest 10 minutes.

Add butter to milk and heat to lukewarm, or until butter is melted. Cool 5 minutes. Stir and add yeast. Beat egg with salt and stir into the yeast mixture.

Add flour gradually, while stirring, until you have a soft, non-sticky dough. Sprinkle a good 1/2 cup (125 mL) of flour on the work surface, turn dough on top and knead until elastic and not sticking to the hand — add a little more flour if necessary. Place the dough in a large bowl, cover with a towel and let rise until doubled in bulk, about 1 hour.

Now prepare the cream filling (recipe follows).

Vanilla Cream:

³/₄ *cup (190 mL) light*   ¹/₄ *cup (60 mL) sugar*
    cream   *1 tsp. (5 mL) vanilla*
4 egg yolks

Heat light cream. Beat egg yolks with sugar and vanilla. Pour a bit of the hot cream in it, stir well and pour into the rest of the hot cream. Cook over low heat until creamy, stirring most of the time so it does not curdle. Stir for a few seconds more, remove from heat, cover and let cool.

When the dough is ready, punch down. Divide dough into 2 pieces, sprinkle work area with a little flour, roll out each piece with a rolling pin until it is about ¹/₃ in. (0.83 cm) thick. With a round cookie cutter the size of a doughnut cut out rounds. Place on a greased baking sheet and put about 1 tsp. (5 mL) of the cooled cream filling in the middle of each round. Cover with another round and pinch the edges together to enclose the filling. Cover with a cloth and let rise again for 30 to 45 minutes. Brush lightly with a little milk and sprinkle with sugar when ready to bake.

Bake in a preheated 375°F. (190°C) oven 25 to 30 minutes, or until golden brown. Cool on rack or serve hot. *Yield: 18 to 20.*

Krumkake

Whenever you are in Norway, you will see these artistic paper-thin wafers, crisp and tasty — served with jam, just as they come out of the iron; crimped while still hot to fit into a four-corner dish and filled with ice cream; or rolled over the handle of a wooden spoon to form delicate cylinders. All variations are good, but you must have a *krumkake* iron, found in specialty shops. It is somewhat like an elegant waffle maker, but round with beautiful designs inside the plates. As it is not automatic, it is set on gas or electric heat.

3 eggs
¹/₂ cup (125 mL) sugar
6 tbsp. (90 mL) melted
butter
¹/₂ tsp. (2 mL) ground
cardamom

¹/₂ tsp. (2 mL) grated
lemon rind
³/₄ cup (190 mL)
all-purpose flour

Beat eggs and sugar until light and creamy. Add melted butter, cardamon and lemon rind. Stir until well mixed. Add flour gradually, beating well at each addition.

To bake, place the iron directly over medium heat. Heat one side until a few drops of water poured on top sizzle. Flip the iron over and heat again to sizzle. Open iron and brush lightly with melted butter. Spoon a large tablespoon of batter into the center, close and press the handles together. Flip the iron and scrape any batter that might have flowed out. Bake, flipping the iron every 20 seconds. After 40 seconds, open to check for doneness. As soon as it is golden and crisp, quickly lift out with a spatula. Cool on cake rack, reheat iron and repeat process till all batter is used. *Yield: 12 to 14.*

Finnish Food:
Secrets from Marta and Lempi

Summer Vegetable Soup

A delicate cream of vegetable soup, delectable when made from garden fresh vegetables or those from the farmers' market.

In Sweden leeks, carrots and radishes are used. In Finland young carrots, fresh green peas and small early cauliflower are preferred; this is also my choice.

3-5 young carrots, scrubbed and sliced	¹/₄ tsp (1 mL) sugar
1 lb. (500 g) fresh green peas, shelled	2 tbsp. (30 mL) butter
	2 tbsp. (30 mL) flour
1 small head of cauliflower, cleaned and sliced	3 cups (750 mL) milk
	8-10 large shrimps (optional)
2 cups (500 mL) boiling water	salt and pepper
	a bowl of fresh parsley, chopped

Place prepared vegetables in boiling water. Stir in sugar. Boil, uncovered, 8 to 10 minutes.

In another saucepan, melt butter, add flour and stir until well mixed. Add milk and bring to the boil while stirring. When smooth, pour in vegetables and their water. Salt and pepper to taste. Add shelled shrimps and simmer 5 minutes.

Serve piping hot — everyone can add as much parsley as desired to the soup — the more the better. I like to mix the parsley with some chopped fresh chives, although this is not Finnish. *Serves 6.*

Lempi's Sillsalad

Lempi was a Finnish woman who worked with me for many years. She worked like a Finn, which means to "perfection." We had lots of fun together — I showed her how to cook Canadian and she showed me how to cook Finnish. This is her recipe for authentic herring salad.

4 fresh salted herring
fillets
1 cup (250 mL) milk
1 1/2 cups (375 mL)
pickled beets, diced
1 1/2 cups (375 mL)
freshly boiled
potatoes, diced
1/3 cup (80 mL) dill or
sweet pickles, diced

1/2 cup (125 mL)
unpeeled apples, diced
1/2 cup (125 mL) celery,
diced
1 onion, finely diced
4 tbsp. (60 mL) cider
vinegar
2 tbsp. (30 mL) water
2 tbsp. (30 mL) sugar
1/4 tsp. (1 mL) pepper
3 hard-boiled eggs

Soak herring fillets in milk overnight. Next day, remove them from the milk, drain well, remove any skin and cut into tiny pieces with scissors. Place in a bowl and add beets, potatoes, pickles, apples, celery and onion. Mix well with a fork until salad is a deep pink.

Shake cider vinegar, water, sugar and pepper together in a bottle until sugar is dissolved. Stir gently into the salad, then taste for salt. Rub a mold with salad oil and pack salad into it. Cover and refrigerate a few hours or overnight. Unmold on serving plate 1 hour before serving and garnish the top with sliced hard-boiled eggs, and the sides with quartered eggs and sprigs of fresh dill or parsley. *Serves 8 to 10.*

Gravlax

Gravlax is pickled, uncooked salmon. A superb treat when prepared with a large piece of fresh salmon from the early spring catch, when the waters are still very cold. Marta told me that the salmon caught in the early spring in the very cold rivers of northern Sweden is the very best, so I taught her how to replace it with the early spring Gaspé salmon.

This is a Scandinavian delicacy, though many feel it originated in Sweden. Since my Finnish friend showed me how to make it I like to think of *gravlax* as Finnish.

about 3 lb. (1.5 kg)	*2 tbsp. (30 mL) sugar*
fresh salmon	*12 crushed white*
2 tbsp. (30 mL) coarse	*peppercorns*
salt	*lots of fresh dill*

Wash the fish and dry thoroughly. Remove as many bones as possible but do not remove the skin.

Place a thick layer of long stems of dill, fresh of course, on a dish long enough to hold the piece of salmon. Mix together salt, sugar and peppercorns. Rub salmon, inside and out, with the mixture. Place fish on the thick bed of fresh dill, then cover with more dill until the fish is completely covered. Cover fish completely with a long wooden board, cover with a clean cloth, then place a weight of your choice over the entire wooden board as all the fish must be weighted down. Place in the refrigerator and let stand 24 hours, turning the fish once, making sure that it is completely covered with the dill.

To serve, cut into very thin slices on the bias or slantwise toward the skin. Serve on black or rye bread, with unsalted butter, and a glass of ice-cold aquavit. Superb.

Finnish Jellied Beef Tongue

To cook veal or lamb tongues the Finnish way simply follow this recipe using 2 to 3 calf tongues or 6 to 10 lamb tongues. Simmer until they are tender and easy to peel. Once peeled, cool in their own cooking broth. This is a precious recipe if you like boiled tongue — I have never found a better one. Jellied tongue is a main item on the Scandinavian cold table.

1 fresh beef tongue	*4 cups (1 L) cold water*
2 tbsp. (30 mL) sugar	*2 tbsp. (30 mL) coarse*
1 tbsp. (15 mL) coarse	*salt*
salt	*1 tbsp. (15 mL) sugar*
8 cups (2 L) hot water	*1 envelope unflavored*
1 bay leaf	*gelatine*
1 unpeeled lemon, thinly	*juice of 1 lemon*
sliced	*1 cup (250 mL) sour*
5-6 slices fresh ginger	*cream*
root	*fresh dill or parsley*

Mix the 2 tbsp. (30 mL) of sugar and the 1 tbsp. (15 mL) of salt together and rub evenly over tongue. Cover and refrigerate overnight.

The next day, place tongue in a large saucepan with the hot water and add bay leaf, sliced lemon and ginger root. Bring to a fast rolling boil, skim off the foam, then cover and simmer over low heat for 2 to 3 hours until the tongue is tender. Skin the tongue while hot and let it cool in its broth.

In the meantime, bring to a boil the 1 quart (1 L) cold water with the 2 tbsp. (30 mL) salt and the 1 tbsp. (15 mL) sugar. Let cool, then add the cooled peeled tongue. Refrigerate for 12 hours. Drain thoroughly and place on a flat platter.

Soak the unflavored gelatine in the lemon juice for 5 minutes and then dissolve over hot water. Slowly add to the sour cream, while stirring. Wipe cold tongue with absorbent paper and place attractively on the serving platter. Spread with jellied cream and refrigerate for 1 hour to set the gelatine.

To serve, garnish with sprig of dill or parsley. Slice thin. *Serves 6 to 8.*

Apple Meatloaf

In Finland meat and dry fruits or fresh apples are often combined and the result is very interesting. Lempi showed me how to make this in the sixties and it is now one of my summer favorites.

2 eggs	*2 tsp. (10 mL) salt*
2 lb. (1 kg) lean ground	*1 tsp. (5 mL) dill seed*
pork	*OR 2 tbsp. (30 mL)*
1 medium onion,	*chopped fresh dill*
chopped fine	*¹/₄ tsp. (1 mL) ground*
1 garlic clove, chopped	*allspice*
fine	*1 cup (250 mL) apple*
¹/₂ cup (125 mL) grated	*juice or light cream*
raw turnips or carrots	*3 medium apples*
1 tbsp. (15 mL)	*1 tbsp. (15 mL) butter*
cornstarch	

Beat eggs in a bowl, add meat, onion, garlic, turnips or carrots, cornstarch, salt, dill, allspice and apple juice or cream. Mix thoroughly.

Core and slice apples, but do not peel. Arrange a layer of apples in a greased 9 × 5 in. (22.5 × 12.5 cm) loaf pan. Top with half of the meat mixture. Place another layer of apples over the meat and top with the remaining meat, pressing well on each layer as it is completed. Top with the remaining apple slices. Dot with butter here and there. Bake in a preheated 350°F (180°C) oven for 1¹/₄ hours. Serve hot with baked potatoes and pickled beets. *Serves 6 to 8.*

Rolled Loin of Pork

Like so many of the Finnish dishes this one may sound odd but, believe me, it is worth any time you put into it. Another plus is the fact that once cooked it can be kept for four to six weeks, refrigerated.

a 2-3 lb. (1-1.5 kg) loin
  of pork
1 tsp. (5 mL) freshly
  ground pepper
1 tbsp. (15 mL) sugar

1 tsp. (5 mL) ground
  ginger
1 tsp. (5 mL) coarse salt
3-5 lemon slices,
  unpeeled
1 tbsp. (15 mL) salt

Ask the butcher to bone the loin and reserve the bones for you. Spread the loin on wax paper. Spread all over one side ground pepper, sugar, ginger and coarse salt. Rub well into the meat with your hands. Roll the meat and tie with string as tightly as you can 5 to 6 times around the roll.

Place bones in a saucepan, set meat over them, cover with cold water and add lemon slices and the salt. Bring to a fast rolling boil, then simmer over low heat, covered, until tender. This may take 1 to 2 hours, depending on the meat. Do not overcook.

When done, remove the meat to a bowl. Strain enough of the cooking juices over the meat to completely cover it. Cool. Cover and refrigerate. When cold, skim off the fat. Slice the meat thinly and serve with hot new potatoes and Finnish mustard. *Serves 4 to 6.*

Finnish Mustard

This recipe came from Marta's old Finnish cookbook. I have been making Finnish mustard for a good ten years and I serve it at my table along with Dijon mustard — with ham it is perfect.

8 tbsp. (120 mL) dry
  mustard
3 tbsp. (50 mL) sugar
1 tsp. (5 mL) salt

8 tbsp. (120 mL) boiling
  water
2 tbsp. (30 mL) cider
  vinegar

Combine mustard, sugar and salt. Mix thoroughly.

In a saucepan, mix water and vinegar. Stir in the dry ingredients. Stir until well mixed, then cook, stirring over low heat, until it becomes a smooth, creamy paste. It will be a bit runny at first, then thicken only slightly, but it will thicken more as it cools. The cooking time is about 10 to 12 minutes.

Pour into small jars. Cover. *Yield: ²/₃ cup (160 mL).*

Finnish Spinach Pancakes

I serve these as a vegetable or piping hot as appetizers or cold (room temperature) with cold cuts or green salad. Sometimes, for a light lunch, I make small, round half-inch (1.25 cm) thick beef patties and serve them between two of the pancakes with a bowl of Finnish mustard.

If possible, shape them into small pancakes and cook them in a Swedish cast-iron *plätter* pan, otherwise a pancake griddle or cast-iron frying pan will do nicely. I have not seen these pancakes made anywhere other than Scandinavia.

a 10-oz. (283.5 g) bag of spinach, washed and coarsely chopped or 1 lb. (500 mL) cooked fresh spinach	*1 cup (250 mL) flour*
	2 tbsp. (30 mL) butter, melted
1¹/₂ cups (375 mL) milk	*2 eggs*
1 tsp. (5 mL) salt	*¹/₂ tsp. (2 mL) sugar*
a pinch of nutmeg	

Pack spinach tightly into a saucepan, cover and cook 2 minutes over high heat, with only the rinsing water clinging to the leaves as liquid. Turn once after 1 minute. Drain and squeeze as dry as possible.

Combine in a bowl milk, salt, nutmeg, flour and melted butter. Beat with a whisk until smooth.

In another bowl beat melted butter, eggs and sugar. Add spinach. Mix well and add to flour mixture. Mix thoroughly and cook in a *platter* pan,* as you would any pancake, turning only once. Keep warm. *Yield: 10 to 25, depending on size.*

*See Swedish "Platter Pan" Pancakes, p.78.

Fried Onions with Currants

Another unusual and very tasty way to serve onions. In Finland they are popular served with fried fish. I also like them with roast of veal or sausages.

Fried Onions:

1 large Spanish onion	*2 tbsp. (30 mL) cold*
4 cups (1 L) boiling	*water*
water	*1 cup (250 mL) fine dry*
½ tsp. (2 mL) salt	*breadcrumbs*
¼ tsp. (1 mL) sugar	*2 tbsp. (30 mL) butter*
1 egg, beaten	

Cut the onion into thick slices and break into rings. Place in a colander, pour boiling water on top. Let stand a few minutes. Rinse under cold running water. Drain and place rings on absorbent paper.

Stir together in a large plate salt and sugar, add beaten egg and the cold water. Mix.

Place breadcrumbs in another plate. Heat butter in a large frying pan until it becomes a nutty color. Dip each onion ring into the egg mixture, then roll lightly in breadcrumbs. Place in hot butter immediately and fry over medium heat, turning only once. As the rings become cooked, place on a hot dish. Serve with currant sauce (recipe follows).

Currant Sauce:

½ cup (125 mL) dry	*1½ tbsp. (20 mL) flour*
currants	*juice and grated rind of*
2 cups (500 mL) water	*1 lemon*
2 tbsp. (30 mL) butter	

Bring water to the boil with currants. Boil uncovered for 6 to 8 minutes.

Knead together into a ball butter and flour. When currants are cooked, add lemon rind and juice to them, then the flour ball, stirring rapidly over low heat until sauce is creamy. Salt to taste. Serve separately.

Lempi's Ginger Cookies

No one could bake bread or make ginger cookies like Lempi. Her strong hands and arms seemed to make no effort when she baked. The result — always perfect.

¹/₂ *cup (125 mL) sugar*	¹/₂ *tbsp. (7 mL) ground*
1 ¹/₂ cups (375 mL)	*cinnamon*
molasses	¹/₂ *tbsp. (7 mL) ground*
1 cup (250 mL) butter	*ginger*
or shortening	*1 tsp. (5 mL) ground*
4 cups (1 L) all-purpose	*cardamom*
flour	¹/₂ *tsp. (2 mL) salt*
1 tsp. (5 mL) baking	*1 cup (250 mL)*
soda	*buttermilk*
	2 egg whites

Place sugar and molasses in a saucepan. Stir over low heat until sugar is melted. Add butter or shortening and continue to stir over low heat until the butter is melted. Remove from heat and cool.

Sift 3 cups (750 mL) of the flour with baking soda, cinnamon, ginger, cardamom and salt. Measure the last cup (250 mL) of flour and set aside.

Add the dry ingredients to the molasses mixture alternately with the buttermilk, then mix thoroughly until you have soft dough. If needed, use some of the reserved flour. Turn dough onto a floured table and knead for 5 minutes. Wrap and refrigerate for 5 to 8 hours.

Roll out dough ¹/₄ in. (0.625 cm) thick. Cut into rounds. Brush each round with slightly beaten egg white. If you wish, sprinkle each one with a pinch of sugar.

Place 1 in. (2.5 cm) apart on buttered cookie sheets. Bake in a preheated 350°F. (180°C) oven for 15 to 20 minutes. *Yield: 4 dozen.*

Lempi's Brandy Cream

When fresh strawberries were in season, Lempi made this cream which she surrounded with cool sweetened straw-berries. I also make it with raspberries or blueberries or sliced peaches, depending on the season.

3 egg yolks	*3 tbsp. (50 mL) cold*
¹/₄ cup (60 mL) sugar	*water*
1 cup (250 mL) cream	*3 egg whites, beaten*
a vanilla pod	*2-3 tbsp. (30-50 mL)*
1 envelope unflavored	*brandy*
gelatine	

Beat together in a saucepan egg yolks, sugar and cream. Add vanilla pod. Heat over low heat, stirring often.

Soak gelatine in cold water and let stand 5 minutes. Add gelatine to hot egg yolk mixture and keep cooking and stirring until it turns into a light cream. Remove from heat and beat for a few minutes to cool.

Beat egg whites and add to hot mixture, folding in gently. Stir in brandy. Pour into a glass serving dish. Cover and refrigerate until ready to serve. In winter serve it with homemade jam. *Serves 4 to 5.*

Pulla Coffee Cake

A moist, rich, fragrant coffee bread, served hot, cold or toasted. It is usually shaped into a large braid, but since it is served at every festive occasion it can be a Christmas star or a bishop's wig or a Lucia's crown. Lempi taught me all about Pulla and for the last fifteen years I have never ceased to make and enjoy it.

1 envelope active dry	*1 tsp. (5 mL) salt*
yeast	*8-12 whole cardamom*
¹/₂ cup (125 mL) warm	*pods, seeded and*
water	*crushed with a*
1 tsp. (5 mL) sugar	*wooden mallet*
2 cups (500 mL) hot tap	*4 eggs, well beaten*
water	*6-8 cups (1.5-2 L)*
1 cup (250 mL) instant	*all-purpose flour*
powdered milk	*¹/₂ cup (125 mL) melted*
³/₄ cup (190 mL) sugar	*butter*

Stir together yeast, the ¹/₂ cup (125 mL) of warm water and the 1 tsp. (5 mL) of sugar. Let stand 10 minutes.

In a large bowl stir in the hot tap water, powdered instant milk, the ³/₄ cup (190 mL) of sugar, salt, cardamom and beaten egg. Mix thoroughly. Stir yeast, add to the liquid mixture, then add 3 cups (750 mL) of the flour. Stir until well mixed and smooth looking. Add melted butter. Beat until dough looks glossy again. All of this can be done in an electric mixer if you have a dough hook.

Add the remaining flour 1 cup (250 mL) at a time, beating well at each addition. I usually keep 1 cup (250 mL) of the flour to knead and roll the dough, as it must be soft.

Turn onto a lightly floured board, cover with inverted bowl or a cloth, let the dough rest 10 to 15 minutes, then knead until smooth. Place in a large, lightly greased bowl. Cover with a cloth and let rise in a warm place until double in bulk, about 1 hour. Punch down and let rise again but only until almost double in bulk, about 30 to 40 minutes.

Punch down and turn dough onto a lightly floured board and divide into 3 parts, then divide each part into 3 more parts. Shape each part into a strip about 15 to 16 in. (38 to 40 cm) long; this is easy to do if you roll the dough on the board with your palm. Before braiding the strips, place them on a greased baking sheet (as lifting braids is difficult). Braid 3 strips together, pinching the ends and tucking them under. Repeat process for other two braids. If you do not wish to make 3 braided breads you can shape some of the dough as you please or even bake it as a bread loaf in a loaf pan.

Let the shaped braid or bread rise about 20 to 30 minutes, or until puffy, but not double in size.

Beat an egg with 1 tbsp. (15 mL) milk. Use to brush top of bread and sprinkle top with coarse sugar and a few thinly sliced almonds.

Bake in a preheated 400°F. (200°C) oven 20 to 30 minutes, or until golden brown. Unmold onto cake rack as soon as baked.

I prefer to bake them 1 braid or loaf at a time. If they brown too fast, lower the heat of the oven. Keeps and freezes very well.
Yield: 3 braids.

Finnish Cardamom Cake

A specialty of my Finnish friend Marta. A cake with an exciting cardamom flavor, speckled with raisins, it can be served as is, dusted with icing sugar and thinly sliced. Well wrapped it will keep fresh four to six weeks. It is better to let it ripen three to four days before cutting.

¹/₂ cup (125 mL) soft butter or margarine	2 tsp. (10 mL) baking soda
1 cup (250 mL) sugar	2 cups (500 mL) commercial sour cream
2 eggs	
¹/₂ cup (125 mL) molasses	
2¹/₂ cups (625 mL) flour	¹/₂ cup (125 mL) chopped walnuts
1 tsp. (5 mL) cinnamon	³/₄ cup (190 mL) seedless raisins
¹/₄ tsp. (1 mL) salt	
2 tsp. (10 mL) ground cardamom	

Butter two 9 × 5 in. (22.5 × 12.5 cm) loaf pans or a 10-in. (25 cm) Bundt pan. Cream the butter or margarine in an electric mixer at high speed until light. Gradually adding sugar, beat until creamy and light. Add eggs, one at a time, beating well after each addition. Add molasses and beat at high speed to mix.

Meanwhile, sift together twice or mix thoroughly flour, cinnamon, salt, cardamom and soda. Add all at once to the creamed mixture and pour sour cream on top. Mix with a spatula just enough to cover the flour, then beat at high speed for 2 minutes. Add walnuts and raisins and beat by hand until well mixed.

Divide the batter equally between loaf pans, or pour into Bundt pan, and bake in a preheated 325°F. (160°C) oven 40 to 50 minutes. Test for doneness. Unmold and cool on cake rack.

The Netherlands

Thinking of Holland brings back many a memory. My first trip there was at the close of World War II in 1945, and I lived for almost a year in Amsterdam and The Hague with my husband, who was still in the army. It was a life full of unbelievable experiences. I was billeted by the Canadian army and used their rations, since foreigners as well as army personnel could not buy anything in Dutch shops. But we could look and ask questions, and that I did, so consequently I learned about many aspects of food in Holland.

The only thing we could buy were fresh flowers — and how I enjoyed them at the time!

I was astounded at the number of bicycles on every street, most of them without rubber tires because of the shortage during the War. Between the rubberless bicycle wheels and the wooden clogs, both moving fast on the cobblestones, I will never forget the noise. It had the ring of "I will not be defeated." I also travelled quite a bit across the country with my husband, in a military jeep. And I remember how nervous I was going even only forty miles an hour on the narrow dyke roads, with water on each side.

Another feat of ingenuity by the Dutch is the man-made islands, where they grow flowers, small lilac trees, etc. That summer, my husband took me to a summer cottage on a lake near Hilversum. We had to take a rowboat to get to the cottage — an enchanting corner. When I got up the first morning, I went out to see the lovely lilac trees all in bloom on a small island near our house, which I had seen the night before, but to my amazement, they were nowhere to be seen. I asked Bernard, "Am I crazy? I was sure I had seen those lilacs." He laughed and told me all about the man-made moving islands that the tides brought back and forth.

The Dutch have an extraordinary love and understanding not only for flowers, but also for the soil and its culture. They always had to put up such a struggle against nature and against the sea; over the centuries, large parts of the country have been reclaimed from the sea. To keep that reclaimed land dry and arable, it must be drained continuously, using dykes, which explains the famous windmills of Holland. Today, the work is done with electric hydraulics; more efficient, yes, but so much less romantic. Windmills can still be seen across the country, but few are actually used.

I will always have a vivid recollection of the deep green grass that grows on the damp polders and the numerous black and white Dutch cows, now mixed here and there with the white French cows. They are so glossy, so well cared for and so fat. It may be simply that Dutch grass is so good.

My first taste of golden creamy Gouda was in 1945, when I met at the Flower Market, in Alkmaar, a Dutch woman named Hilda who spoke English and made country cheese of the Gouda type. My husband had a Dragon sailboat, lent to us by a Dutch friend. When the winds were good, we went sailing, taking with us fruits, some of Hilda's cheese, freshly baked country bread and a bottle of wine or some beer. Quite a feat, at the time, to be able to have such food. All of it was made possible through our friendly, pleasant Hilda. Sometimes we sailed for hours, since we were at the whim of the winds from the Ysselmeer (formerly Zuiderzee), which could change so fast without rhyme or reason.

A few years ago, in the early seventies, I was invited to Holland by the "Cheese People," as they are referred to—it was a beautifully planned trip and very exciting. It was really at that time that I learned to appreciate the subtlety of the Dutch cheese, which has a clean, buttery taste, a conventional texture and excellent keeping qualities. I was also impressed by the fact that Holland, which manufactures only a few types of cheese, all of similar texture, has done more than any other country, except France, to convince her people of the importance of eating Dutch cheese every day.

The best known Dutch cheeses are Edam, in the shape of a round red ball, and the large flat round Gouda, which is known as Leiden cheese when cumin seeds are added.

On a third trip, I again saw the flowers and the neatness of the land and witnessed once more the hospitality of the Dutch people and their very unique and interesting foods — the way they use spices (probably influenced by their Indonesian connections), their super, small yellowish potatoes, which they know how to cook to perfection, the fresh herring, raw or salted or smoked, their breads, all the buns they serve with coffee, and good coffee it is as they know how to make it. Not to mention the honey and ginger cakes one can keep for months, the hard candy made with coffee and demerara sugar.

I always return from Holland with a peaceful, pleasant feeling, since my natural taste runs to the beauty of nature, the good country life, the pastoral scenes — and Holland has all of these.

Cream of Cucumber Soup

A spring specialty of Amsterdam, this should be served the Dutch way, in a nice soup tureen with two heads of fresh dill floating on top. Serve piping hot or chilled.

1 long or 2 average-size cucumbers	*salt and pepper*
2 tbsp. (30 mL) butter	*¹/₂ tsp. (2 mL) chopped fresh dill*
¹/₄ cup (60 mL) flour	*1¹/₂ cups (375 mL) milk*
2¹/₂ cups (625 mL) diluted canned consommé or water	*1 egg*
	¹/₂ cup (125 mL) heavy cream

Peel cucumber and cut in half lengthwise. Remove the seeds with a teaspoon and cut the cucumber into small dice.

Melt butter in a saucepan, add flour and stir until well mixed. Add consommé or water and stir until creamy (it will have the consistency of a light cream sauce). Add cucumber, salt, pepper and dill. Cover and simmer 30 minutes. Cool, then pass through a sieve to purée the cucumber or use a blender or food processor.

Return to the pan and taste for seasoning. Add milk and slowly bring to the boil. When ready to serve, beat the egg and the cream together and pour the boiling soup on top, while stirring with a whisk. Garnish with dill and serve. *Serves 4 to 6.*

Marinated Herring

In Holland, herring is more than just a fish. In 1953, I attended the celebration of "Flag Day," sometimes referred to as "Herring Holiday," at the end of May, just before the herring fleet sets sails for the yearly catch. All the ships are decorated with hundreds of flags and they sail in a parade along the coast. Quite a spectacle!

After the festivities, I had a feeling that every Dutch person was waiting for the first catch to come in, as in Norway, where it is announced throughout the country that the "New Herring" are in. People look for the small, spotlessly clean stalls to appear on the streets — this is the moment when all herring lovers rush out to try the new herring, and discuss at length the merit and quality of this year's over last year's.

We were filming this great event, and of course our Dutch host insisted that we taste the new herring. I shivered, as I had not yet been to Norway and had never at any time eaten herring, cooked, smoked, salted and, much less, raw. I wondered if I would be able to follow the rules and swallow the raw herring fillet — by holding one end of the fillet with the thumb and the first finger, bending my head back, holding the fish high over my mouth and gradually swallowing it. Well, my curiosity for food got the better of me, and I swallowed the herring, while our host was telling me that the first batch is always more expensive, but no real herring lover minds, and he pays with a smile. As of that day, I became appreciative of a perfect fillet of raw herring.

Try their way to marinate herring which will keep ten to fifteen days refrigerated. Serve them with a small glass of ice-cold Dutch Genever gin.

10-12 fresh herring fillets	*15 peppercorns*
10-12 small gherkins or dill pickles	*10 juniper berries**
1 lemon, unpeeled and thinly sliced	*1 1/2 cups (375 mL) white or cider vinegar***
1 medium onion, thinly sliced	*1/4 cup (60 mL) cold water*
3 bay leaves	*2 tsp. (10 mL) pickling salt*

Ask your fish merchant to fillet the fresh herrings, unless you know how to do it. Roll each fillet around a gherkin or dill pickle (this explains why they must be small — if unavailable, cut larger pickles into finger-size pieces). Place the rolls in a sterilized glass jar, one over the other, in such a way that they do not open. As you fill the jar, divide equally between rows the lemon slices, bay leaves, peppercorns and juniper berries.

Bring to the boiling point vinegar, water and salt. Remove from heat and cool. Then pour over the herring rolls and cover the jar. Refrigerate at least 1 week before serving. *Serves 6 to 8.*

*See note, p. 138.

**Cider gives milder flavor.

Hussar's Salad

In all small, large and quick food restaurants in Holland, you will find the *Huzarensla* salad; with a bock of cold beer it is a pleasant lunch, and a good way to use leftover veal, pork or beef roast. I found this salad reminiscent of the Finnish herring salad in its composition, although in Holland meat replaces fish.

1-2 cups (250-500 mL)
    cooked pork, veal or
    beef, diced
2 firm apples, peeled
    and diced
1 beet, cooked and diced
1 hard-boiled egg, finely
    chopped
2 small dill pickles,
    chopped
1 onion or 6 green
    onions, finely chopped

2-3 cups (500-750 mL)
    potatoes, cooked and
    diced
3 tbsp. (50 mL)
    vegetable oil
3 tbsp. (50 mL) fresh
    lemon juice or wine
    vinegar
1/2 tsp. (2 mL) salt
1/4 tsp. (1 mL) pepper
1/4 cup (60 mL)
    mayonnaise

In a large bowl, toss together the first 7 ingredients.

Stir in a jar oil, lemon juice or vinegar, salt and pepper. Pour over the salad ingredients and toss until the meat and vegetables are well coated with the dressing.

Set salad on a platter in a nest of lettuce leaves and top with mayonnaise. In summertime, sprinkle the mayonnaise generously with fresh minced chives. Cover and refrigerate 1 hour before serving. *Serves 6.*

Bitterballen

Like the Hussar Salad, the *Bitterballen* are prepared from cooked veal or pork and are a daily part of Dutch life. They are served at cocktail time, usually with a glass of "Old Genever" and a jar of French or Dutch mustard. I like them also for a quick lunch, with a green salad and cheese.

3 tbsp. (50 mL) butter	*2 tbsp. (30 mL) fresh*
4 tbsp. (60 mL) flour	*parsley, chopped*
1 cup (250 mL)	*salt and pepper*
chicken or beef	*1 tsp. (5 mL) A-1 sauce*
consommé	*2 egg whites, lightly*
1-1½ cups (250-375	*beaten*
mL) cooked ground	*¾ cup (190 mL) fine*
veal or pork	*dry breadcrumbs*

Heat butter in a saucepan, add flour and cook over medium heat for 2 to 3 minutes, stirring most of the time. Add consommé and stir until a thick paste is formed. Remove from heat, add the next 4 ingredients and stir until well blended. Spread this mixture on a platter, cover with waxed paper and refrigerate 2 to 4 hours. Shape the mixture into 1-in. (2.5 cm) balls. Dip each one in the beaten egg whites, then roll in the breadcrumbs.

Pour vegetable oil into a saucepan to a depth of 2 to 3 in. (5 to 7.5 cm) and heat. Deep fry a few meatballs at a time for about 2 minutes, or until golden brown. Drain on paper towels and set on a cooling rack. Serve hot with wooden cocktail picks, with mustard for dipping. *Yield: 30 to 40.*

Hutspot, Slavinken, Kaassechotel: Main Course Dishes

Hutspot

The meat and vegetables in the Dutch boiled dinner are slowly simmered together; then mashed vegetables thicken the broth into a delicious sauce.

2 lb. (1 kg) beef short rib	*3 onions, sliced*
4 cups (1 L) cold water	*5-8 carrots, sliced*
2 tbsp. (30 mL) salt	*6-8 whole potatoes, peeled*
1 bay leaf	*2 tbsp. (30 mL) butter*
¼ tsp. (1 mL) thyme	*freshly ground pepper*

Cover meat with the water, add salt and bring to a boil. Boil 5 minutes and with a perforated spoon remove any scum that rises. Then cover and simmer 1½ hours.

Add bay leaf, thyme and vegetables and simmer, covered, another 1½ hours, or until meat is tender.

Remove meat to a warm platter, strain broth and reserve. Mash vegetables, add butter and enough broth to make a thick purée, then taste for seasoning. Slice meat and serve over vegetable purée in deep plates. The broth can be used for soup, and any leftover meat can be used to make a Dutch beef salad. *Serves 4.*

Slavinken

Whenever I am in Holland, I find new ways to prepare ground meat, each one original and different. Most of the year this recipe is referred to as *Slavinken,* except in the spring when I have seen it referred to as "Salad Birds," on menus in hotels. Perfect served with a bowl of Dutch mustard, a bock of cold beer and thick slices of Dutch black bread or, as a hot meal, with mashed potatoes and milk gravy.

Slavinken:

2 slices black or white bread	*¹/₈ tsp. (0.5 mL) nutmeg*
¹/₄ cup (60 mL) milk or flat beer	*¹/₄ tsp. (1 mL) allspice*
1 lb. (500 g) ground pork	*1 small onion, finely chopped*
salt and pepper	*6 thin bacon slices*
	1 tsp. (5 mL) butter

Crumble bread, pour milk or beer on top and let stand for 10 minutes. Squeeze bread to remove excess liquid, if any. Place in a bowl. Add ground pork, salt, pepper, nutmeg, allspice and onion. Knead mixture until well blended.

Form into 6 cylinders and wrap a slice of bacon around each one. Secure with a wooden pick.

Melt butter in a cast-iron frying pan. Fry the *slavinken* over medium heat, 6 minutes on each side. Remove to a hot platter as they become cooked, and keep warm. *Serves 6.*

Milk Gravy:

1 tbsp. (15 mL) flour	*¹/₄ cup (60 mL) light cream*
pan fat from slavinken	*parsley*
¹/₂ cup (125 mL) milk	

Stir flour into the remaining fat in the pan used to make the *slavinken* and cook over medium heat until it becomes a caramel color. Add milk and light cream. Stir until creamy. Add parsley and season to taste. Pour over meat or serve separately.

Altmaar Potato Special

The little golden oval Dutch potatoes are recognized every-where as the very best there are. Even in France, they are a favorite. The combination of potatoes and cheese in this dish is particularly delicious. Use Idaho-type potatoes — very good ones are grown in western Canada, especially those from the sandy lands of Brandon, Manitoba.

Serve this specialty with thinly sliced roast beef and a good pot of mustard, or by itself as a main dish.

6-8 medium potatoes	*2 tbsp. (30 mL) butter*
¹/₂ cup (125 mL) hot	*2 tbsp. (30 mL) parsley*
light cream or milk	*or chives, chopped*
¹/₂ cup (125 mL) grated	*4 eggs, separated*
Gouda cheese	

Boil the potatoes over medium heat—beware of overcooking—drain and dry them. Mash, then add remaining ingredients, except eggs, and mix thoroughly. Beat egg yolks until thick and pale yellow, about 2 minutes, then fold into potatoes. Beat egg whites until stiff, then fold in potato and egg yolk mixture.

Pile gently into a 2-quart (2 L) buttered casserole. Bake in a 375°F. (190°C) oven 25 minutes, or until puffed and slightly browned on top. *Serves 4.*

Kaassechotel

Kaas means cheese, and *chotel*, casserole. A casserole made with their own cheese, and served at least once a week, is a must for the Dutch.

¹/₄ cup (60 mL) butter	*3 eggs*
6 slices bread, crusts	*1 cup (250 mL) milk or*
removed	*light cream*
¹/₂ lb. (250 g) thinly	*¹/₄ tsp. (1 mL) salt*
sliced Edam or Gouda	*¹/₈ tsp. (0.5 mL) savory*
cheese	*or a pinch of nutmeg*

Butter generously a 1-quart (1 L) casserole and each slice of bread. Place bread in casserole, overlapping slightly, and top with sliced cheese.

A pleasurable way to enjoy teatime in the summer. I like to use English Stoneware of the Botanical Garden series — each piece represents a different medieval garden design.

Pour the Café Liégeois in front of your guests and let them enjoy its rich darkness while they munch on a nutty macaroon.

While I was looking at the fresh sardines, crayfish, "puffballs" and so much more in the Nice market, the friendly marchande *asked me in French, "Do you want a fish for an elegant dish or a simple daily fare?" Unfortunately I was just looking.*

Beat remaining ingredients together, pour over bread and let stand 30 minutes. Then place dish in a pan of hot water and bake in a 350°F. (180°C) oven 30 to 40 minutes, or until golden brown and puffed. The result is creamy bread covered with a thick layer of melted cheese, held together by a creamy sauce. *Serves 4.*

Cheese Pancakes

The Dutch have many types of pancakes, each one quite differ-ent. I had these for lunch on the first day of my "cheese trip," in a little restaurant in the woods near Arnheim. The batter is best if it stands for an hour or two before being cooked. These pancakes come out crisp on top, with just the right soft creamy texture inside. The molasses-lemon addition is my idea; fruit syrup or jam is used in Holland.

4 eggs
2 cups (500 mL) milk
2 cups (500 mL)
  all-purpose flour
1 tsp. (5 mL) salt
¹/₂ cup (125 mL) water

2 cups (500 mL) grated
  Gouda or Edam
  cheese
1 cup (250 mL)
  molasses
juice of 1 lemon

Beat eggs until light, then add 1 cup (250 mL) of the milk. Mix flour and salt in a bowl and stir into egg mixture. Blend, then gradually add remaining milk and cold water while beating with a rotary beater or whisk. When batter is thin and smooth, set aside.

Use a large iron frying pan or a griddle for cooking. Heat, buttering generously, and ladle out ¹/₃ cup (80 mL) of batter for each pancake. When brown on one side, turn and brown other side.

Place 1 or 2 pancakes on a hot platter and sprinkle each with 1 tbsp. (15 mL) of cheese. Repeat, stacking pancakes on top of each other with cheese between. When completed, cut in wedges or in half and lay sideways on plates.

Serve with a jug of the molasses that has been heated with the lemon juice (this may be omitted) and pour over the pan-cakes. *Yield: about sixteen 5-in. (12.5 cm) pancakes.*

Leyden Smothered Mushrooms

Leyden is Rembrandt's birthplace. The world-famous University of Leyden has a superb collection of Dutch antiques, a small part of which I have seen.

The smothered mushrooms are a well-known specialty of this interesting town. The addition to the sauce of a couple of dried wild mushrooms gives the dish its distinctive flavor.

1 lb. (500 g) fresh mushrooms
2 dried mushrooms*
1 cup (250 mL) commercial sour cream
1 tbsp. (15 mL) chopped parsley

3 French shallots, chopped fine
1 tbsp. (15 mL) butter
¼ tsp. (1 mL) each salt and pepper
1 tbsp. (15 mL) lemon juice
2 tbsp. (30 mL) grated Parmesan

Butter a covered casserole. Place mushrooms in a colander and wash quickly under running water. Shake hard to remove as much water as possible. Cut a bit off the stem end. Place stem-side down in the buttered casserole.

Break or cut the dried mushrooms into small pieces. Sprinkle over the fresh mushrooms. Mix the remaining ingredients except the cheese. Pour over the mushrooms.

Sprinkle cheese on top. Cover tightly. Bake in a preheated 350°F. (180°C) oven about 30 minutes. *Serves 4, as a meal, or 6, as a vegetable.*

*Many types can be found in specialty shops. They are sold packaged in small quantities, and are expensive. They can be omitted.

Greenhouse Carrots and Peas

I love vegetables, and nowhere else other than in Holland have I eaten a better mixture of these two popular vegetables. In early spring, many greenhouses that grow vegetables sell baby carrots and fresh green peas. The custom is to top the basket with a few sprigs of fresh parsley and fresh chives. Depending on the type of vegetable you use, this dish may vary in perfection, but it will always be good.

1 lb. (500 g) baby carrots	*3 tbsp. (50 mL) light cream*
1/2 tsp. each (2 mL) sugar and salt	*1 tbsp. (15 mL) butter parsley or chives*
2 lb. (1 kg) fresh green peas, hulled	

Place carrots, sugar and salt in a saucepan. Pour boiling water over, cover and simmer 15 to 20 minutes, or until carrots are tender. Drain and set aside.

Shuck green peas and place in a jam jar. Cover and place jar in a deep saucepan. Pour hot water (not boiling) in the pan, high enough to cover 1/2 to 3/4 of the jar. Cover pan and boil 35 minutes. Do not drain peas—the small amount of water in the bottom of the jar is the natural water from the vegetables.

Place in a saucepan cream and butter and simmer until butter is melted. Add carrots and green peas. Simmer over low heat about 15 minutes, stirring a few times. Add parsley or chives. Taste for seasoning and serve. *Serves 4 to 6.*

Dutch Treats

Dutch Gingerbread

Dutch women have a great talent in the use of spices. For many centuries, spices have had a priority in their kitchens because of the Netherlands' association with Indonesia. Here's a very special and most enticing gingerbread.

¹/₂ cup *(125 mL) pure lard*	¹/₂ tsp. *(2 mL) salt*
¹/₂ cup *(125 mL) brown sugar*	2 tsp. *(10 mL) ground ginger*
1 egg	1 tsp. *(5 mL) crushed coriander seeds*
²/₃ cup *(160 mL) treacle or molasses*	2 tsp. *(10 mL) caraway seeds*
grated peel of 1 orange	1 tsp. *(5 mL) baking soda*
2¹/₂ cups *(625 mL) all-purpose flour*	1 cup *(250 mL) boiling water*
2 tsp. *(10 mL) baking powder*	

Cream lard, sugar and egg until light and foamy. Add treacle or molasses and orange peel. Sift together flour, baking powder, salt, ginger, coriander seeds, caraway seeds and soda. Add to the creamed mixture, mix well and add the boiling water. Mix until smooth and do not add any flour if the batter seems very thin — it should be thin.

Pour into a greased bread pan and bake at 325°F. (160°C) for 50 to 60 minutes, or until well done. Cool, unmold on cake rack and let it rest a day or two before eating, well wrapped in foil or transparent paper.

Rice and Fruit Porridge

The Dutch have a way with rice that is unusual. Again, this may be the Indonesian influence. On a beautiful Sunday in the summer of 1961, I was invited for brunch to the home of a bulb grower, whom I had met in the post-war period in Holland. There was a big, beautiful earthenware soup tureen filled with the rice porridge and two lovely silver filigree baskets on each side—one with *oliebollen*, or Dutch doughnuts, the other with rye honey spiced bread and cardamom rusks — lots of dark black coffee and, to finish, *advocaat* eggnog or liqueur, delicious and potent (also hard to describe) and served in white wine glasses.

3 cups (750 mL) sweet
white wine
2 cups (500 mL)
long-grain rice*
1 cup (250 mL) currants

8 apples, peeled, cored
and sliced
a bowl of beaten
unsalted butter
a bowl of brown or
Demerara sugar
a shaker of cinnamon

Place in a heavy metal saucepan wine, rice, currants and apples. Bring to a boil over medium heat, stirring. Cover, lower heat to simmer and cook 30 to 35 minutes, or until rice is tender. Stir gently. Serve hot. Each person can add butter, sugar and cinnamon to taste. Thick cream or yogurt can replace the butter. *Serves 6.*

To whip butter: Beat until creamy in a blender or food processor or by hand with a whisk. Pour into a serving dish. Refrigerate until ready to serve.

*The rice can be cooked the day before, then covered and refrigerated. When ready to use, warm up in a double boiler over low heat. Stir with a fork.

Advocaat

Some call it dessert, others, a liqueur. To me it is a sort of French *sabayon* . . . whatever, it is delectable.

5 eggs
a pinch of salt
³/₄ cup (190 mL) sugar

1 cup (250 mL) brandy
1 tsp. (5 mL) vanilla

Beat eggs, salt and sugar with an electric beater in the top of a double boiler until very thick and pale yellow. Then add brandy a tablespoon (15 mL) at a time, beating constantly.

Boil water in the bottom of the double boiler, place mixture over it, lower the heat, then beat, without stopping, until the mixture is warm, thickened and creamy.

Remove from heat and stir in the vanilla slowly and gently. Pour into a glass pitcher or into individual glasses. Eat *slowly* with a spoon. *Serves 6.*

Belgium

Too often Belgian food is forgotten or considered inferior to French cooking. Personally, I strongly disagree. Belgium has created and perfected a cuisine very much its own, despite the fact that it is a country with two distinctive types of table, the Flemish in the north, Walloon in the south, and influenced by Germany, Holland, Luxembourg and France. Once you travel through Belgium, you cannot ignore its individual cuisine. Do not let anyone tell you that it is German or Dutch or that it does not compare to French cooking. Certainly, there is less variety, but there is always stress on the quality of the ingredients used. We become aware of it when we eat the *asperges de Malines* or the *jambon des Ardennes* or the *beurre de Namur*— such butter! In the best restaurants, hotels and homes, they are very particular about the quality of the butter (only the very best is used), and they cook mostly with butter!

I thought no one could make as a good a ham as the Danish, until I tasted the "Ardennes ham." Barely a year ago, I spent some time again in Belgium, and was thrilled by the fact that the quality of the food being offered was still first class. I had thought that now that it had become the center of many international communities, such as NATO, the Common Market, etc., it would perhaps be different, but I noticed that the shoppers were taking as much care in choosing their foods as ever. I have always thought that home cooking in Belgium was superior to that in France. I know many will disagree, so I will add: Did you ever taste their chicken, their mussels, their pastry, their chocolate or nougat and their fancy-shaped marzipan? If ever you stay in Brussels long enough, take a day to go to the St. Catherine Market—everything is beautiful to look at —color, shape, quality, and presented with taste. Do not miss the fish market — you will be amazed at the variety and freshness of the displays.

To close the door on all this beautiful food, end the visit by going to the Flower Market on the Grande Place in Brussels. If you are like me, you will wish you had twenty rooms to fill with all the beautiful flowers.

In America we have hundreds of fast-food outlets; in Belgium, no matter where you go, whatever the time of day or night, you will find little places, referred to as *fritures,* where you can have french fries, a bowl of superb stewed mussels and beer. Another food largely used is mayonnaise. I sometimes felt its use was overdone.

To end this speedy gourmet tour of Belgium, I would like to pay homage to their one typical cheese, the Hervé. There are the mild (*doux*) and the strong (*fort*) varieties. My preference goes to the mild, which is like thick unctuous cream, melting on your tongue. I have not seen it in our country, but I never fail to enjoy it when in Belgium.

Soup and Seafood

Fish Soup of Ostend

While travelling through Belgium in 1963, I went to Ghent, or Gant — a charming city, and well worth the visit. Its architecture is ancient Flemish, and the whole city has an air of yesteryear. It is famous for its chicken *Waterzooi* and one of its best restaurants is the St. Jorishof, built in the thirteenth century in the Gothic style. The city has a reputation for the beauty of its interior and the quality of its food.

From Ghent, we drove to Bruges. Had it been only to visit the Municipal Museum with the most important collection of Flemish paintings, it would still have been well worth the kilometers. On the Quai du Rosaire, one can find a few pieces of Bruges lace and some very interesting small restaurants. If you drive on a little more, you will reach Ostend on the North Sea, where seafood is super. On my first trip there I had the specialty of Ostend, fish soup filled with little pink shrimps, sweet, tender and so tasty. All you need after a bowl of Ostend Soup is a few paper-thin slices of *jambon des Ardennes* and a glass of cool dry white wine.

1 head and the bones of a seawater fish*	*3 tbsp. (50 mL) flour*
6 cups (1.5 L) water	*2 cups (500 mL) small cooked shrimps*
2 lemon slices, unpeeled	*1 tsp. (5 mL) tomato paste*
6–8 sprigs of parsley	*juice of ¹/₂ lemon*
1 leek, cleaned and thinly sliced	*¹/₂ cup (125 mL) light cream*
1 carrot, peeled and sliced	*1 tbsp. (15 mL) fresh chervil or parsley, chopped*
1 tsp. (5 mL) salt	
6 peppercorns, crushed	

Place fish head and bones in a saucepan. Add the water, sprigs of parsley, lemon slices, leek, carrot, salt and peppercorns. Bring to a fast rolling boil, lower the heat, cover and simmer 30

---

*If you cannot use fish bones, replace with 1 bottle of clam juice poured into a measuring cup and add enough water to make the 6 cups required.

minutes. Strain through a fine sieve and discard fish and vegetables.

Mix flour with ½ cup (125 mL) of the broth until creamy and smooth. Add to the remaining broth, stirring with a whisk.

Place 1 cup (250 mL) of the shrimps in a food processor or blender with tomato paste, lemon juice and half the cream. Cover and blend until the whole is a purée. Add to the soup, along with the remaining cream. Heat over low heat, stirring often, but do not boil. Add the remaining shrimps and chervil or parsley. Heat again. Serve very hot. *Serves 6.*

Soup Chantrier

I have a weakness for all soups, but when my refrigerator contains the combination of leeks, barley and chicken stock, I play it fast! In Brussels, you can enjoy this soup at Le Cygne, one of the best restaurants on La Grande Place.

4 bacon slices	*¼ cup (60 mL) pearl*
2 large leeks	*barley*
4 cups (1 L) chicken	*3 tbsp. (50 mL) chopped*
broth	*parsley*
1 tbsp. (15 mL) butter	*½ cup (125 mL) heavy*
	cream

Chop bacon and fry until golden brown and crisp. Wash leeks and slice fine, using as much of the green as possible. Add to the bacon fat and stir over medium heat, about 2 minutes. Add chicken stock.

Melt butter in a frying pan, add barley and stir constantly until it becomes a nutty brown color. Add to soup. Bring to boil, lower the heat and simmer for 1 hour.

Add parsley to cream and simmer over *very low heat*, until reduced by half. Set aside. Add to soup when ready to serve. *Serves 4.*

Trout Bruxelloise

Any small whole fish can be cooked in this manner and many restaurants in Belgium offer these on the lunch menu. A simple but interesting way to serve fish. The traditional fish is the whiting.

4 small trout or whiting
3 tbsp. (50 mL) milk
¹/₄ cup (60 mL) flour
1 cup (250 mL) fine dry
  breadcrumbs
3 tbsp. (50 mL) butter
1 small onion, chopped
  fine

1 French shallot,
  chopped fine
  (optional)
¹/₄ cup (60 mL) white
  wine
1 tbsp. (15 mL) wine or
  cider vinegar

Wash fish, roll in milk, then flour and finally in breadcrumbs. Let stand 10 minutes.

Melt butter in a large frying pan. (In Belgium, they use an enamelled cast-iron pan.) Cook the fish 4 minutes on each side, over high heat, turning only once. After you turn the fish, lower the heat to medium. When done, set on a warm platter.

To the remaining butter in the pan add onion and shallot and stir over medium heat until soft. Add white wine and vinegar. Boil 1 minute and pour over the fish. Serve with steamed potatoes rolled in parsley. *Serves 4.*

Mussels Bruxelloise

Throughout Belgium, mussels are cooked in the following manner and served in large, deep soup plates, with a bowl of french fries, or *frites*, as they are called.

5 lb. (2.5 kg) mussels	*1 medium onion, thinly*
3 tbsp. (50 mL)	*sliced*
unsalted butter	*1 cup (250 mL) dry*
¹/₂ cup (125 mL)	*white wine*
chopped celery leaves	*10 crushed peppercorns*
10 parsley sprigs,	
chopped	

Clean mussels one by one with a brush. Do not let them soak in water. Rinse quickly under running water.

Melt butter in a large saucepan with a good cover, and add celery leaves, parsley, onion, white wine and peppercorns. Simmer until hot.

Place mussels on top of this mixture and cover the pan. Simmer—do not boil—until the shells open, which should take from 6 to 8 minutes. With a perforated spoon place the mussels in a warm bowl. Strain the broth through a fine sieve over the mussels. Serve immediately. *Serves 4.*

Belgian Vegetables: Asparagus, Endive, Sprouts

Malines Asparagus Salad (Asperges de Malines)

Malines is a city in the center of Belgium which specializes in growing these big, juicy, snow-white asparagus. They are served with an egg sauce consisting of a hard-boiled egg chopped and stirred into melted butter, a spoonful of lemon juice, a dash of nutmeg and minced parsley.

The salad, an unusual combination of hot and cold ingredients, is a specialty of the Grand Hotel in Brussels.

Lobster Sauce:

2 tbsp. (30 mL) butter
1 tbsp. (15 mL) flour
1 tsp. (5 mL) salt
1/2 tsp. (2 mL) sugar
1/4 tsp. (1 mL) pepper
1 cup (250 mL) light
   cream

1 cup (250 mL) fresh
   cooked or canned
   lobster
1 tsp. (5 mL) fresh
   lemon juice or brandy
1 egg yolk
2 tbsp. (30 mL) dry
   sherry

Melt butter and thoroughly mix in flour, salt, sugar and pepper. Add cream, then whisk and stir over medium heat until mixture has a light, creamy-smooth texture. Add lobster, making sure it is not chopped too fine.

Beat lemon juice or brandy with egg yolk and sherry. Remove hot lobster sauce from heat and stir in egg yolk mixture (it will change the sauce texture). Keep hot over low heat — it must not boil.

Salad:

4 hard-boiled eggs,
   halved
20 fresh asparagus,
   cooked and cooled

3 tbsp. (50 mL) grated
   Swiss cheese

Arrange egg halves and cold asparagus on a warm platter, pour hot lobster sauce on top and sprinkle with cheese. *Serves 4.*

Endive Salad

Endives are often referred to in Belgium as *chicous* or *chicorée Witloof*. They are perfect, yet unusual, served as a salad. In our country, they are a costly gourmet pleasure and are often served braised. They are fairly easy to find from January to April, imported, and in September, when home grown.

To serve as a salad the leaves may be separated and simply left whole, or the whole head may be cut into half-inch slices (1.25 cm) — as they do in Belgium. It is a refreshing, crunchy, tangy salad, as well as being low in calories. Endives are also often served tossed with boiled beets that have been diced or sliced.

Salad:

1 lb. (500 g) endives	*2–3 green onions, thinly sliced*

Remove the first 2 to 4 leaves from each endive, then cut the whole head into ¹/₄ to ¹/₂ in. (.62 to 1.24 cm) slices. Break up in a salad bowl and sprinkle with green onions.

Dressing:

¹/₃ cup (80 mL) olive or vegetable oil	*¹/₄ tsp. (1 mL) pepper*
juice of 1 lemon	*1 tsp. (5 mL) Dijon mustard*
grated rind of ¹/₂ lemon	*a pinch of sugar*
¹/₂ tsp. (2 mL) salt	

In a bowl whisk together olive or vegetable oil, lemon juice and grated rind, salt, pepper, Dijon mustard and sugar. When ready to serve the salad, whisk the dressing once more and add by spoonfuls, tossing after each addition. *Serves 4.*

Endive Sandwiches

In August you will find many tea rooms serving these with a
bowl of *frites* and a glass of beer.

2 heads of endives
2 hard-boiled eggs,
  chopped
1/2 cup (125 mL) celery,
  diced
1/4 cup (60 mL) green
  onions, chopped

1/4 cup (60 mL) parsley,
  chopped
mayonnaise
1 tsp. (5 mL) wine or
  cider vinegar

Mince whole heads of endives, add chopped hard-cooked eggs,
then celery, green onions and parsley. Stir lightly. Add just
enough mayonnaise to bind the whole, and stir in the vinegar.
Salt and pepper to taste. Use whole-wheat bread to make the
sandwiches. *Yield: 6 sandwiches.*

Brussels Sprouts Purée

The Belgians, as well as the French, are masters at turning any type of vegetable into an attractive and delectable purée. I have even used this one as a filling for crêpes, topped with a sprinkling of grated cheese, and heated in the oven when ready to serve.

4 cups (1 L) Brussels sprouts	*¹/₄ tsp. (1 mL) nutmeg*
1 bread slice, toasted	*¹/₄ tsp. (1 mL) curry powder*
¹/₄ tsp. (1 mL) sugar	*salt and pepper*
4 tbsp. (60 mL) butter	*2 egg yolks*
1 tbsp. (15 mL) flour	*¹/₄ cup (60 mL) light cream*
1 cup (250 mL) of cooking liquid from the sprouts	

Remove top leaves of each sprout, place in a saucepan, set toasted bread on top and sprinkle bread with sugar (the sugared bread prevents a cabbage flavor from developing). Then pour in enough boiling water to completely cover the vegetables. Bring back to boil, then boil, uncovered, for 10 to 12 minutes, or until sprouts are tender. Reserve a cup (250 mL) of the liquid and drain the rest.

Melt butter, add flour and mix well, then add the reserved cup (250 mL) of water. Stir until bubbly and creamy. Add seasonings and stir until well blended. Place the drained sprouts and bread in a blender or food processor, pour sauce on top and mix until creamy.

Beat egg yolks with cream. Place in a saucepan over low heat, gradually pour in the Brussels sprouts purée, stirring constantly with a wire whisk. Heat thoroughly, but do not let it boil. The egg and cream can be added to the purée even a few hours after it is cooked. In this case, warm up the purée and slowly add the beaten egg and cream, over medium heat, beating until hot. *Serves 4 to 6.*

Chicken Dishes

Ostend Chicken Breasts Glacés

This is a classic of the Belgian cuisine in the Flanders on the North Sea, and is served hot or cold, depending on the season. The delicious oyster crouton stuffing is a bit costly nowadays, but well worth it. Ostend is known for its delicious oysters.

3 whole chicken breasts,	*¹/₂ cup (125 mL) melted*
with skin	*butter*
2 cups (500 mL) small	*3 tbsp. (50 mL) butter*
bread cubes	*3 tbsp. (50 mL) flour*
1 tsp. (5 mL) salt	*2 cups (500 mL) milk*
¹/₂ tsp. (2 mL) pepper	*1 cup (250 mL) oysters*
¹/₄ tsp. (1 mL) mace or	*soft butter*
nutmeg	*¹/₂ cup (125 mL) red*
¹/₂ cup (125 mL) fresh	*currant jelly*
parsley, chopped	*grated peel and juice of*
1 small onion, diced	*1 orange*

Split breasts into halves and salt and pepper both sides. Cut off bread crusts and dice bread. Place on a baking sheet and bake for 5 to 10 minutes at 350°F. (180°C), or until golden brown. Let cool.

Put bread cubes in a bowl with salt, pepper, mace or nutmeg, parsley, onion and the melted butter. Stir until well blended.

Make a wine sauce with the 3 tbsp. (50 mL) butter, flour and milk. When creamy and smooth, add well-drained oysters. Let cool, then pour over bread cube mixture. Toss lightly with 2 forks.

Place each breast on its own square of foil, skin-side down, and fill with ¹/₃ cup (80 mL) of stuffing. Turn breasts so stuffing will be on foil and turn foil up, but do not cover top of breasts. Set side by side in a shallow roasting pan and brush the tops with soft butter.

Bake uncovered at 325°F. (160°C) for 30 to 40 minutes. After 25 minutes, beat red currant jelly with a rotary beater until smooth, brush each breast with it and continue to roast, brushing 3 to 4 more times.

When breasts are done, remove foil and set breasts on a hot dish. Add orange peel and juice to drippings. Stir until hot, strain and pour over breasts. Serve with fine noodles, lightly buttered. *Serves 6.*

Bruges Chicken Casserole

When I got married at twenty, my veil was held by a little bonnet of *dentelle de Bruges*, given to me by a Belgian friend of my mother's. I used it for the baptism of my daughter Monique and my granddaughter Susan. So, for many years I had a desire to go and see the laces in Bruges. Finally it happened, but, alas, it was after the First War, and much of it had disappeared. Today, finding authentic Bruges lace is difficult, and it is a costly treasure. However, last year in Brussels I saw some in a beautiful linen and lace shop on the Grande Place. How romantic if one could eat this Bruges Chicken Casserole wearing a lace cap!

Because this is a Flemish specialty, beer is used instead of wine.

a 3¹/₂-lb. chicken (1.5 kg) or 3 whole chicken breasts, halved	*1 tsp. (5 mL) salt*
	¹/₂ tsp. (2 mL) pepper
	1 tbsp. (15 mL) brown sugar
3 tbsp. (50 mL) butter	*3 bacon slices*
1 large onion, diced	*1¹/₂ cups (375 mL) light beer*
2 medium carrots, chopped	*juice of ¹/₂ lemon*
2 celery stalks, finely chopped	*1 tbsp. (15 mL) cornstarch*
¹/₄ tsp. (1 mL) marjoram	*2 tbsp. (30 mL) brandy*

Cut chicken into individual serving pieces. Melt butter in a casserole (enamelled cast iron would give it the true Flemish touch). Stir in vegetables and marjoram over low heat until well buttered. Mix in salt, pepper and brown sugar. Stir well, add chicken and stir again.

Top with bacon slices and cook uncovered in a 400°F. (200°C) oven 20 minutes. Add beer, cover and cook 30 to 40 minutes, or until chicken is tender.

Blend remaining ingredients, stir into sauce until slightly thickened, simmer 5 minutes over low heat and taste for seasoning. *Serves 6.*

Gand Mustard Chicken

One day I drove to Gand, or Ghent (depending on whether you say it in Flemish or Belgian) just to see the renowned triptyque or altar piece, *Agneau Mystique*, at the Cathedral of St. Bevon —a pure joy, well worth the miles you may have to travel. Then we lunched at a very elegant small restaurant (six tables in all), where all the food was cooked to order. We needed time to silently absorb the beauty of the Cathedral that still filled our eyes, so we were happy to wait.

I had the Mustard Chicken with a plate of cold *Asperges de Malines* as an appetizer. Allowing that the quality of chicken in Belgium is outstanding, the finished dish was still "three stars." It must be made with Dijon or top quality German mustard, as none of our ordinary mustards will give good results.

a 3-4 lb. (1.5-2 kg) broiler, whole	*3 tsp. (50 mL) olive or peanut oil*
½ lemon	*brandy or chicken broth*
½ tsp. (2 mL) salt	*or light cream*
Dijon-type mustard	

Rub the chicken all over, inside and out, with the cut lemon— squeeze the lemon as you work—then sprinkle with salt. Truss and tie the chicken and place on a rack. Using a pastry brush, spread mustard all over. Place breast-side down on the rack and brush underside of chicken with mustard. Leave chicken breast-side down on the rack (it is the classic way to roast chicken in Belgium). Dribble the olive or peanut oil all over the chicken.

Roast in a preheated 450°F. (230°C) oven for 8 minutes, then turn on its side, baste the chicken with drippings and roast 7 minutes. Lower the heat to 350°F. (180°C) and continue roasting for 10 minutes. Turn chicken breast-side up, and roast another 5 to 7 minutes.

Untie and place the chicken on a hot platter. Add a little brandy or chicken broth or light cream to roasting pan. Scrape well over low heat. When boiling, strain into a bowl. Serve chicken surrounded with french fries. *Serves 4.*

Three Meals-in-a-Pot

Oxtail Hochepot

The addition of pig's feet gives a special flavor to this oxtail. In Belgium, I learned to serve it cold, removing all the bones from the sauce and mixing the meat, vegetables and juice into one golden, jellied mold. It forms its own jelly because of the pig's feet. So take your choice—hot or cold—both ways equally good.

1 or 2 oxtails	1 can consommé or
2 pig's feet (1¹/₂-2 lb.)	onion soup, diluted
(750 g-1 kg)	1 tsp. (5 mL) salt
1 small cabbage,	¹/₄ tsp. (1 mL) pepper
coarsely chopped	1 bay leaf
10 small onions, peeled	¹/₄ tsp. (1 mL) thyme
1 small turnip, diced	¹/₄ cup (60 mL) celery
6 carrots, diced	leaves, minced
2 tbsp. (30 mL) bacon	¹/₄ cup (60 mL) parsley,
fat	minced
	1 garlic clove, crushed

Ask the butcher to cut the oxtail in pieces, and to chop each pig's foot in 3 pieces. Prepare the vegetables. Spread the bacon fat thickly in the bottom of a Dutch oven or enamelled cast-iron casserole and place the oxtail and pig's feet over it. Place on top cabbage, onions, turnip and carrots. Pour in consommé or onion soup (diluted according to directions on the can), salt, pepper, bay leaf, thyme, celery leaves, parsley and garlic.

Cover tightly, simmer over low heat for 3 to 4 hours, or bake the same length of time in a 300°F. (150°C) oven. The cooking period is determined by the tenderness of the oxtail.

To mold it, cool, then remove all the meat from the bones and place in a mold of your choice. Bring the vegetables and juices to a full rolling boil. Boil uncovered 5 minutes. Pour over the meat. Cool. Cover and refrigerate 24 hours before unmolding. *Serves 6 to 8.*

Waterzooi Gantoise

The most traditional and best-known dish of Belgium, originating from the Flanders part of Belgium. It is made with fish, or just vegetables, or with chicken, the latter being the most famous. It is lots of work, but when done, you will have two or three different meals. It is hard to describe as it is somewhere between a stew and a soup; as a matter of fact, it is traditional to serve it in large soup plates. A superb party dish.

1 lb. (500 g) beef short rib	*1 tbsp. (15 mL) coarse salt*
2 lb. (1 kg) veal shank	*1 tsp. (5 mL) thyme*
1 lb. (500 g) chicken giblets	*12 cups (3 L) water*
4 carrots, peeled and left whole	*a 4–lb. (2 kg) chicken*
3 leeks, white part only	*2 egg yolks*
4 medium onions, left whole	*1 cup (250 mL) heavy cream*
3 sticks celery, cut in half	*salt and pepper*
	¹/₄ tsp. (1 mL) nutmeg

The day before cooking the chicken, place in a large saucepan the first 10 ingredients. Bring to a fast rolling boil. Cover and simmer over low heat 4 hours. Cool and let meat stand in bouillon all night. The next day remove meat and strain the consommé. You should have 8 cups (2 L) left. If there is more, boil uncovered until consommé is reduced to 8 cups (2 L). Add the well-trussed chicken, bring back to boil, cover and simmer until chicken is tender, about 1 hour.

In a large soup tureen or bowl, beat egg yolks, cream, salt, pepper and nutmeg. Cut the hot chicken into pieces (not slices). Pour 1 cup (250 mL) of the boiling stock over egg mixture, stir well with a whisk, add chicken pieces, then more stock. Stir well and taste for seasoning. Serve with boiled rice. The vegetables are sometimes cut into large pieces and added to the consommé. *Serves 6.*

Suggestions for Leftovers
Boiled beef: Slice thinly and serve cold with a potato salad. Or, warm up in some of the remaining consommé, without boiling, and serve with boiled potatoes and a herb vinaigrette or French dressing, thick with finely chopped fresh parsley and green onions.

Veal shank: Dice and stir into a medium white sauce, made partly with milk, partly with remaining consommé or some white wine. Place in a casserole and top generously with grated cheese, such as a mild Cheddar. Bake 20 minutes in a 350°F. (180°C) oven.

Vegetables: Dice and add to the remaining consommé, along with fine noodles or leftover rice.

Pork and Ale Sauerkraut

My husband and I had this robust, tasty dish in a small café-restaurant in Liège. As we were in a rush, we stopped at the first place that was on our way. Once more we realized that in Belgium even small unpretentious restaurants not only give you your money's worth, but also good food. As in England, there is a beer on tap most of the time, and the beer, even if potent, is good. The *plat du jour* was the Pork and Ale Sauerkraut, served with a big basket of thick slices of assorted dark brown bread — that was super.

For dessert, the lightest, most delicious lemon crêpes, and to top it all, a perfect cup of *Café Liégeois*.

2 lb. (1 kg) sauerkraut	salt and pepper
1 pt. (500 mL) ale	3 garlic cloves, minced
1 tbsp. (15 mL) brown	4 apples, unpeeled and
sugar	grated
10 juniper berries*	3 potatoes, peeled and
6 pork shoulder steaks	coarsely grated
2 tbsp. (30 mL) bacon	
fat or butter	

Place in an enamelled cast-iron saucepan sauerkraut, ale, brown sugar and juniper berries. Cover and simmer 40 minutes over low heat.

Brown the steaks in bacon fat or butter.

Put a layer of sauerkraut in a casserole and place pork steaks on top. Sprinkle with garlic and grated apples. Cover with half the remaining sauerkraut. Set potatoes over this and cover with the remaining sauerkraut and all its juice.

Cover and bake in a preheated 350°F. (180°C) oven 40 to 50 minutes. *Serves 6.*

*Juniper berries are sold at supermarkets, in the herb section. There are lots to be found in the Canadian woods. Gather and dry them in the summer sun.

Dessert and Coffee

La Cramique

A sort of large raisin bread, cut into thick slices and served hot with coffee. There are varied recipes for it, but the following is my favorite.

1–2 cups (250–500 mL) *seedless raisins*	*¹/₂ cup (125 mL) melted* *butter*
2 envelopes active dry *yeast*	*2 eggs, well beaten* *6 cups (1.5 L)*
2 tbsp. (30 mL) sugar	*all-purpose flour*
¹/₄ cup (60 mL) *lukewarm water*	*1¹/₂ tsp. (7 mL) salt* *1 cup (250 mL) small*
2 cups (500 mL) *lukewarm milk*	*sugar cubes**

Cover raisins with boiling water. Let stand 15 minutes and drain.

Stir together yeast, sugar and lukewarm water. Let stand 10 minutes.

Stir together in a large bowl lukewarm milk, melted butter, eggs and well-stirred yeast mixture. Mix well, add the salt and stir. Add flour gradually, 1 cup (250 mL) at a time, stirring at each addition until you have a smooth soft dough. Stir the raisins with 1 cup (250 mL) of the flour and knead into the dough, then fold in small sugar cubes.

Turn dough on a floured board and knead 2 to 3 minutes, sprinkling dough with flour if it gets sticky. When sugar cubes are well incorporated, cover dough and let rise in a warm place about 1 hour, or until double in bulk. Knead lightly, then divide in 2 equal pieces.

Butter 2 round 8-in. (20 cm) pans. Shape the dough in round loaves and place in pans. Cover with towel and let rise 45 to 50 minutes. Brush tops gently with milk and sprinkle with sugar. Bake in a preheated 375°F. (190°C) oven about 30 to 40 minutes, or until golden brown on top. Unmold on cooling rack. Cool 20 to 30 minutes and serve.

---

*If small ones are not available, break up regular size cubes.

Lemon Crêpes Liégeoise

Light, refreshing, different — a perfect dessert to serve after a heavy meal.

¹/₄ cup (60 mL) soft	*¹/₂ cup (125 mL) milk*
unsalted butter	*¹/₂ cup (125 mL)*
¹/₄ cup (60 mL) sugar	*all-purpose flour*
2 eggs, separated	*¹/₂ cup (125 mL) sugar*
grated rind of 1 lemon	*2 lemons, cut in wedges*

Cream butter and sugar until well blended. Beat egg yolks lightly, add to butter mixture and beat until very creamy. Add half of the grated lemon rind and the milk. Stir to mix, then beat in flour until the batter is smooth and creamy. Beat egg whites until stiff, then fold into the batter.

To cook the crêpes, drop by generous tablespoons (15 mL) into a well-buttered, heavy, hot frying pan or a crêpe pan. Brown the crêpes on both sides, turning only once. As they are ready, fold them into quarters and set on a warm platter.

Have ready the last ¹/₂ cup (125 mL) of sugar and the remaining half of the grated lemon rind, well mixed. Sprinkle a few pinches of this mixture over each folded crêpe after you place them on the platter.

To keep them piping hot, place the platter over a pan of simmering water. Set the lemon wedges around the cooked crêpes — each person squeezes lemon juice as desired over the crêpes. *Yield: 16 to 18 small crêpes.*

Café Liégeois

Whenever I am in Belgium, on the first day I must have my *Café Liégeois*. Do not let the vanilla and the cream stop you from making it. It is smooth, delectable and at its best when the coffee is black mocha-java freshly ground and filtered.

1/4 *tsp. (1 mL) vanilla*
1/2 *cup (125 mL) heavy*
   cream, whipped
1 egg white, beaten stiff

4 cups (1 L) hot coffee of
   your choice
a bowl of Demerara
sugar

Combine vanilla and cream. Blend in the beaten egg white. Fill 6 to 8 coffee demitasses 1/3 full with the cream mixture. Slowly fill cups by pouring the boiling hot coffee on top of the cream. Do not stir. Serve — each person adds the desired amount of sugar. It can also be served with a liqueur glass of brandy, sipped alternately with the coffee. *Yield: 6 to 8 demitasses.*

France

To the French people, the pleasure of good food and wine is really part of their daily lives — it is the expression of years of tradition, the center of their family and social life. The Sunday family lunch, even today, has not lost its importance; some families eat together at home, many others go out to eat at the bistro or at a favorite restaurant away from the city, which explains the number of cars leaving the city on Sunday, filled with *papas*, *mamans*, small and grown-up children and even grandparents. The restaurant they go to has always been dependable for them. I have, through the years, gone to many of these family restaurants, some of which do not even have a written menu. They describe to you what you will eat, and do it with such verve that you get hungrier by the second; so you wait eagerly for whatever will come. I have never been disappointed. I always found that it was in the provinces, at little out-of-the-way places, that eating was at its best. If you are a guest at friends' who live in the provinces, there is but one problem — too much food, too much wine and long hours at the table to enjoy it all.

What has fascinated me for years about French cooking is their unbelievable collection of regional dishes and cooking ideas. Yet tourists are not usually aware of the regional cuisine, or they are not attracted by it. But the great French chefs of today look to all the different regional recipes for inspiration. By giving these recipes a little something different, they create still another way of cooking specific foods.

Think of Normandy: it is a region of lush green fields, fat cattle, rich cheese and large apple orchards — a nature's delight to visit in early spring when in bloom, and then more enjoyment in autumn when the very potent cider and Calvados can be sampled. Brittany, on the other hand, is a much poorer province, much of it swept by the strong winds blowing off the ocean. How cold it can be in the winter! But what seafood they have, and how well they prepare it! Unforgettable to me is the deep old-fashioned soup plate of Breton fish soup served with large thin buckwheat pancakes, piping hot and folded in four. And let's salute their spring asparagus, cauliflower and super artichokes — the best to be had in France.

Turning to Perigord, the very first French province I visited at the age of eighteen — it was a culinary paradise; the women in their costumes were fascinating. Some of it has changed, but the Perigord remains the great land of geese and *confit d'oie*, which is goose cut in pieces, slowly braised in large brown earthenware pots (a familiar sight everywhere in Perigord) and left in these pots the entire winter, preserved in their fat. I ate this delectable dish at its best at a friend's house in Bagnères-de-Bigorre. It was served as an entrée, with large slices of fresh dark bread. We spread the bread with the fat and topped it with slices of goose, and drank a *vin du pays* that was at the peak of its perfection. The Perigord is better known around the world for its truffles, or black diamonds, as they are often referred to, undoubtedly because of their cost.

When travelling through France, I have stopped very often at farms or small restaurants where only the locals go. I have, at times, been disappointed, but I've been much more often delighted at discovering exciting foods or ideas. For instance, one day in the fifties I stopped at a most attractive farmhouse, where men, women and children wore the *costume du pays*. After chatting together for a while, they asked me to *déjeuner* (lunch) with them. I saw a large dark wooden table with benches all around. In the middle of the table were two large flat baskets, one filled with assorted fresh fruits, another with lots of bread. At one end of the kitchen there was a huge fireplace with iron pots over it suspended on chains. The mother went out and came back with a basket of eggs mixed with truffles, a lot of them. She set them near her little bench, pulled down one of the iron kettles and set it over the fire along with a long-handled black frying pan. She picked out a dozen or more eggs which she broke in the pan which had butter melting in it, then with a wooden stick she quickly scrambled the eggs, and then promptly set them on a piece of marble at the end of the table. At the other end, on another piece of marble, she put an iron pot filled with assorted vegetables simmering in chicken bouillon, with lots of parsley. The subtle flavor of the truffles in the eggs, the flavor of the garden vegetables, a perfect farm-made cream cheese — another unforgettable meal! You may wonder why the truffles were mixed in the basket with the eggs, but not used. I did, and asked why. The women pick them to sell for good money, around $40 a pound, so they do not eat any. However, left in the egg basket for a day or two, the truffles' flavor is absorbed by the eggs, making them a gourmet's delight out of our reach.

Another interesting province is the Gironde, known by many for the great Bordeaux wines it produces, which are considered by connoisseurs the best in the world. They surely are my preferred wines. Who can resist a lightly chilled Médoc, the assertiveness of a vintage St. Emilion, which was my mother's favorite, the beautiful dry white Entre-Deux-Mers and so many others? At the Restaurant Dubérie, situated in a private hotel built in 1895, you will find not only excellent food, but also one of the best cellars in the district—the heart of Château du Médoc, the Graves and St. Emilion. At the Dubérie, you will find what they refer to as an English bar, with whiskey, etc. Another restaurant I always enjoy in Bordeaux is the Saint James, expensive but worth it. It faces the Victor-Louis Theatre, which usually presents interesting plays.

If we think only of the Bordeaux wines, we easily forget that high-quality gastronomy exists in the Gironde, with its largest city, Bordeaux, considered by many to have one of the leading cuisines of France. There is a saying in Bordeaux that it is neither the cook nor the lady of the house who decides the menu, but the bottle of wine chosen by *Monsieur*, and it should be served with a dish that does not contrast nor overpower the chosen wine. Another unchanging rule is that a dish prepared with wine should be accompanied at the table with the same wine.

Before a meal, if you wish to follow their tradition, you will serve a true apéritif, the "Kina Lilet," not easy to take out of France, but worth the try. Refrigerate a few hours before serving.

Another delight is the *caviar de Gironde*. I first became aware of it around 1918–1920, through Mr. Prunier's restaurants in Paris and London, still to this day excellent fish places. Prunier was the one who discovered the sturgeon eggs of the Gironde River. They were sold at the time for a few *centimes*, and used as bait for sardines. Prunier was acquainted with a Russian who had migrated to France from the Caspian Sea. He showed Prunier how to make caviar, named in France *caviar Volga*, which you can eat at Prunier's and occasionally find in fancy groceries. About seven to nine tons of it are made in France every year, which is very little considering that the French eat twenty-five tons a year. Occasionally in Bordeaux, and in many places in the Gironde, you will see it on the menu under the name *caviar de Gironde*. Try it.

Yet another table pleasure of this province is *les petits royans*. They are beautiful tiny sardines eaten either highly salted and raw or unsalted and cooked over a wood fire. They are served on a slice of buttered (unsalted) French bread and accompanied by a cool glass of white Graves wine. How many I have eaten! The famous *agneau du Pauillac,* a *pré-salé* type, comes from the Gironde River, and is the Parisian favorite.

If you visit Bordeaux in early autumn, do eat *les cèpes*—they are part of every cuisine during that season and Bordeaux is still the place to eat these mushrooms, beautifully prepared, so delectable, and fresh, of course.

May I close this inadequate description of culinary delights of La Gironde with a word about their famous liqueurs? I have more than once enjoyed the "Anisette Marie Brizard," one of their better-known liqueurs, which I like to serve in their traditional way — poured into a liqueur glass filled with crushed ice. For the stronger soul, the "Vieille Cure de Cénon" is a brandy produced in Cénon, a small suburb of Bordeaux. Many consider it the very best produced in France.

While studying the history of art in my convent days, I became intrigued with and strongly attracted by *l'art roman*

(Norman art), in whatever form it was. I learned that in Poitou they had numerous "Romane" cathedrals and monasteries built during the Middle Ages, mostly dating from the eleventh and twelfth centuries. Sitting on my convent bench, I decided that if ever I went to France it would be a must to take a quiet, well-organized, comprehensive trip through Poitou, Vendée and les Deux Sèvres, which I did, by *autocar* (bus), and I had more than my share of unforgettable moments.

To see and understand *le Poitou*, one must drive, armed with a good map, on side roads and country roads, rather than on the *Nationale*, or else travel by *autocars*, which are a well-organized and informative mode of transportation for tourists. Too often we bypass many beautiful parts of the French provinces for Paris.

Poitou is also where I met my first French chef, Abélard, who had a most romantic restaurant in Thouards, the Héloïse. He showed me how to make his famous *orange Héloïse*, which I still enjoy. During dinner, he recited poems about Héloïse, and everyone was enthralled. I also discovered that it was a part of France where food was not to be ignored. This is where I learned all about autumn game birds — not only that one should eat them, but also how to cook them, according to their traditions. Les Deux Sèvres, part of Poitou, offers all kinds of river fish, and Le Vendée, facing the Atlantic, brings in seafood in large quantities.

One of their traditional desserts is named *tourteau fromage*, and would you believe that it is the ancestor of our well-known cheesecake, which we think of as American? Their *fromage blanc* (cottage cheese) is said to be the best in France.

Though I thought I would discover a prize dish in *poulet sauté Niortais,* it turned out to be one my mother made every spring with young chicken, potatoes and sweet red onions. Of course, the French-Québec cuisine has long included Poitou dishes brought to Canada by those who came from La Rochelle and many other parts.

At "Noirmoutier" there are large salt pans. At eighteen, I learned that salt was more than a white powder you poured over food. There was not only the *sel gris*, grey salt, used to season long-cooking food, but also a delicious sea salt, pale pink in color and exquisite in taste. I cannot exaggerate its perfection. Whenever I travel in France and can find it, I come back with a kilo.

Every Christmas I am reminded of Le Poitou when I use another one of their specialties, *l'angélique de Niort*, to decorate my fruit cake.

As we keep travelling south, we reach the Pyrenees mountains where the influence of the Basques and Spaniards is evident — more oil, tomatoes, peppers and spices in their dishes. Who can ignore the *potage Basque*, a sort of cream of potato and fresh green beans, the *ouliat Béarnais*, an interesting onion soup, or the baked calf liver of well-known Biarritz, or the chicken legs of Bayonne? An interesting fact for Canadians whose ancestors came from that part of France is that as early as 1680 the Basque fishermen were going as far as Newfoundland to fish for cod. Cod to this day remains a popular meal, and the way they prepare it in Bayonne remains my favorite. I have never seen it made in this manner anywhere in Canada.

Can anyone while in France resist visiting La Provence, where the pungent and piquant aroma of fresh herbs and the fragrant perfume of flowers mingle together begging you to stop? Their food is as exuberant as the pungent scent of their herbs and as colorful as their flowers. Their famous *aioli* sauce is said to be the oldest on earth, brought to their shores by the Phoenicians sailing the Mediterranean even before the birth of King Solomon.

There is so much about French cuisine that is is impossible to say it all, but I cannot stop here without saluting Lyon, recognized as *the* gastronomical city of the world. This is where you will find the really great chefs: Paul Bocuse at Coulonges-au-Mont d'Or, very near Lyon; Alain Chapel, my favorite chef among the best, in Mionnay, eighteen kilometres from Lyon; "Les Frères Troisgros"; "La Mère Blanc" and so many others. A salute should go to the Great Master, Monsieur Point at Vienne, who led the way for so many of these great chefs. Since he died the restaurant is under the care of Madame Point, and the same perfection reigns. I remember a lunch my husband and I had there in 1963; the eating and wine drinking lasted three hours—hours of sheer delight. After we left and got into the car, my husband felt he had to take "thirty winks," which went on for three hours! This gave me time to visit the rest of Vienne, and our dinner that night, to the disgust of the *restaurateur*, consisted of a tiny piece of cheese, a green salad and a *tisane*!

I am convinced that the French secret of success in cooking lies in the good quality of the produce and the fact that housewives and *restaurateurs* are most critical and difficult to please when it comes to selection for buying. They also have such patience when cooking, since they are, most of the time, seeking perfection. Then when the time comes to eat their creations and drink their chosen wines, they know how to take their time for the full enjoyment of it all. To acquire all this expertise takes more than a lifetime—the knowledge of their ancestors has given their cuisine a strong foundation.

Two Traditional Soups

Potage Tourin

Each province has its own way to make a *tourin*—in Gironde it is a sort of onion soup made with milk, eggs and cream, equally good hot or cold.

6-8 medium onions	*1 tbsp. (15 mL) flour*
2 tbsp. (30 mL) bacon	*1 cup (250 mL) light or*
fat	*heavy cream*
2 tbsp. (30 mL) butter	*4 slices toasted French*
1 tsp. (5 mL) sugar	*bread*
3 cups (750 mL) milk	*a bowl of grated Swiss*
2 egg yolks	*cheese*

Peel and slice onions into thin shreds. Melt bacon fat and butter together. Add onions and sprinkle with sugar. Cook over medium heat, stirring often, until lightly browned here and there. Pour into a strainer, set over a bowl and let the fat drain out. Heat milk, then add the drained onions. Simmer over low heat until milk is hot. Beat egg yolks with flour, then gradually add cream. Mix well and add slowly to the soup while stirring. Simmer 2 to 4 minutes over low heat, stirring well.

Place a slice of toasted bread in each plate and pour hot soup on top. Let each person sprinkle grated cheese to taste. *Serves 4.*

Ouliat *"Béarnais"*

Pau, capital of the Béarne, has many interesting castles from the thirteenth and fourteenth centuries. My interest, of course, centered around Henry IV, who created so many legends with food, such as the *poule-au-pot*. The bouillon from the *poule-au-pot* is used to make this excellent soup. I first ate it in Bigorre, where it was named *"toulia,"* on a beautiful summer day, at a garden lunch. The *toulia* was served in hot grass-green earthenware bowls, set in a basket filled with straw to keep the bowls warm.

6–8 medium onions	2 tbsp. (10 mL) salt
⅓ cup (80 mL) olive or peanut oil	1 tsp. (5 mL) pepper
	3 egg yolks
6 thin slices French bread	1 cup (250 mL) grated Swiss or Cheddar cheese
¼ cup (60 mL) flour	
8 cups (2 L) chicken bouillon	¼ cup (60 mL) brandy

Peel and thinly slice onions.

Heat the oil in the pan to be used for soup. Brown slices of bread in hot oil. Remove with a fork, drain off excess oil and place bread on plate. Reserve.

Add onions to oil and stir over high heat until lightly browned here and there. Add flour and mix thoroughly. Add 4 cups (1 L) of the chicken bouillon. Beat with a whisk until boiling, add the remaining bouillon, salt and pepper.

Bring to the boil while stirring, then cover and simmer 30 to 40 minutes.

Pass through a sieve or blend to make a cream soup.

When ready to serve, heat egg yolks with grated cheese in a soup tureen or a saucepan. Pour in 2 cups (500 mL) of boiling hot soup while beating with a whisk. Add remaining hot soup. Do not heat again after eggs are added. Pour in brandy. Stir and serve, topping each plate with a slice of fried bread.

The *ouliat* can be cooked ahead of time and, when ready to serve, simply heated up and poured over the eggs and cheese. The latter mixture should not be heated until you are ready to serve. *Serves 6 to 8.*

Faire Chabrot

An amusing tradition that all Bordeaux people enjoy. The evening soup is served piping hot in large old-fashioned plates and a bottle of good red Bordeaux wine is set on the table. When there is only a bit of bouillon or potage left in everyone's plate, each person pours in some red wine, swirls it gently and drinks right from the plate.

Don't think it silly to *faire chabrot*. Do it once and you will see how pleasurable it is.

Eggs Lorraine

Another classic of the Alsatian table. Not only is it scrumptious for brunch, it is also quick and easy to prepare. This recipe is for two, but it is as easily made for ten.

butter	*salt and pepper*
2 thin slices Swiss or Dutch cheese	*2 tbsp. (30 mL) rich cream*
2 slices cooked bacon, crumbled	*2 tbsp. (30 mL) grated cheese*
2 eggs	

Use 2 individual shallow pottery dishes, little ramekins, or small breakfast cups. Butter dishes and place a slice of cheese in bottom of each. Top with crumbled bacon, then break an egg over the bacon.

Season to taste, pour 1 tbsp. (15 mL) of cream over each egg and top with grated cheese. Bake in a 400°F. (200°C) oven 5 to 7 minutes, or until eggs are set to your liking. *Serves 2*.

Fish Entrées

White Wine Court Bouillon

A perfect stock for poaching fish, especially salmon, trout or halibut. Following the "Golden Rule" of Bordeaux, serve with the fish the same dry white wine used to poach it — the dry Graves is the favorite.

The following quantities can be doubled or halved or quartered, according to the amount of fish you wish to cook.

2 cups (500 mL) dry
    white wine
8 cups (2 L) cold water
½ tsp. (2 mL) thyme
2 bay leaves
4 sprigs of parsley, left
    whole

2 medium carrots,
    peeled and sliced
1 medium onion, sliced
1 tsp. (5 mL) salt
¼ tsp. (1 mL)
    peppercorns

Simmer all the ingredients for 35 minutes, then cool.

When ready to cook the fish, heat the stock before adding the fish. Cook it uncovered, 10 minutes to the inch (2.5 cm), measured in its thickest part.

After using the *court bouillon*, strain, bottle, cool and refrigerate. It can be used 2 to 3 times, even with different types of fish. Serve the fish hot or cold.

Roasted Fresh Tuna

The ports of the Vendée coast are referred to as *ports thoniers* because of the large quantity of tuna brought back by the fishermen, which is then mostly canned. Their very simple way of roasting fresh tuna is superb.

2 fresh tuna steaks,
    1 in. (2.5 cm) thick
¼ cup (60 mL) each
    butter and olive oil
1 onion, peeled and
    thinly sliced

salt, pepper and paprika
1 large tomato, peeled
    and diced
1 tbsp. (15 mL) heavy
    cream

Rub both sides of fish steaks with lemon juice. Melt butter and olive oil in a baking dish and mix in onion.

Place in preheated 400°F. (200°C) oven for 5 minutes. Remove from oven, stir and spread onion evenly. Place fish steaks on top. Sprinkle with salt, pepper and paprika. Place diced tomato around the fish. Bake 15 to 18 minutes, uncovered. Remove from oven, and let stand covered for 5 minutes. Remove fish to a hot platter, add heavy cream to onion and stir well over medium heat. Pour over fish. *Serves 4.*

Fillet of Sole Chapon Fin

The Bordelais people say that this sole, served with a dish of
very fine noodles, which are mixed with lots of slivered fresh
mushrooms and little green onions, along with a glass of cool
Sauternes, is pure perfection.

*2 lb. (1 kg) fresh fillets
   of sole
salt and pepper
unsalted butter
3 medium tomatoes
1 small onion, chopped
   fine*

*2 French shallots,
   chopped fine
¹/₄ cup (60 mL) parsley,
   minced
4 tbsp. (60 mL) white
   wine
3 tbsp. (50 mL) heavy
   cream*

If you have an oval metal dish that is long enough, leave the
fillets whole, otherwise cut them and make rolls. Rub salt
and pepper on each piece of fish.

Peel and dice tomatoes and mix with onions, French shallots
and parsley. Spread in bottom of generously buttered pan.
Place fillets on top, slightly overlapping each other, or roll
the pieces and place one next to the other. Cover dish with a
sheet of foil and place cover on top. Set directly over high heat
to start cooking. After 3 minutes place dish in a preheated
400°F. (200°C) oven. Bake 10 minutes.

Gently remove fish to a hot platter. Place pan over direct
heat, add white wine and a generous piece of butter. Beat with
a wire whisk until reduced by half. Gradually add cream, while
still beating. Add salt, if needed, and pour over fish. *Serves 6.*

Meat Entrées

Frog Legs "Relais de Poitiers"

In Poitiers you can visit three beautiful "Romane" churches, Saint-Hilaire, Notre-Dame-la-Grande and Sainte-Radegonde.

The Relais de Poitiers at Chasseneuil, one of my favorite restaurants in Poitou, near Poitiers, prepares these extraordinary frog legs.

16–18 frog legs	*1 large garlic clove,*
4 cups (1 L) cold water	*minced*
3 tbsp. (50 mL) wine	*¹/₂ cup (125 mL) minced*
vinegar	*parsley*
4 tbsp. (60 mL) milk	*1 tsp. (5 mL) savory*
2 tbsp. (30 mL) flour	*salt and pepper*
¹/₃ cup (80 mL) butter	

Rinse frog legs under cold running water. Mix in a bowl cold water and vinegar. Add frog legs and let stand 20 minutes. Drain, dry and roll each leg in milk, then dip in flour.

Melt butter in a large frying pan until nutty brown in colour. Add frog legs, one next to the other, and brown on both sides, turning only once. Cook them for a total of 5 to 7 minutes. Remove to a hot platter. Add the remaining ingredients to the pan and stir constantly for a minute or two. Pour over frog legs and garnish with lemon quarters, which can be squeezed on the legs to taste. *Serves 4.*

Baked Beef "aux Poivrons"

While driving from Paris to Alençon in 1962, we stopped for lunch at the Hostellerie du Clos in Verneuil, situated in a little castle of Norman-English architecture. We enjoyed it so much that we stayed on for two days.

While there, I ate this very interesting version of English beef stew.

1-1¹/₂ lb. (500-625 kg)
stewing beef, diced
2 green peppers
2 large onions
8 small potatoes, peeled
2 tbsp. (30 mL) tomato
paste

1 cup (250 mL) beef
consommé
¹/₂ tsp (2 mL) each
sugar and thyme
salt and pepper

I like to peel green peppers the way they do in France — place peppers on a baking sheet under the oven grill, about 3 in. (7.5 cm) from the flame. When blistered on one side, turn over (this takes about 3 minutes in all). Place in a bowl, cover tightly, let cool, then peel skin away. Remove seeds and cut into slivers. Peel onions and also cut into long slivers.

In a casserole, first place the meat, top with onions, then with peppers. Cover with potatoes which have been left whole.

Place the remaining ingredients in a saucepan and bring to the boil, while stirring. Pour over meat and vegetables and cover tightly (foil can be used). Bake in a preheated 250°F. (120°C) oven for 2¹/₂ hours.

To prepare this dish ahead of time, uncover after cooking and stir ingredients until well blended. Cover again, and keep at room temperature for 3 to 6 hours, then reheat in a 300°F. (150°C) oven for 20 to 25 minutes. *Serves 4.*

Rondelles de Boeuf Provençales

When the tourist season is in full swing on the Côte d'Azur, these *rondelles* are served everywhere. They are nicely sea-soned pan-fried hamburgers.

1 lb. (500 g) ground beef	*1 tbsp. (15 mL) cream of wheat, uncooked*
2 slices stale bread	*1 tsp. (5 mL) salt*
4 tbsp. (60 mL) milk or light cream	*¹/₄ tsp. (1 mL) pepper*
1 tsp. (5 mL) vegetable oil	*¹/₈ tsp. (0.5 mL) grated nutmeg*
1 onion, minced	*¹/₄ tsp. (1 mL) thyme*
1 garlic clove, chopped fine	*2 tbsp. (30 mL) butter*
2 eggs, beaten	*¹/₄ cup (60 mL) dry red wine*
	chopped parsley

After removing the crusts, crumble the bread in a bowl, pour milk or cream on top and let stand for 10 minutes.

Heat vegetable oil, add onion and cook until light brown. Pour this into a bowl and add ground beef, beaten eggs, cream of wheat, salt, pepper, nutmeg and thyme. Add the soaked bread and knead the mixture with your fingers, then cover and refrigerate for 2 hours.

Shape the meat into 6 small patties. In a heavy iron frying pan, heat the butter until light brown. Add the patties and cook over medium heat 2 to 3 minutes on each side. Place the patties on a heated platter.

Add red wine and parsley to butter in the pan. Stir for 1 minute over medium heat and pour over the patties. *Serves 4 to 6.*

Roast Veal "Thouars"

Served with buttered long-grain rice and Green Peas Vendéen, this makes a special dish. I like to use a rib roast of veal.

a 4-lb. (2 kg) veal rib
roast or rolled
shoulder
2 tbsp. (30 mL) diced
fat, removed from
roast
1/4 cup (60 mL) butter
or vegetable oil
1 large orange, peeled
and thinly sliced
1/2 cup (125 mL) dry
port wine

1 tbsp. (15 mL) brandy
1/4 tsp. (1 mL) sugar
1 tsp. (5 mL) salt
1/4 tsp. (1 mL) each
cinnamon and
nutmeg
grated rind of 1 orange
juice of 2 oranges
1/3 cup (80 mL) dry
muscatel raisins

In a Dutch oven (called a *calin* in Poitou), melt fat from roast, then add butter or vegetable oil. When quite hot, brown meat over medium heat on all sides. This should take 25 to 30 minutes, as the meat must be firm. Cool. With a sharp knife, cut meat into thin slices. Place in an enamel frying pan (*sauteuse*) and top with orange slices.

To the remaining juice in the Dutch oven, add the rest of the ingredients. Simmer 10 minutes, stirring often. Pour over meat. Simmer, uncovered, over very low heat 30 to 40 minutes. Do not stir. *Serves 6.*

Roasted Calf Liver

A creation of "Mère Brazier," one of the first *"mères célèbres."* In 1953, the year the *Guide Michelin* started to give "stars" to best restaurants, she was not only the first woman to receive a star, but also the first recipient of an award from *Guide Michelin*, and she is still the only woman who has ever received "three stars" from them.

I am happy to have known her and to have received this perfect recipe from her. I was young then, and she told me something I never forgot: "If you work eighteen, even nineteen, hours a day, you will succeed, but if you sleep eight hours a night, you will be late everywhere." At the time, I thought that would be an impossible task, but now I know she was right.

1–1¹/₂ lb. (500–750 kg) lamb or calf liver, in one piece	*¹/₂ tsp. (2 mL) salt*
	¹/₄ tsp. (1 mL) pepper
	2 tbsp. (30 mL) chili
1 large onion, peeled and slivered	*sauce**
	1 tbsp. (15 mL) A-1
1 leek, some of the green part and all of the white (optional)	*sauce*
	¹/₂ tsp. (2 mL) thyme
	¹/₃ cup (80 mL) dry port
3 tbsp. (50 mL) butter	*wine*

Both onion and leek should be cut into slivers. Fry in butter without browning too much.

Rub liver all over with salt and pepper. Place in a baking dish just large enough to hold the liver. Add the remaining ingredients, except port wine, to onions. Stir until hot and well mixed. Pour over the liver.

Pour port wine into the frying pan and heat, scraping the pan at the same time, but do not boil the port. Pour around the liver. Bake uncovered in a preheated 325°F. (160°C) over 30 minutes.

To make the gravy, add to the pan ¹/₄ cup (60 mL) hot or cold tea or coffee. Scrape the pan with a spoon. In no time you will have a deep brown gravy. *Serves 4 to 6.*

*Mère Brazier used a fresh, well-spiced tomato purée. I found chili sauce gave the same result, with half the work.

Beef Kidney *"Vieille Cure"*

Cooked in 6 minutes, flamed with brandy and topped with a light red wine sauce — a favorite of my dear teacher Dr. de Pomiane. He was a great admirer of *cuisine bordelaise.*

Vieille Cure is considered by connaisseurs as one of the best of all brandies.

1 beef kidney	*salt and pepper*
2 tbsp. (30 mL) butter	*¹/₈ tsp. (0.5 mL) nutmeg*
¹/₄ cup (60 mL) brandy	*1 tsp. (5 mL) Dijon*
3 bacon slices, diced	*mustard*
2 French shallots, diced	*1 cup (250 mL) small*
1 tbsp. (15 mL) flour	*mushrooms*
³/₄ cup (190 mL) red	
wine	

Cut kidneys into thin slivers, discarding the white middle part. Work around this part — it doesn't matter if the slices are not uniform in size; but it is important that they be thin.

In a cast-iron frying pan heat butter until it has a nutty color. Add kidney and stir constantly over high heat, about 3 minutes. At that point the kidney will almost be cooked. Leave it over high heat, without stirring, for another minute. Then, pour the brandy on top, stir, flame, stir again and transfer to a hot platter.

Add bacon to the frying pan and stir until it is crisp, then add shallots and red wine. Add salt, pepper and nutmeg and bring to the boil over medium heat. Mix in Dijon mustard and mushrooms, and stir until creamy — this should take about a minute. Place kidney back in the sauce, simmer for a minute and serve. *Serves 4.*

Oxtail Vinaigrette

If your love of cars takes you to Le Mans for the great car races, you will find that Oxtail Vinaigrette is a favorite local dish because one can "eat quick and enjoy." It is served everywhere with hot crusty French bread. This is also popular in Paris as a quick, tasty family lunch; many butchers sell the oxtail already cooked and ready to be prepared in vinaigrette. The oxtail can be served as a main course, the bouillon as a light, tasty consommé which can be garnished to your liking.

Oxtail:

1 oxtail, cut into pieces
1 onion, sliced
1 carrot, peeled and
   sliced
2 stalks celery, coarsely
   cut
1 bay leaf

¹/₄ tsp. (1 mL) thyme
1 tsp. (5 mL) salt
¹/₄ tsp. (1 mL) pepper
2 thick lemon slices,
   unpeeled
2 quarts (2 L) water

Place all the ingredients in a saucepan and bring to a full rolling boil. Cover and simmer 3 to 4 hours over low heat, or until the oxtail is tender. Let it cool in its consommé. Serve with a simple vinaigrette (recipe follows).

Vinaigrette:

¹/₄ tsp. (1 mL) dry
   mustard
¹/₂ tsp. (2 mL) salt

¹/₄ tsp. (1 mL) pepper
a pinch of sugar
¹/₂ cup (125 mL)
   vegetable oil

Shake all the ingredients together in a bottle.

To serve, dice 3 cups (750 mL) of cooked potatoes, mix them with a few spoonfuls of vinaigrette and place them on a serving platter. Place the cooled oxtail in a bowl and blend with vinaigrette to taste. Sprinkle with finely minced parsley or green onion tops. *Serves 4.*

Ham Girondine

In France, *jambon de Bayonne* is used, a ham recognized as the very best and eaten mostly raw, sliced paper-thin. Elsewhere, we can replace it with a top quality precooked ham. When travelling in France, it is a must to sample the ham, as they have many types and interesting ways of cooking it. The Girondine way is one of my favorites.

3 center slices of	*3-4 French shallots,*
precooked ham, ¹/₄ in.	*chopped fine*
(.625 cm) thick	*3 tbsp. (50 mL) sugar*
3 tbsp. (50 mL) butter	*¹/₄ cup (60 mL) red*
	wine or cider vinegar

Cut each slice of ham in 2 or 4 pieces, whichever you prefer, for serving. Remove rind. Melt 2 tbsp. (30 mL) of the butter on a baking sheet or in a shallow roasting pan. Roll each piece of ham in the melted butter. Cover pan with foil and *warm up* ham 15 minutes in a preheated 300°F. (150°C) oven. Set on a warm platter. Reserve the juice.

Melt the remaining butter in a frying pan, and add shallots and sugar. Stir together over medium heat until caramelized to a golden color. Add vinegar and reserved juice of the ham. Stir just to heat; do not let it boil. Pour over ham. Surround with steamed potatoes sprinkled with chopped parsley. *Serves 6.*

Alsatian Spareribs and Sauerkraut

I am very fond of Alsatian wine, so when time permits I go to Colmar or Strasbourg. Halfway between the two cities there is a small hotel, Le Clos St-Vincent, surrounded by vineyards and right in the middle of the Alsatian wine route. They specialize in *dégustations* of Alsatian wine and liquor and serve excellent food. As there are only nine rooms, it is wise to plan ahead and make reservations.

My choice there was this very good dish, prepared with their homemade sauerkraut and home-grown juniper berries.

3 lb. (1.5 kg) pork spareribs	*16 juniper berries**
	3 garlic cloves, minced
2 lb. (1 kg) sauerkraut	*4 apples, unpeeled and grated*
2 cups (500 mL) Alsatian wine or light white wine	*3 potatoes, peeled and grated*
1 tbsp. (15 mL) brown sugar	

Place in a saucepan half the sauerkraut, wine, brown sugar and juniper berries. Cut spareribs into individual portions and put on top of the mixture. Sprinkle the ribs with garlic and apples and cover completely wtih the remaining sauerkraut. Top with potatoes. Pour a bit of sauerkraut juice over the ingredients. Cover and simmer 1 hour over medium to low heat. *Serves 6.*

*See note, p. 138.

Fowl Entrées

Chicken Sauté "Niortais"

You might like to know that in Niort you can find beautiful leather gloves. I have some hand-stitched ones that I bought fifteen years ago, still supple and perfect. This is because of the high quality of Niort leather.

This recipe is another example of Niortais quality.

1 broiler, cut into individual pieces	¼ cup (60 mL) minced green onions
4 tbsp. (60 mL) butter	¼ cup + 1 tbsp.
salt and pepper	(80 mL) dry port wine
½ lb. (250 g) fresh mushrooms, thinly sliced	2 tbsp. (30 mL) flour
	1 cup (250 mL) milk

Melt 2 tbsp. (30 mL) of the butter in a heavy metal casserole. Add chicken pieces gradually and brown lightly on both sides. Salt and pepper to taste. Add mushrooms and green onions, and stir to mix. Add 2 tbsp. (30 mL) of the port wine. Cover tightly and simmer over low heat until chicken is tender, about 30 to 45 minutes. When chicken is ready, place the pieces on a platter and keep warm. Make a white sauce with the remaining 2 tbsp. (30 mL) of butter, 3 tbsp. (50 mL) of port, flour and milk.

Meanwhile, boil over high heat the juice of the chicken; when only a few spoonfuls remain, pour in the white sauce and stir until well mixed. Taste for seasoning. Add chicken pieces and cover them with the white sauce. Simmer over low heat until chicken is hot. *Serves 4.*

Citrus Chicken Mionnay

Spending a few days at Alain Chapel's place, "Mionnay," is an unforgettable and expensive experience. He is my most favorite of all the French *grands chefs*: creative, shy, with a true flair for flavors and presentation. Of course, Mionnay *is* near Lyon! I ate this citrus chicken prepared with young, tender two-pound broilers and fresh citrus fruits.

3 whole chicken breasts, split or two 3-lb. (1.5 kg) broilers, quartered	$^1/_3$ cup (80 mL) white wine
$^1/_4$ cup (60 mL) fresh lime juice	1 garlic clove, crushed
	1 tsp. (5 mL) salt
$^1/_4$ cup (60 mL) fresh lemon juice	$^1/_4$ tsp. (1 mL) pepper
	$^1/_2$ tsp. (2 mL) tarragon, fresh if possible
	3 tbsp. (50 mL) butter

Blend lime and lemon juice with white wine, garlic, salt, pepper and tarragon. Place the chicken pieces side by side in a shallow casserole and pour the lime mixture on top. Refrigerate for 2 hours, or overnight.

Remove chicken from the marinade and arrange the pieces in a shallow casserole or baking pan, without overlapping. Dot with butter and bake uncovered at 350°F. (180°C) for about 40 minutes, or until tender. Baste with the marinade every 10 minutes.

When cooked, cool the chicken before serving or wrap it in foil and keep in a cool place. Strain and refrigerate the drippings. To serve, remove the hardened fat from the top of the cold drippings. Serve the golden-colored jelly underneath with the chicken. *Serves 6.*

Chicken Legs Biarritz

After World War I, many Canadian soldiers came back raving about the seaside of Biarritz and the beauty of French women. My father's brother, an officer in the forces, was one of them. He not only taught me how to prepare these famous chicken legs, but also how to cook and eat French artichokes, which I had previously seen at the Greek food shop of the Basil Brothers — I had never known what to do with them.

4 whole chicken legs
juice and rind of 1
    lemon
1 garlic clove, sliced
2 bay leaves

salt
freshly ground pepper
2 tbsp. (30 mL) each
    butter and vegetable
    oil

For perfect results, the chicken legs should be boned, leaving only an inch (2.5 cm) of the end piece, but they can also be cooked without being boned.

Place in a bowl lemon juice and rind, garlic, bay leaves, salt and pepper. Roll chicken pieces in the mixture until well coated. Cover and marinate 3 to 5 hours.

To cook, drain well, then roll each leg in the flour. Heat butter and oil in a frying pan. Add the chicken legs and cook over medium heat, turning once or twice, until cooked and browned all over, about 30 to 35 minutes. Serve piping hot with cold Watercress Mayonnaise (recipe follows). *Serves 6.*

Watercress Mayonnaise:

1 cup (250 mL)
    mayonnaise, not the
    sweet type
³/₄ cup (190 mL)
    watercress or
    parsley, chopped

1 tsp. (5 mL) dry
    tarragon
1 tsp. (5 mL) lemon
    juice
1 tsp. (5 mL) grated
    onion

Place all the ingredients in a blender or food processor and mix thoroughly until green. Taste for salt and pepper. Serve cold with piping hot chicken legs.

Duck Vendéen

I prefer to use commercial duck, as wild duck does not lend the same intriguing flavor. The famous Tour d'Argent Restaurant in Paris, owned by Claude Terrail, son of the founder, prepares only "Challans" duck. Challans, in the center of Vendée, holds an agricultural show every autumn which focusses on its famous ducks. It is amazing what the little duck contributes to the welfare of man; for instance, duck liver is used to make iron pills and the Chinese use the legs and head in their medicines.

1 domestic duck
4-6 apples (not too ripe)
2 tbsp. (30 mL) butter
1 tbsp. (15 mL) brandy
grated rind of 1/2 orange
salt and pepper
juice of 1 orange
1/4 cup (60 mL) brandy
3 tbsp. (50 mL) Grand
Marnier (optional)

4 tbsp. (60 mL) sugar
1/3 cup (80 mL) red
wine or cider vinegar
grated rind of 1 orange
1/2 cup (125 mL) fresh
orange juice
1 orange, peeled and
thinly sliced

Wash duck inside and out with a cloth dipped in vinegar.

Peel and core apples and cut into quarters. Melt butter in a saucepan. Add apples, stir until each piece is well buttered, then simmer 10 minutes over very low heat. Add the 1 tbsp. (15 mL) brandy and grated rind of half an orange. Stir well, cool and use half of the apples to stuff the duck. Salt and pepper. Place in a dripping pan. Roast 25 minutes in a pre-heated 400°F. (200°C) oven. Place the remaining apples around the duck, add the juice of 1 orange, the 1/4 cup (60 mL) brandy and Grand Marnier. Stir. Lower the heat to 350°F. (180°C) and roast the duck another 40 minutes, basting once or twice.

Meanwhile, place in a frying pan sugar and vinegar, boil, stirring until sugar is melted, then cook over high heat until it starts to caramelize. Then add the grated rind of 1 orange and the 1/2 cup (125 mL) fresh orange juice, and stir over medium heat until it comes to the boil.

When the duck is cooked, remove from pan to a hot platter. Pour the vinegar mixture into the gravy and add the orange slices. Stir well over direct heat until hot. Place the orange slices over the duck and serve the gravy separately. *Serves 4.*

Monsieur Point's Pheasant

Fernand Point was one of France's great chefs for fifty years, until his death in the early seventies. Most of today's famous French chefs were trained at his world-renowned restaurant in Vennes. This was one of the best meals I had there.

Pheasant:

2 hen pheasants	*3–4 lemons*
3/4 cup (190 mL)	*paprika*
unsalted butter	*watercress or parsley*
1 tsp. (5 mL) tarragon	

Season each bird inside and out with salt and pepper to taste. Place 1/4 cup (60 mL) butter in each cavity and sprinkle 1/2 tsp. (2 mL) tarragon inside each. Place birds side by side in a roasting pan and roast uncovered in a 450°F. (230°C) oven 30 minutes, basting 3 times with the pan juices. Then reduce heat to 300F. (150°C) and roast another 20 to 30 minutes, or until birds are tender and juice from the breasts runs clear.

Meanwhile, peel lemons, cut into quarters and sprinkle generously with paprika. When cooked, place pheasants on a large platter, surrounded with watercress, or parsley, and the paprika-coated lemon.

Sauce:

1 cup (250 mL) red	*1/4 cup (60 mL) French*
currant jelly	*cognac*

Heat jelly and cognac over very low heat—do not boil. Remove from heat while little pieces of the jelly still remain undissolved. Pour in the pan gravy, mix and serve in a gravy boat. *Serves 4.*

Poule-au-pot in Casserole

I have cooked and enjoyed the famous *poule-au-pot* in several ways, but this one is my favorite. I ate it for the first time in a funny little restaurant in Pau, where the dining room consisted of a few tables in the kitchen and on the veranda, every inch of it spotless. The chef was dressed in white, the other staff, mostly women, in pale blue, their heads covered with a very attractive *coiffe Béarnaise*.

They not only cooked, but also served at the table.

a 4–5 lb. (2.5–3 kg) chicken	3 whole carrots, peeled
2 tbsp. (30 mL) brandy	2 medium onions, peeled
5–6 branches of tarragon, chopped or 1 tbsp. (15 mL) dry tarragon	2 whole cloves
	4 tbsp. (60 mL) flour
	1/4 cup (60 mL) light or heavy cream
3 tbsp. (50 mL) butter	salt and pepper
4 cups (1 L) chicken bouillon	

Rub the chicken inside and out with brandy. Cream together tarragon and butter. Shape in a ball and place inside the chicken. Tie legs with a string. Place in a saucepan large enough to hold the chicken, bouillon, carrots, onions and cloves. Salt and pepper to taste. Bring to the boil, then add the chicken which should be only partly covered by the bouillon. Cover and simmer over medium heat 40 to 50 minutes, or until tender.

Remove chicken to a warm platter. Cover to keep warm. Boil the bouillon uncovered over high heat, until reduced to almost half. Stir together flour and cream, add to the bouillon and whisk until creamy. Season to taste. Cut chicken into pieces, and add to the sauce. Serve in a nest of parsleyed long-grain rice. *Serves 4 to 5.*

The Butters

Flavored butters, or *beurres composés*, play such an important role in French cuisine that one should definitely learn how to prepare them. Though there are hundreds of them, the following are the most popular and useful.

After preparing, place butter in jam jars, cover tightly and refrigerate — it will keep from two to three months. You will soon learn which type of butter to add to your favorite recipe to give it a special touch.

Bercy Butter:

1 cup white wine (250 mL)
2 tbsp. (30 mL) French shallots, finely chopped
1 cup (250 mL) unsalted butter, creamed

1 tbsp. (15 mL) minced parsley
juice of ¹/₂ lemon
1 tsp. (5 mL) salt
¹/₄ tsp. (1 mL) pepper

Boil wine and shallots until reduced to ¹/₂ cup (125 mL). Add remaining ingredients and blend in an electric mixer. Keep refrigerated.

Note: ¹/₂ lb. (125 g) of beef marrow, chopped fine, is usually added. As it is rich and not readily available, it can be omitted without affecting the butter.

Lemon Butter:

grated rind of 1 lemon and juice of ¹/₂ lemon
¹/₂ tsp. (2 mL) freshly ground pepper

1 cup (250 mL) unsalted butter, creamed

Stir together lemon rind, pepper and salt, then add butter to the mixture. Place in a glass container and top with lemon juice. As the juice stays on top, spoon out a little each time some butter is used.

Lemon Butter Fines-Herbes:

½ cup *(125 mL) butter*	*1 tsp. (5 mL) chopped*
juice of 1 lemon and	*parsley*
grated rind of	*1 green onion, finely*
½ *lemon*	*chopped*
½ *tsp. (2 mL) each*	
basil and tarragon	

Cream butter, add remaining ingredients and stir until thoroughly blended. Pack in a dish, cover and refrigerate.

Use it on vegetables, chicken breasts, toasted muffins—even a plain boiled carrot will come alive with this beautiful butter.

Chive Butter:

½ cup *(125 mL) fresh*	*1 cup (250 mL) butter,*
chives, finely chopped	*creamed*

Blend ingredients together (use a food processor if you have one) — the butter will be a beautiful green. Excellent with poached fish and chicken. (Variation: Add ½ cup (125 mL) finely chopped parsley to chives.)

Montpellier Butter:

½ cup *(125 mL) each*	*2 hard-boiled egg yolks,*
chervil, tarragon and	*chopped*
finely chopped parsley	*1 raw egg yolk*
1 cup (250 mL)	*1 small garlic clove,*
watercress and	*chopped*
spinach, finely	*1 cup (250 mL)*
chopped	*unsalted butter*
3 small sour pickles,	½ *tsp. (2 mL) each salt*
finely chopped or 1 tsp.	*and pepper*
(15 mL) capers,	*3 tbsp. (50 mL) olive oil*
well-drained	

Place chervil, tarragon, parsley, watercress and spinach in a saucepan, pour in boiling water and boil 1 minute. Drain, and press in a cloth.

Place mixture in a bowl, add pickles or capers, egg, garlic and butter. Beat by hand or in a food processor, gradually adding salt, pepper and oil, until creamy and well blended. Store in a glass jar. Delicious on cold veal, fish or shrimps.

Salads

While I was studying in France in the twenties, two student friends and myself ate a lot of salads, as the greens were cheap and plentiful in the market. We each took turns going there at 6 A.M. to buy our needs, including a *baguette*, hot from the baker's oven, and a good-sized piece of cheese. I have never forgotten those green salad lunches, so good to eat, and so filled with laughter and friendship. A "boyfriend" who sometimes joined us is now a *membre de l'Académie Française*.

Once the greens were washed and dried in the salad drier, we sprinkled them with chopped parsley or basil or chives (whichever was cheapest in the market that day) and set them in the "ice box" to cool.

Then we mixed the **Dressing**: 1/4 cup (60 mL) *huile d'arachide* (peanut oil), 2 tbsp. (30 mL) red wine vinegar, salt and pepper to taste and 1 tsp. (5 mL) Dijon mustard. We stirred, and stirred, and left the bowl on the kitchen counter. The cheese, still wrapped, was kept at room temperature until lunchtime. Of course, we had no butter. Then, like all the other students, we ran to our eight A.M. class, but were back home at one A.M. for our salad feast. Fifteen minutes before eating, we tossed the lettuce with the room-temperature dressing in a salad bowl, which had been well rubbed with garlic, and chilled it again before sitting at the table.

Lunch was accompanied by tea or coffee, depending on how much money we had, since tea was a luxury in Paris at the time. Fortunately, we had friends in London who never had time to write, but would always send us little packets of tea. Without realizing it, we were eating the best salad we would ever taste, but we all still remember how we enjoyed those meals.

To make a perfect salad, one should learn about two important ingredients, oil and vinegar.

Always pour the vinegar first, because if the oil is added first it coats the greens, preventing the vinegar from penetrating. Fresh lemon and lime juice can always replace vinegar in any salad.

All vinegars have an alcohol base, the nature of which determines the character of the particular vinegar, but in the fermentation process it becomes non-alcoholic.

Distilled Vinegar: This is our white vinegar. It is fermented from grain alcohol and is strong, with a sharp aroma, so should be used mainly for pickling.

Cider Vinegar: A base of hard-apple cider gives it its full-bodied aroma and its slightly fruity flavor, although the taste is actually sharp. This golden-colour vinegar is good with coleslaw or other similar types of salad.

Malt Vinegar: This type is processed by fermenting malt alcohol or beer, which explains its distinctive flavor and light beer aroma. It ranges from pale to dark ginger in color. Use with fish, ham or root vegetable salads.

Red Wine Vinegar: Its flavor and color vary greatly, depending on the variety of grape used in the wine and the degree of dilution — the full-bodied flavor of the wine comes through. A good red wine vinegar is excellent for making herb vinegar. Simply add a few branches of fresh tarragon or sweet basil or dill or a few peeled uncut garlic cloves. If you make a pint bottle of each, you can then vary the flavor of your salads, or give a new zip to your stews, throughout the year by adding two or three tablespoons (30 to 50 mL) of your favorite vinegar.

White Wine Vinegar: Much the same applies here as for the red, except that its color is light golden yellow, its aroma delicate and subtle. It can also be used to make herb vinegar. Plain or flavored white wine vinegar is an excellent choice for salads.

Olive Oil: It varies greatly even among the French types alone —the very best being the oil marked *pression à froid*. It is also expensive, but a little goes a long way. The Spanish oil is deep gold, as opposed to the French pale gold, in color, with a strong olive flavor. The Italian oil is strong and very oily in the south, milder and lighter in the central and northern regions. Greek oil can range from "three stars" to poor quality, the oil from Calamata olives being the best.

Corn Oil, Peanut Oil (*huile d'arachide* in France): Both are mild in flavor and excellent in salad dressing if you do not want a particular oil flavor in your salad. Corn oil is not as delicate as it can be a mixture of up to seven oils, and the French peanut oil is more delicate than ours.

Vegetable Dishes

Ali-Bab Turkey Rice Salad

Babinsky was a French engineer who worked on the Suez Canal in the twenties. When the chef suddenly died and could not be replaced, Babinsky gave up his job to cook for the other men. Ali-Bab (as he is known) became and still is one of the great masters of French cuisine. His book *Encyclopédie Gastronomie Pratique* (available in English) is a classic.

Though this salad is prepared with leftover turkey, it is in every way a gourmet dish. Like all Ali-Bab's creations, there is a lot of preparation, but the result is a most elegant luncheon salad.

1 tbsp. (15 mL) butter
1 small onion, diced
1 tsp. (5 mL) curry powder
1 tbsp. (15 mL) tomato paste
4 tbsp. (60 mL) red wine
1 tbsp. (15 mL) fresh lemon juice
2 tbsp. (30 mL) apricot jam, sieved
1 1/2 cups (400 mL) mayonnaise
2 tbsp. (30 mL) heavy or sour cream
salt and pepper

2–3 thin slices of turkey or chicken for each serving
1 cup (250 mL) long-grain rice
2 cups (500 mL) boiling water
1 tsp. (5 mL) salt
2 tbsp. (30 mL) cider or wine vinegar
3 tbsp. (50 mL) olive oil
1/4 cup (60 mL) toasted slivered almonds
1 cup (250 mL) fresh green grapes, halved and seeded
watercress or parsley

Heat butter in a frying pan, add onion and simmer over low heat until onion is soft but not brown. Add curry powder and stir until well blended with the onion. Add tomato paste, red wine, lemon juice and apricot jam. Stir over medium heat 3 to 4 minutes. Cool.

Pour mayonnaise into the cooled mixture and stir well, then add cream. Taste for seasoning.

Place sliced or diced cooked turkey on individual plates. Coat generously with the mayonnaise mixture.

Cook rice in the boiling water 18 to 20 minutes, or until tender. Rinse under cold running water to cool. Drain thoroughly. With a fork, gently stir in vinegar, oil, salt and pepper.

Fold toasted almonds and green grapes into the rice. Surround each plate of turkey with a portion of this rice. Garnish with watercress or parsley. If preparing a few hours ahead of time, cover and refrigerate. *Serves 6.*

Luncheon Potato Salad

Try this summer special of the Côte d'Azur for a summer lunch. Use a large crisp lettuce leaf for each person and fill it with a good portion of the potato salad. Set leaves side by side on a platter, and fill the spaces with celery sticks or hearts. In May of 1979 I ate this salad at the Hôtel de Paris in Monaco, served with long shreds of chicken breast and large pieces of fresh lobster. Very good!

5 large potatoes, unpeeled	1/4 cup (60 mL) minced
2/3 cup (160 mL)	green onions
consommé or dry	2 tbsp. (30 mL) chopped
white wine	parsley
1/3 cup (80 mL) olive or	salt and pepper
vegetable oil	1/4 cup (60 mL) melted
1 tbsp. (15 mL) wine	butter
vinegar	

Scrub and boil potatoes until just tender, then drain and peel. Dice or slice them, and place in a bowl with remaining ingredients while still warm. Toss gently, cover and let marinate 2 to 3 hours at room temperature. Do not refrigerate because the potatoes harden and the butter coagulates if chilled. *Serves 4 to 6.*

Ratatouille Niçoise

A recipe that can range from bad to excellent even if made with the same types of vegetables. In the thirties, while travelling through the south of France, I was served this *ratatouille* cold, at one of my favorite hotels, La Réserve de Beaulieu. It was accompanied with hot baked herbed rice, and was superb!

1 medium to large eggplant	*2 small carrots*
1 large or 2 medium onion(s)	*¹/₄ cup (60 mL) olive or peanut oil*
2 celery stalks	*1 large garlic clove, chopped*
1 green pepper	*1 tsp. (5 mL) thyme*
¹/₂ lb. (250 g) fresh mushrooms	*1 tsp. (5 mL) basil*
1 small cucumber	*1 tbsp. (15 mL) sugar*
3-4 zucchini	*¹/₄ cup (60 mL) chopped parsley*
4 tomatoes	*juice of 1 large lemon*

Peel and cut eggplant into small cubes. Dice onion and celery. Cut green pepper into thin strips. Thinly slice mushrooms. Peel, seed and quarter cucumber, then cut in thin slices. Trim ends of zucchini and cut into ¹/₂-in. (1 cm) slices. Peel and quarter tomatoes. Peel and thinly slice carrots.

Heat vegetable oil in a heavy metal casserole. Add garlic and stir for a second. Add eggplant. Stir over high heat for a few minutes, then remove from pan with a slotted spoon. Add onion, celery, green pepper and mushrooms. Cook 4 to 5 minutes, stirring often. Add cucumber, zucchini, tomatoes and carrots. Stir until blended with the rest. Return eggplant to casserole. Season with salt and pepper to taste. Add thyme, basil, sugar, parsley and lemon juice. Cover and simmer over low heat 40 to 50 minutes, or cover and bake in a 325°F. (160°C) oven for 1 hour (do not uncover during cooking period.)

This dish can be prepared ahead of time and baked when ready to serve, or serve it chilled, sprinkled with the juice of 1 lemon and ¹/₄ cup (60 mL) vegetable oil It will keep, refrigerated, for 3 to 4 days. Serve with Baked Rice (recipe follows). *Serves 4 to 6.*

Baked Rice:

*1 cup (250 mL)
long-grain rice
2 cups (500 mL) boiling
water
1 tsp. (5 mL) salt
1 tbsp. (15 mL) butter*

*¹/₄ cup (60 mL) fresh
minced parsley
¹/₂ tsp. (2 mL) dried
tarragon
2 French shallots,
minced*

Place rice in a casserole, pour in water, add salt and butter and mix. Cover and bake in a 350°F. (180°C) oven for 45 minutes.

Add parsley, tarragon and shallots, stir and serve. *Serves 4.*

Onion Monégasque

Serve as an hors-d'oeuvre, or simply as an interesting relish with meat and poultry. It will keep 3 to 4 months in a glass jar, covered and refrigerated.

On a recent trip to the Côte d'Azur I was offered these as an hors-d'oeuvre with chunks of tuna fish, in a small but excellent restaurant called Le Roquebrune, near Menton. I also drank the very best lemon-verbena tea I had had for years. I saw the leaves being gathered in the garden below; then they were brought, so fragrant, to the table in a little basket, with a pot of boiling water, so I could make my own tea.

*1 lb. (500 kg) small
white onions
1¹/₂ cups (375 mL)
water
¹/₂ cup (125 mL) cider
or white wine vinegar
3 tbsp. (50 mL) olive oil
or peanut oil*

*3 tbsp. (50 mL) tomato
paste
1 bay leaf
¹/₂ tsp. (2 mL) thyme
1 tsp. (5 mL) salt
¹/₂ tsp. (2 mL) pepper
¹/₂ cup (125 mL)
seedless raisins*

Peel onions and place in a saucepan. Add the remaining ingredients. Stir well, cover and simmer over medium-low heat 1¹/₂ hours, or until the onions are tender (test with the point of a paring knife) and the sauce is thick and somewhat reduced. Pour into a jar and cool. Cover and refrigerate. *Yield: 1 pint (500 mL).*

Celery Root Purée

When we lived in France, my husband could not let more than a week slip by without travelling to Chailly-en-Bière near Paris, to go riding in the forest, or else we would go to l'Hôtellerie du Bas Breau in Barbizon, a haunting spot of the impressionist painters, who made the place famous. There one can delight in the food and even live at the *hôtellerie*.

Small chickens were split and broiled, then served on a bed of celery root purée, all thickly sprinkled with finely chopped parsley and tarragon.

2 medium celery roots	1 cup (250 mL) chopped
2 cups (500 mL) milk	parsley
¹/₂ tsp. (2 mL) each salt	2 tbsp. (30 mL) butter
and sugar	

Peel and slice celery roots. (Immediately after slicing, place them in a bowl of cold water to prevent discoloration.)

Warm up milk with salt and sugar. Drain celery roots and add to the hot milk. Bring to the boil, lower the heat, cover and simmer until tender, about 25 minutes. After 15 minutes add parsley.

When ready, remove celery and parsley with a perforated spoon. If you prefer, the celery can be drained in a strainer, reserving the milk.

Place celery and parsley in a food processor or blender and purée the mixture, adding the butter in 2 parts. If purée is too thick, add a little milk. Warm up over low heat. Serve garnished as suggested above or serve as a vegetable. You can also add part of the purée to the remaining milk to make a very good cream of celery root soup. Top the soup with buttered croutons. *Serves 4.*

Purée Soubise

This superb classic French onion or leek purée can be used as a creamed vegetable, a thick sauce for garnishing, or to pour over poached fish or to top broiled veal or chicken. It is a must in the repertoire of the great chefs' cuisine, and freezes very well. I keep some in my freezer in half-cup (125 mL) and one-cup (250 mL) quantities, to have on hand as needed. Try adding half a cup (125 mL) of the purée to a can of mushroom, tomato or celery soup, when the soup is ready to be served. It can also be added frozen to the soup, then simmered slowly until melted.

7 cups (1 ½ L) roughly chopped peeled onions or leeks	3 tbsp. (50 mL) flour
	1 cup (250 mL) beef or chicken consommé
3 tbsp. (50 mL) butter	½ tsp. (2 mL) salt
1 tbsp. (15 mL) vegetable oil	a pinch of freshly ground pepper
1 ⅓ cups (330 mL) beef or chicken consommé	¼ tsp. (2 mL) nutmeg
2 tbsp. (30 mL) butter	¼ cup (60 mL) rich cream

Pour prepared onions or leeks in a bowl of boiling water and let stand 5 minutes. Drain thoroughly. Melt the 3 tbsp. (50 mL) of butter and the oil in a saucepan, add onions and stir for 5 minutes over high heat, until moisture has evaporated. Add the 1⅓ cups (330 mL) consommé. Bake in a 375°F. (190°C) oven for 35 minutes. The mixture should be dry at this point, but if not, continue cooking.

While the onions are cooking, make the sauce. Melt the 2 tbsp. (30 mL) of butter, add the flour and stir until well mixed. Add the 1 cup (250 mL) of consommé all at once and stir over medium heat until sauce is thick and creamy. Season with salt, pepper and nutmeg. Add the cooked onions to the sauce, then put it through a food mill or processor, or beat with a wire whisk to make a smooth purée. Pour purée back into saucepan, and add the cream bit by bit, stirring constantly over medium heat. *Yield: 3 to 3½ cups (750 to 875 mL).*

Artichokes *"Barigoule"*

One of these, with a good crusty bread and Cheddar as dessert, is a meal. Reading the recipe, one might think it involves a lot of work, but in reality it is very easy. This is a well-known Provençale recipe, and as the people there say, "Once tasted, desired forever."

6 medium or large globe artichokes	¹/₄ cup (60 mL) red wine or cider vinegar
1 tsp. (5 mL) salt	¹/₂ cup (125 mL) dry white vermouth
1 cup (250 mL) diced onions	1¹/₂ cups (375 mL) canned consommé, undiluted
¹/₃ cup (80 mL) olive or vegetable oil	
2 garlic cloves, minced	1 bay leaf
salt and pepper	¹/₂ tsp. (2 mL) thyme

Trim each artichoke by cutting the prickly tip of each leaf. Split in 2. Cut off stem end. Rub all over with a piece of cut lemon to prevent discoloration. Remove the prickly part of the heart with a teaspoon. Place in a large pot of boiling water, add salt and boil uncovered for 10 minutes. Drain.

In the meantime, brown onions in oil in a large shallow pan, referred to in France as a *sauteuse*. Stir in garlic, salt and pepper to taste, and place the artichoke halves side by side, cut-side down, over the onions. Cover and simmer 10 minutes over low heat.

Add wine vinegar and vermouth and boil uncovered over high heat 3 to 6 minutes, or until liquid is reduced by about half. Then add consommé, bay leaf and thyme. Cover with a cheesecloth or a J-cloth (to keep the artichokes from floating). Cover the pan. Cook in a preheated 325°F. (160°C) oven 1¹/₄ hours. Set aside at room temperature for a few hours, removing the cover but not the cloth. The artichokes are best when eaten at room temperature.

Serve 1 or 2 halves to each person, and pour a spoonful of the tasty onion gravy over each.

They will keep 12 to 24 hours in a cool place, and 2 to 4 days refrigerated. Warm up by steaming if they are too cold. *Serves 4 to 6.*

Green Peas Vendéen

Vendée is the region of Poitou that produces superb vegetables, especially the potatoes from Noirmoutier Island, which is also a delightful sea resort in summer. The green peas and beans are cultivated in the northern part of Vendée, and sent to Nantes, which has one of the best canneries in France.

2 lb. (1 kg) fresh
  green peas OR 2 cups
  (500 mL) frozen green
  peas
3 tbsp. (50 mL)
  unsalted butter
a sprig of fresh thyme OR
  1/4 tsp. (1 mL) dry
  thyme

2 green onions, thinly
  sliced
1/4 cup (60 mL) fresh
  parsley, minced
a pinch of summer
  savory
1/2 tsp. (2 mL) sugar
2 cups (500 mL) lettuce,
  shredded
salt and pepper

Shell peas, and boil shells 30 minutes in 2 cups (500 mL) of water. Reserve the water.

Melt butter in a saucepan, then add thyme, green onions (use both white and green parts), parsley and savory. Stir together a few seconds. Add green peas and stir over low heat until peas are well coated with the butter. Sprinkle with sugar, and add lettuce. Stir again until all the ingredients are coated with the butter.

Add just enough hot water, drained from the shells, to barely cover the mixture. Bring to the boil and continue boiling over medium heat, uncovered, about 10 minutes, or until peas are tender. Drain (reserve the delicious broth to use in soup or sauce) and serve. *Serves 4.*

Strasbourg Mashed Beets

One of my favorite recipes for beets, given to me years ago by the owner of a little inn in Strasbourg. Unfortunately, it no longer exists. I can see the woman now, in a large black taffeta head-dress and a long black skirt which she wore summer and winter. A fabulous cook, she served the beets with a roasted and cured smoked loin of pork, *Kasseler-Rippenspeer*, a specialty which can be purchased in German delicatessens. The roast sat on a bed of thick unsweetened applesauce and was topped with a good piece of unsalted butter. You might like to try it yourself.

6-10 medium beets | *1 tbsp. (15 mL)*
juice of 1 lime | *cornstarch*
pinch of ground cloves | *¹/₃ cup (80 mL) dry red*
1 tsp. (1 mL) sugar | *wine*
salt and pepper | *1 tsp. (5 mL) butter*
| *chives or parsley*

Boil or steam-bake beets until tender. Peel and mash in a blender, or pass through a food mill. Return to the saucepan and add lime juice, cloves, sugar, and salt and pepper to taste. Mix the cornstarch with the red wine. Add to the beets. Cook over medium heat, stirring constantly until hot and creamy.

Remove from the heat and stir in butter and chives or parsley to taste. *Yield: about 6 servings.*

True French Brioche

Did you ever sigh with ecstasy and delight over breakfast in a French country inn or a Paris bistro, as you took in the smell and warmth of the golden *brioche*, topped off with its jaunty little hat? If so, you will want to know how to make it, even though it is readily available at good pastry shops. Learn to make it "at home," as the cost is much lower and the quality superb. If you do not have fluted *brioche* pans, use muffin tins. One of my easy recipes for *brioche* follows.

A *brioche* is one of the glories of the French cuisine. It is a light, fancy yeast bread, rich in butter and eggs, and can be made in various shapes and sizes, plain or garnished. When baked as a roll it looks like a big beautiful mushroom.

△ *This is a meal of colorful* sukiyaki, gohan *with a "heart" of shrimps, and the green* matcha, *to be sipped after some tasty, warm* sake. *I hope it gives you a feeling for what the Japanese call perfection, or* kisetsukan. *I had to go to Japan to understand it.*

▽ *Fish, rice, tomatoes and black olives are all typical ingredients of the Greek flavor.*

Whenever I travel in the south of France, I always make at least one trip to a fruit market. There are not only countless unusual and tropical fruits, but also many varieties of each type, each one with its own distinct flavor. I usually keep a good supply in my hotel room.

You can freeze *brioches* without losing any of their quality. They will keep for six to eight months if well wrapped. To serve, warm them up, unwrapped but not thawed, at 350°F. (180°C).

1 envelope dry yeast	*1 tbsp. (15 mL) fine*
½ cup (125 mL) warm	*sugar*
water	*1 tsp. (5 mL) salt*
3 cups (375 mL)	*4 eggs, lightly beaten*
all-purpose flour,	*1 cup (250 mL)*
sifted twice	*unsalted butter*

Stir together yeast and warm water. Stir in ½ cup (125 mL) of the flour. Beat with a whisk until smooth, then form into a ball. Place in a bowl of warm water and cover bowl with a cloth. Let it rise until double in bulk (about 30 to 40 minutes).

Place the remaining flour in a large bowl, and make a well in the center. Pour sugar, salt and beaten eggs into the well. Knead thoroughly together to make a smooth dough. When the sponge of dough rising in the water is ready (it will rise to the surface of the water), add it to the egg dough and work it in until well incorporated. Knead butter with your hands until soft, then work it into the dough until well blended. Sprinkle lightly with flour. Cover with a cloth and let rise until double in bulk — it will take from 2 to 3 hours. Then punch down the dough. Cover again and refrigerate overnight.

Grease individual fluted *brioche* pans or muffin tins, enough for 12 to 18 *brioches*. Shape dough into balls that half fill the pans. Cut a cross into the top of each ball and insert a small ball of dough which will make the crown of the *brioche*. Let rise in a warm place until double in bulk.

Beat 1 egg with 1 teaspoon (5 mL) water. Brush top of each *brioche* with this glaze.

Bake in a preheated 400°F. (200°C) oven 15 to 20 minutes, or until golden brown. When cooked, unmold immediately. Cool on cake rack. *Yield: 12 to 18 brioches.*

Note: You can also make 2 large, or 4 small, brioche loaves from this recipe. Cut chilled dough in half, shape and place in two 5 × 9 × 3 in. (12.5 × 22.5 × 7.5 cm) or four individual bread loaf pans, well greased. Let rise until double in bulk and brush with egg glaze. Bake in a 375°F. (190°C) oven, 50 minutes for large loaves, 35 minutes for small ones. Unmold and cool. Serve hot or cold.

Desserts

Gâteau Pithiviers

For many years I thought I made the best "Golden Pithiviers" because I had adapted the recipe from that of the "Great Carême," who, during the period of Louis XVIII, was the first chef to create French pastry. This was after the French Revolution. *Pâtisserie* was his forte; he designed each piece like an architect designing a beautiful home, but he didn't do it at the expense of taste. My illusions were destroyed the day I went to Gien with my husband to visit the Château de la Chasse à Tir et de la Fauconnerie — the first to be constructed in the Loire. This château (translated "Hunting and Falconry Castle") was built in 1484 by Anne de Beaujeu and was practically destroyed in World War II. After the war it was reconstructed; its beautiful Gothic doors, unbelievable roof framework and its many turrets all perfectly rebuilt. However, what is most fascinating to many, especially those interested in hunting, riding and falconry, are the numerous authentic collections of arms and of paintings and tapestries relating to these sports.

The *faience de Gien* (Gien stoneware) was another great attraction for me, especially since the craft was first started there by an industrious Englishman, in 1823. At first, simple baking and cooking ware were made, then, later on, elegant tableware, now world renowned, was produced. I cherish every piece I own.

All this leads me back to the subject of *Gâteau Pithiviers,* as it was in Gien, in a small tea room facing the castle and the old bridge, overlooking the gently flowing Loire River, that I discovered they served my favorite cake. I ordered it, *quite* convinced that it couldn't be as perfect as Carême's recipe. Well, it was the very best I had ever eaten, and the pastry chef gave me the recipe.

In 1977, my husband and I entertained the Trompes du Musée de la Chasse de Gien (Hunting Horns of Gien's Museum) who are recognized as the very best in France! They were on tour in Canada, participating in a competition. I made the Pithiviers, which I served to them at high tea in our garden (I baked four but they could have eaten eight). I was happy they could enjoy a specialty of Gien which they were all familiar with. In gratitude the group picked up their hunting horns and played a *merci,* as they called it. The horses, sheep and dogs were so fascinated by the sound of horns, they came down from the fields and stood at attention. It was an extraordinary sight — instinctively they knew it was a hunting call!

rich pastry or puff pastry (optional)	*3 tbsp. (50 mL) melted butter*
¹/₂ cup (125 mL) almonds, toasted and ground	*2 egg yolks*
	2 tbsp. (30 mL) heavy cream
¹/₂ cup (125 mL) fine granulated sugar	

Buy or make the puff pastry; or use your favorite pastry—also good but not as perfect. Roll out large enough to cover a 9-in. (22.5 cm) pie plate. Refrigerate until ready to use.

Place almonds, in their skins, on a baking sheet. Roast in a 300°F. (150°C) oven until lightly toasted, about 15 minutes. This is to bring out the almond flavor. Cool for 10 minutes, then grind in a food processor or blender until fine, but not so that it is like butter. Mix the almonds with sugar, butter, egg yolks and cream. Beat in an electric mixer or food processor until thoroughly blended and creamy.

Pour into the pastry-lined plate, but do not let it cover the rim. Brush the rim of pastry with a beaten egg. Top with a round lid of the same pastry used for the bottom, pressing it down gently around the edges. Make a small hole in the middle, brush the top pastry with the beaten egg and refrigerate 15 minutes. Then, with a knife, nick the edge of the pastry at regular intervals (about 10 to 12 nicks), then push up the pastry on either side of each nick to form a scalloped rose petal edge. (This last operation can be omitted, leaving the pastry plain all around.)

Bake in a preheated 450°F. (230°C) oven 10 minutes, then lower the heat to 400°F. (200°C) and bake until browned and puffed, about 25 to 30 minutes. Remove from the oven, sprinkle top of cake with fine granulated sugar and return to oven for 4 to 6 minutes, or until sugar becomes a dark brown glaze. Cool, serve and delight. *Serves 6 to 8.*

Alsatian Blueberry Torte

In France blueberries are called *myrtilles* — such a romantic name. This large torte makes a beautiful dessert for eight, and keeps very well. Serve it with a cool Alsatian white wine.

I adapted this recipe from one given to me by the chef at the Château d'Isenbourg, near Colmar. The château, built in the thirteenth century, is surrounded by vineyards and has a superb view of the Alsatian plain and the Vosges mountains. During my stay there, I managed to enjoy this torte three times in ten days!

1¹/₂ cups (375 mL)
  all-purpose flour
¹/₂ cup (125 mL) sugar
¹/₂ cup (125 mL)
  unsalted butter
1¹/₂ tsp. (7 mL) baking
  powder
1 egg
1 tsp. (5 mL) vanilla
    * * * * *
3-4 cups (750 mL-1 L)
  fresh blueberries
grated rind of 1 lime or
  lemon
2 tbsp. (30 mL) sugar

    * * * * *
2 cups (500 mL)
  commercial sour
  cream
2 egg yolks
¹/₂ cup (125 mL) sugar
2 tbsp. (30 mL) lime or
  lemon juice

Butter generously a 10-in. (25 cm) spring-form cake pan.

Mix together in a bowl with your fingers flour, sugar, butter (make sure it is soft), baking powder, 1 egg and vanilla. Pat evenly in the bottom of cake pan.

Mix lightly blueberries, lime or lemon rind and sugar. Sprinkle evenly over dough.

Mix in a bowl the remaining ingredients. Pour evenly over the berries. Bake in a preheated 350°F. (180°C) oven for 1 hour, or until golden brown on top. Cool on a cake rack for 20 minutes. Unmold and slip cake onto a serving plate using a spatula. *Serves 8.*

Tarte Bourdaloue

This creation of classic French cuisine is not an everyday type of dessert, but a buffet or dinner party sweet. There are variations of the recipe for this "pie"; the following is my adaptation of the Ali-Bab creation.

a 9- or 10-inch pastry
shell, baked
4 ripe pears
1 cup (250 mL) dry or
sweet white wine
¹/₄ cup (60 mL) honey
3 whole cloves
1 cup (250 mL) heavy
cream
1 tbsp. (15 mL)
cornstarch

3 egg yolks, beaten
3 tbsp. (50 mL) brown
sugar
2 tsp. (10 mL) almond
extract
2 tbsp. (30 mL) brandy
¹/₂ cup (125 mL)
currant jelly
2 tbsp. (30 mL) orange
juice

Peel, halve and core pears. Gently boil wine, honey and cloves 2 minutes, then add pears; cover and poach until just tender, about 10 minutes — do not let pears boil.

Remove pears with a slotted spoon and boil syrup uncovered 5 to 6 minutes. In a saucepan, blend cream with cornstarch, add 1 cup (250 mL) of the syrup and cook over low heat, stirring most of the time, until creamy.

Beat egg yolks with brown sugar, then beat into cream mixture. Stir over medium heat for 1 minute, but do not let it boil. Remove from heat, cover and let cool thoroughly. When cooled, stir in almond extract and brandy.

Fill pie shell with cream mixture, then arrange pears over it in a circle, cut-side down and pointed end toward the middle.

Over low heat, melt currant jelly with orange juice until bubbly. Spoon carefully over pears and in the center of the pie. Let set for a few hours at room temperature. *Serves 8.*

Pumpkin-Apricot Pie

Throughout my years of travelling and eating in France, I have learned to make more dishes with pumpkin, from soup to dessert, than one can imagine. All European, Asiatic and South American people make use of pumpkin in so many tasty ways, but in North America, where it is also easy to grow, people seem to forget the golden fruit except when mashing or puréeing it. The combination of pumpkin, dried apricot, citrus fruits and brandy makes this pie a truly elegant, tasty dessert.

1 1/2 cups (400 mL)
pumpkin purée
1 cup (250 mL) dried
apricots, stewed and
mashed
1/3 cup (80 mL) unsalted
butter
3/4 cup (200 mL) light
brown sugar
1/3 cup (80 mL) light
cream

1/2 tsp. (2 mL) mace
1/4 tsp. (1 mL) nutmeg
grated peel of 1 orange
and 1 lemon
1/4 cup (60 mL) brandy
3 eggs, separated
1/4 tsp. (1 mL) salt
a 9-in. (22.5) pie shell,
unbaked

Beat all ingredients, except eggs, salt and pastry, until thoroughly mixed. Beat egg yolks and blend in. Beat egg whites with salt, then fold into mixture.

Pour into pie shell and bake in a 400°F. (200°C) oven 15 minutes. Lower heat to 325°F. (160°C) and bake 30 to 35 minutes, or until filling is set. Do not overbake—filling thickens as it cools. *Serves 6.*

Macaroons

True almond paste macaroons are hard to find and very expensive, but easy to make if almond paste is readily available. If you keep them in a metal box with a good cover, a sheet of waxed paper between each row, they will stay fresh for three to four months.

¹/₂ lb. (250 g) almond paste*	1 cup (250 mL) fine granulated sugar
2-3 egg whites**	¹/₂ cup (125 mL) icing
¹/₄ tsp. (1 mL) salt	sugar (approximately)

Knead almond paste with your hands until soft, then break into small pieces. Put egg whites and salt in an electric mixer or food processor (with the latter use the steel blade). Adding sugar and almond paste, a little at a time, beat until the mixture is smooth and thick.

Beat in icing sugar, a tablespoon (15 mL) at a time—it may take ¹/₂ cup (125 mL) or a little less, but use just enough to make a batter thick enough to hold its shape.

Cover baking sheet with *2 layers* of brown paper. Drop batter onto the paper by teaspoons (5 mL) (or more, depending on the size you want), leaving about 2 in. (5 cm) between each macaroon.

Bake in a preheated 300°F. (150°C) oven until lightly browned, about 20 to 25 minutes. Remove from oven, slide the paper off with the macaroons and place it on a baking sheet covered with a damp dish towel. Let stand until macaroons are cool, about 15 minutes. Remove them from paper with a small metal spatula. Continue to cool on a cake rack. *Yield: about 3 to 4 dozen.****

*Use commercial or homemade almond paste.
**Eggs vary in size and moisture content. Sometimes you may only need to use 2 to 2¹/₂ eggs.
***The size of macaroons you make will also determine the yield.

Apples Normande

Many years ago, I visited Paternostre, a small city in Normandy where my ancestors came from. I arrived at a little inn at dinnertime and was offered a soup of cream of celery root, cheese and this compote — a simple applesauce, but what flavor! I promptly decided to find the recipe. *La voilà.*

2 lb. (1 kg) apples	¹/₂-1 cup (125-250 mL)
¹/₃ cup (80 mL) unsalted	whipping cream
butter	2 tbsp. (30 mL) fine
³/₄ cup (190 mL) sugar	granulated sugar
3 tbsp. (50 mL)	
Calvados or brandy	

Peel, core and cut apples in thick slices. Melt butter in an enamelled cast-iron pan. When light brown, add apples and cook over medium heat, stirring often, for about 10 minutes. The apples should then be softened. Add the ³/₄ cup (190 mL) of sugar and Calvados or brandy. Remove from heat. Stir with a whisk until sugar is melted, then pour into a serving dish. Cool, then cover and refrigerate until ready to serve.

Whip the cream, adding the 2 tbsp. (30 mL) of sugar. Spread on top of the cold applesauce. Run the tines of a fork over the top of the cream to make little ridges. *Serves 6.*

Strawberry Sabayon

The French *Sabayon* is the most perfect of sauces to serve with all types of small fruit. When served over strawberries, it's an unforgettable dessert.

4 cups (1 L)	¹/₄ cup (60 mL) liqueur
strawberries	(any kind) or brandy
4 egg yolks	¹/₃ cup (80 mL)
2 tbsp. (30 mL) sugar	whipping cream

Rinse strawberries under cold running water, spread on absorbent paper and hull. (This is the perfect way to clean them.) Refrigerate, covered.

The *sabayon* sauce is a hot emulsion, so it must be cooked in a heavy metal saucepan over low heat. The best way to prevent overheating and curdling is to lift the pan often and lightly touch the bottom with your finger. As long as you can do this comfortably, the sauce will not curdle. A double boiler is not recommended, as there is no control over the temperature of the water.

Place egg yolks in the saucepan and beat at medium speed until the yolks are thick and pale yellow. Gradually add sugar, beating until mixture is light and fluffy. It will form soft peaks when the beater is raised.

Place the pan over low heat and beat, slowly adding liqueur or brandy (bourbon can also be used). Continue beating until mixture is fluffy and in mounds, about 5 to 6 minutes. Place pan over ice cubes and continue beating until egg mixture cools.

When cooled, whip cream and fold into the egg sauce. Refrigerate until serving time, stir again and pour over the prepared strawberries. *Serves 6.*

Les Poires

In France a pear is more than just a pear — it has a name and a personality. The Comice, greenish-yellow to yellow with red splashings, and excellent served with cheese, is famous for its great size and beauty. It bakes well if very firm, however, like anything beautiful, it is expensive and not readily available.

The well-shaped Bartlett, yellow or yellow with a red blush, is usually available from July through November. It is equally good eaten raw, or poached and canned, but does not bake well.

Then November brings with it the pear that can be bought well into May — the chunky Anjou, green or greenish-yellow. Bakes, poaches and cans well.

Now I come to my very favorite, the Bosc pear, green or brown to golden russet, with a long, tapered neck. When just ripe, it is perfect to eat — a true *poire couteau*, as they say in France, but it also cooks well. There are many more varieties in France, but the above are available in our country.

In France, pears and cheese are very often served as a dessert, without bread of course. One cannot know the finesse of Roquefort cheese before tasting it on or with a slice of ripe pear, both at room temperature.

Poires Hélène

I have had more requests for this special dessert than for any other. It is a classic French dessert, but often misrepresented; for instance, when canned chocolate syrup is poured over a Comice or canned pear, with mounds of canned "whipped cream" surrounding it.

The true *Poire Hélène* is fresh poached pears set on a *crème frangipane*, flavored with almond macaroons, and topped with a brandied chocolate sauce poured warm (not hot) over the cold pear and *frangipane* — and *never* any whipped cream.

The Bosc or Comice pears are the best types to use, available on the market in early autumn and for the first part of winter.

Pears:

3 cups (750 mL) cold water	10 peppercorns
1 cup (250 mL) sugar	3 whole cloves
½ cup (125 mL) honey	6-8 pears, peeled and
2 bay leaves	left whole with their
	stems

Combine the first 6 ingredients in a large saucepan. Bring to boil, stirring to melt sugar, then boil 5 minutes over medium heat.

Place pears in syrup. Cover and simmer 8 to 20 minutes, or until pears are cooked but not mushy. The cooking time will vary with their ripeness. While cooking the pears, swirl them around in the syrup with a rubber spatula (a fork will leave a mark), to cook them evenly. Cover and let them cool in the syrup.

Frangipane:

⅓ cup (80 mL) flour	1 vanilla bean OR 1 tsp.
½ cup (125 mL) sugar	(5 mL) vanilla extract
a pinch of salt	2 tbsp. (30 mL) butter
4 eggs	4 macaroons, crushed
2 cups (500 mL) milk	

Place in a saucepan flour, sugar and salt and mix well. Add 1 whole egg and 1 egg yolk. Mix thoroughly with a wooden spoon. Then stir in another whole egg and 1 egg yolk. Mix again.

Meanwhile, scald the milk (with the vanilla bean, if you are using this rather than extract). When hot, add it little by little to the creamed egg mixture, stirring with a whisk. Place over medium heat and stir until the mixture reaches the boiling point, then cook over gentle heat, about 2 minutes. Discard vanilla bean. Add butter, macaroons and vanilla extract (if you are not using the bean). Mix well, then pour into a dish or jar. Cover and keep refrigerated. It will keep about 4 weeks.

Hélène Chocolate Sauce: This is a must for the true recipe. Use a 13-ounce (370 g) bar of Swiss bittersweet chocolate, the "Lindt Fils" variety. If unavailable, use our usual semi-sweet chocolate which is sold in 8-ounce (227 g) bars. Ignore the difference in weight, as the Swiss type is much lighter in texture and requires more to produce the same results.

one 13-oz. (370 g) bar	*²/₃ cup (160 mL) sugar*
Swiss bittersweet	*2¹/₃ cups (580 mL)*
chocolate OR *one*	*water*
8-oz. (227 g) bar	*3 tbsp. (50 mL) brandy*
semi-sweet chocolate	*1 tsp. (5 mL) vanilla*

Break up chocolate, and combine it in a saucepan with sugar and water and bring to the boil over medium-low heat, stirring often. Simmer over low heat 5 minutes. Remove from heat. Add brandy and vanilla and pour into a jug. It will keep 5 to 8 weeks, refrigerated.

To warm it up, place the covered jar in the top of a double boiler and let it stand over simmering water until it is warm. Open the jar to stir once or twice.

To serve the pears: Place a spoonful of cold *frangipane* cream in the bottom of a low-stem glass. Stand 1 pear upright in the cream. Just before serving, pour the desired amount of warm chocolate sauce over the pear. *Serves 6 to 8.*

Poires Caramel

While in Paris, I attended a fascinating lecture given by the great "Colette" in the twenties. The subject was "How cats learn to live with us." As a cat lover, I fully understood her amusing anecdotes. She mentioned that when she made *Poires Caramel* she had to double the recipe because so much of it had to be shared with her favorite cats. She also explained her recipe, referring to brown sugar as *gervoise*, and heavy cream as *crème double*. Maybe a dessert for cats, but not for dieters!

6 medium pears	*3 tbsp. (50 mL) butter*
²/₃ cup (160 mL) brown	*¹/₂ cup (125 mL) heavy*
sugar	*cream*

Peel pears and cut in halves. Place in a baking dish in a single layer. Sprinkle brown sugar on top and dot with butter.

Bake in a preheated 350°F. (180°C) oven for 30 to 45 minutes (depending on the juiciness of the pears). Baste 2 to 3 times during the cooking period. When done, you should have a fairly heavy syrup.

Set aside pears, add cream to the syrup and stir gently until it turns a deep caramel color. Cool, pour over pears and serve. *Serves 6.*

Italy

On my first trip to Italy, I crossed the border from France at the spectacular High Briançon pass. Suddenly, I felt the sun, which always seems warmer and brighter when one is in Italy! Then I noticed the spectacular grey-green olive trees, their centenary roots growing out of the arid soil, all gnarled, but still giving their bounty of olives each year. I was delighted with the rosemary shrubs growing among the rock walls, and surprised by the vivid color of the scenery around me.

I quickly sensed the difference between the French, with their polite coolness, and the Italians, dark haired and laughing; and, as people differ, so does the food and the attitude toward it. For instance, I found out that with the Italians, if you do not like their food they are sorry for you, but *they* keep enjoying it. On the other hand, the French quickly make you feel they know better and properly snub you.

In spite of the fact that the great Renaissance of food began in Italy with "Lorenzo the Magnificent," whose daughter, Catherine de Medici, brought to France her own chefs and their "secrets" when she married the King and revolutionized French cooking, Italy has never since attained the international fame and the degree of snobbishness of French cuisine. However, if I stay in France for any length of time, I reach a point of saturation with the cuisine. Not so in Italy. "Why?" you may ask, and "Just what is Italian food?"

First, let me say that there is more to it than pizza and spaghetti sauce. It is a cuisine that differs totally from one part of the country to the other. There are so many types of pastas: *alla Firenze, alla Milanese, alla Bolognase, alla Napolitana,* etc., each one distinct from the other. My great favorite is *alla Firenze* (Florentine), none of it buried under heavy spices nor thick tomato sauce. Their amazing pale pink roast of beef, so tender, so tasty; their Fresca cream cheese, light, rich, superb; the fresh figs; the purple green beans served with a dash of oil and lots of minced basil; the tiny green peas, simply served with butter; a *granita di caffe* at 11 A.M., sitting in a tiny café; hot creamy chocolate at Enrico Rivoir's poured from a gold spigot into a tiny cup, and sipped from a little spoon — subtle but so good!

Of course, there is more than just Florence. When you cross the Alps from France you find Torino the delicate, Milano the rich and elegant, Padova and Venezia, full of great history and art, their produce coming from both land and sea. Bologna, or "La Grassa," as it is nicknamed, is regarded by many as offering the best in Italian cuisine, as well as producing the beautiful Lambrusco wine, light and fresh. Genoa, perched on a mountainside, its beautiful Riviera coast below, is home of the piquant aromatic *il pesto*, fresh basil, olive oil, *pignolia*, sharp Parmesan cheese and famous seafood — all to be enjoyed with white wine, produced from the tart grapes growing on the steep hills of "Cinqueterre."

Central Italy is an area of renowned landscapes, where the light is the color of glittering gold. Where else is it the custom to sit in silence to enjoy the sunset? After such moments you can enjoy a glass of their young Chianti, a transparent bright red color, with a fragrance of violets. What delight!

Assisi, in the region of Umbria, is home of the extraordinary Basilic of San Francesco, a formation of two superimposed churches, housing a superb fresco by Giotto. Just in front of the Basilic there is a little sidewalk café where you can sip superb espresso and munch on hot croissants filled with soft almond paste. Umbria is also where you can delight in a spit-roasted kid or young lamb, enjoyed with a dry golden Orvieto wine and a dish of steamed Italian rice, topped with rich tasty gravy.

Rome's table differs for two reasons: the historical one being the Greek cooks, who were brought to Rome during the time of emperors, because they were considered status symbols, as well as the very best cooks of the time. They taught the Italian cooks the arts of pastry and ice-cream making, the latter still a great favorite of Italians. The second reason is the great influx of tourists, which brings a cosmopolitan flair to Roman food.

In the south proper, I find the cuisine heavy, oily, repetitive. So often you still feel and taste the Arabic influence which dominated Sicily in the early Middle Ages.

Let's say a word about Naples, the city of a thousand pizzas, made with dark red spicy tomato sauce, and of pastas of all sizes and types. But the one thing that is exquisite and well prepared is the *frutti di mare* (seafood). The Neopolitans have almost as many varieties of seafood as they do of pastas, all of it served with their volcanic-tasting white wine from Ischia and the slopes of Vesuvius. The best known is the Lacrima Christi, which they serve at room temperature, but I prefer it cool.

May I close with Sicily, where you can eat the very best tuna fresh from the sea, and Italy's best ice cream. To finish, have a glass of their sweet potent Marsala, which is always poured over wild strawberries instead of cream!

Green Minestra Soup

Made the Genoese way, with fresh greens and seasonal vegetables, topped with *pesto* to taste. In the summer, serve chilled, but add *pesto* to hot soup.

¹/₄-¹/₂ cup (60-125 mL) olive oil
1 onion, peeled and chopped
1 large or 2 small leeks, diced
1 garlic clove, minced
¹/₂ cup (125 mL) diced carrots
³/₄ cup (190 mL) diced celery
1 cup (250 mL) unpeeled, grated zucchini

1 cup (250 mL) diced green beans or another vegetable of your choice
a 7¹/₂-oz. (213 mL) can of tomato sauce
1 cup (250 mL) finely shredded cabbage
1 tsp. (5 mL) salt
8 cups (2 L) fresh beef stock or diluted canned beef stock
1 cup (250 mL) bow pasta, cooked
Pesto or grated Parmesan cheese.

Heat oil in a large saucepan. Add leeks, onion and garlic, and stir until soft and barely golden. Add carrots and stir occasionally, about 2 minutes, then add the remaining vegetables, one at a time, using the stirring and 2-minute cooking method for each vegetable. Add the remaining ingredients, except the bow pasta and *pesto*. Simmer covered for 1 to 1¹/₂ hours. Add cooked pasta, simmer 10 minutes and serve. When adding *pesto* to soup, combine it with the pasta. *Serves 6 to 8.*

Pasta

Salad of Cold Sea Shells

In Florence pasta is not served with the meat or fish course; rice is preferred. However, pasta is often served as an entrée or a salad. This is one of my favorites; very attractive when served in a nest of crisp watercress.

8 oz. (250 g) small sea
  shell pasta
1 tbsp. (15 mL)
  vegetable oil
4 tbsp. (60 mL) olive or
  vegetable oil

juice of 1 lemon
4 green onions, chopped
¼ cup (60 mL) fresh
  parsley, minced.

Pour the sea shells in a pot of boiling water with the 1 tbsp. (15 mL) vegetable oil. Add a teaspoon (5 mL) of salt. Boil according to time given on package — do not overcook. Pour into colander and rinse under cold running water. Drain at least 30 minutes. Add remaining ingredients, toss, salt and pepper to taste. Do not refrigerate. Leave at room temperature an hour or so before serving. *Serves 6.*

Pasta Modena

Another specialty of northern cuisine. A fresh, fragrant, uncooked tomato sauce served over very hot spaghettini. Try making it when tomatoes are in season and at their very best.

8 oz. (250 g)
  spaghettini
6 medium or 4 large
  tomatoes
1 garlic clove, finely
  chopped
½ tsp. (2 mL) sugar
1 tsp. (5 mL) salt
½ tsp. (2 mL) freshly
  ground pepper

2 tbsp. (30 mL) fresh
  basil, chopped OR
1 tbsp. (15 mL) dry
  basil
½ tsp. (2 mL) rosemary
¼ cup (60 mL) fresh
  parsley, chopped fine
2-3 tbsp. (30-50 mL)
  olive or vegetable oil
grated Parmesan or
  Cheddar cheese

Cook the spaghettini according to directions on package.

Peel tomatoes and cut in quarters. Place in a food processor or blender with garlic, sugar, salt, pepper, basil, rosemary and parsley. Blend just until it becomes a sauce. Add oil and pour over the *very* hot, well-drained, cooked spaghettini. Toss and serve with the cheese. *Serves 6.*

Noodles from Bologna

The food in Bologna, in northern Italy, is superb, and many of the great Italian chefs have made their reputations in the great restaurants of this city. I first ate this pasta at Pappagallo's.

*8 oz. (250 g) noodles,
 cooked and drained
¹/₄ cup (60 mL) grated
 Parmesan cheese*

*juice of 1 lemon and
 grated rind of
 ¹/₂ lemon
¹/₂ cup (125 mL) hot,
 heavy cream
salt and pepper*

Place hot cooked noodles in a warm bowl, sprinkle with Parmesan, lemon rind and juice. Mix with 2 forks. Pour hot cream over the noodles and mix again. Taste for seasoning. Superb with roast chicken or veal or a green salad. *Serves 4.*

Roman Noodles

Don't be put off by the large quantity of bay leaves in this sauce. This is a very old recipe from the south of Italy, quite unique.

*8 oz. (250 g) fine or
 large noodles
4 tbsp. (60 mL) olive or
 vegetable oil
1 medium onion,
 chopped fine*

*4–5 tomatoes, peeled
 and chopped
10 bay leaves
1 tsp. (5 mL) sugar
salt and pepper
¹/₂ cup (125 mL) finely
 chopped celery leaves*

Cook noodles according to package directions.

Heat oil, add onion and cook over high heat, stirring frequently, until light golden brown. Add tomatoes and stir well. Add the remaining ingredients and stir over medium heat for 3 to 5 minutes. Remove bay leaves. Taste for seasoning. Pour over the hot, well-drained noodles. Serve with or without cheese, according to taste. *Serves 6.*

Napoli Spinach-Ricotta Lasagne

Although I am not very fond of the cuisine of southern Italy (oily and heavily spiced), I did enjoy this meatless lasagne at a small *trattoria* in Naples. It was followed by swordfish, served cold, with a sauce made from olive oil, fresh lemon juice, lots of Italian parsley (*cilentro*) and accompanied with a generous amount of lemon. The recipe was given to me by the "Mama" cook.

8 oz. (250 g) lasagne noodles	*2 cups (500 mL) Ricotta or small-curd cottage cheese*
2 lb. (1 kg) fresh spinach	*1 cup (250 mL) commercial sour cream*
2 tbsp. (30 mL) butter	
salt and pepper	*6 green onions, coarsely chopped*
1 garlic clove, chopped fine	*7-8 slices Mozarella cheese*
¹/₂ tsp. (2 mL) oregano	
1 tsp. (5 mL) basil	*³/₄ cup (190 mL) grated Parmesan cheese*
a 7¹/₂-oz. can (213 mL) tomato sauce	

Cook noodles according to package directions. Drain, rinse under cold running water, drain again and set aside. Wash spinach, place in a saucepan and sprinkle with a bit of sugar. Do not add any water, cover and cook 5 minutes over medium heat.

Melt butter, add the drained spinach, salt, pepper, garlic, oregano and basil. Stir until well blended, then add tomato sauce. Stir until hot.

Combine the Ricotta or cottage cheese, sour cream and green onions.

In a 2-quart (1 L) casserole make alternate layers of noodles, spinach and slices of Mozarella cheese, until all ingredients are used. Sprinkle top with grated Parmesan cheese. Bake in a 350°F. (180°C) oven about 30 to 40 minutes, or until golden brown on top. *Serves 6.*

Genoa Pesto

A specialty of Genoa, where sweet basil grows plentiful. *Al pesto* means "by pounding." *Pesto* was originally made with a black marble mortar and pestle, by pounding the aromatic mixture until it was creamy. (I used the same method until the arrival of the food processor.) It looks like a beautiful deep green creamed butter, and keeps, refrigerated, for one month, or six to eight months if frozen.

Pesto can be added (even frozen, it is easy to spoon out) to soups, hot pasta, rice, oil-and-vinegar dressings, mayonnaise, and is super with tomato sandwiches.

The best dressmaker I have ever known, Ivaldi, was from Genoa, and she taught me how to make Pesto and Green Minestra,* that delicious Genoese vegetable soup, accompanied with *pesto,* either served separately in a bowl or added to the soup.

¹/₄ lb. (125 g) Parmesan cheese, diced	¹/₂ cup (125 mL) pignolia or pine nuts
2–4 garlic cloves, peeled	1 tsp. (5 mL) salt
¹/₄ tsp. (1 mL) freshly ground pepper	³/₄–1 cup (190–250 mL) olive oil
2 cups (500 mL) fresh basil leaves	

If you have a food processor, use the steel blade. Add one ingredient at a time and process each for 2 minutes. Then add the oil gradually and beat until creamy.

If you use a blender, it is better to grate the Parmesan cheese and slice the garlic before blending. Place the oil in the blender first, then gradually add the remaining ingredients. Blend until creamy and well mixed. *Yield: 2 cups (500 mL).*

*See recipe, p. 196.

Risotto

There are almost as many varieties of *risotto* in Italy as there are cooks. Each region has its own way of preparing it, and as a rice lover I was keenly interested in trying many types while in Italy. I can honestly say the Milanese type is my favorite.

Use Italian rice, available in specialty shops, or the long-grain type. Do not use instant or converted rice, as the results would not be nearly as good. While northern Italians always use butter, oil is used in the south.

4 tbsp. (60 mL) butter	*4 cups (1 L) chicken*
1 medium onion, finely	*consommé*
chopped	*a pinch of saffron*
2 cups (500 mL) Italian	*¹/₂ (125 mL) grated*
or long-grain rice	*Parmesan cheese*

Melt butter in an enamelled cast-iron saucepan. Add onion, stir and cook 5 minutes over low heat. Add rice and cook 10 minutes over low heat, stirring often. This will butter the rice and warm it up before adding the liquid.

Add 2 cups (500 mL) of the chicken consommé, bring to boil and continue boiling, uncovered, over medium heat, until most of the consommé is absorbed by the rice. Add the remaining consommé and bring back to boil. Add saffron and stir well. Cover and cook over medium-low heat 15 minutes, or until rice is tender and all the liquid is absorbed. Stir in the cheese or serve separately. *Serves 6 to 8.*

From Osso Buco to Pumpkin Blossoms: Main Course Dishes

Osso Buco

The Milanese, the Bolognese and the Florentines all make *Osso Buco* with veal shanks, but they all have their own method of preparing it. The following is the Milanese type.

1 veal shank, cut into 6 slices	*1 onion, chopped fine*
2 tbsp. (30 mL) butter	*1 cup (250 mL) dry white wine*
½ cup (125 mL) flour	*1½ cup (375 mL) chicken consommé*
1 tsp. (5 mL) salt	*1 garlic clove, chopped fine*
¼ tsp. (2 mL) crushed peppercorns	*grated rind of 1 lemon*
¼ cup (60 mL) each diced carrots and celery	*3 tbsp. (50 mL) chopped parsley*

Melt butter in an enamelled cast-iron pan. Mix flour, salt and peppercorns. Roll veal slices in this mixture, then brown in butter, on both sides, over medium heat. Remove from pan. Add carrots, celery and onions. Stir for 2 minutes over medium heat. Add wine and chicken consommé and bring to boil, while stirring. Add veal shanks and stir gently. Cover and simmer over low heat about 1 hour, or until meat is tender.

Mix garlic, lemon rind and parsley, and place in a dish. This is called a *gremolata*, and each person sprinkles the desired amount on the meat. Serve the veal with *risotto*, as they do in Milan. *Serves 4.*

Fegato con Vino

A specialty of the world-renowned "Harry's Bar" in Venice, where I had my first encounter with lamb liver. It was prepared at our table, in a large copper chafing dish, then served on a bed of paper-thin orange slices on deep pink pottery plates. Then they offered us doll-sized coffee cups filled with hot brandy, which we poured over the liver. A memorable dish, and easy to prepare.

9 thin slices of lamb liver	*¹/₃ cup (8 mL) butter*
1 tsp. (5 mL) dried marjoram	*2 medium onions, thinly sliced*
¹/₂ tsp. (2 mL) salt	*¹/₂ cup (125 mL) dry red wine*
¹/₄ tsp. (1 mL) freshly ground pepper	*¹/₄ cup (60 mL) fresh orange juice*
¹/₄ cup (60 mL) flour	*orange slices*

Mix dried marjoram, salt, pepper and flour. Roll liver slices in mixture until well coated. Reserve remaining mixture.

Melt butter in heavy metal frying pan, add onions and stir over high heat until softened and light brown here and there. Remove from pan with a perforated spoon. Place liver in the hot fat remaining in the pan and brown over high heat for 1 minute. Turn and brown other side over medium heat for 2 minutes. Place liver on a bed of orange slices arranged on a hot platter.

Stir remaining flour mixture into the orange juice and mix well. Add this to wine, mix and pour into skillet. Stir well again and add onions. Stir over medium heat until slightly thickened. When boiling hot pour over liver and serve. *Serves 4 to 6.*

Pork Chops Modena

Modena cuisine is from the north of Italy. The way they cook pork chops makes them moist and very tender.

*4-6 pork chops, 1 in.
(2.5 cm) thick
1 tsp. (5 mL) butter or
vegetable oil
1 tsp. (5 mL) fresh sage
OR ½ tsp. (2 mL)
dried sage*

*1 tsp. (5 mL) rosemary
1 garlic clove, crushed
salt and pepper
¼ cup (60 mL) dry
white wine or dry
white Martini or cider*

Grease an enamelled cast-iron frying pan with the butter or oil. Place pork chops in it without overlapping them. Sprinkle with sage, rosemary, garlic, and salt and pepper to taste. Pour just enough hot water over the chops to cover them. Simmer over medium heat, uncovered until the water is evaporated and the underside of the chops is browned — this may take 15 to 20 minutes. Turn them and brown the other side. Remove chops to a hot platter. Add the wine, cook briskly over high heat for 2 minutes, or until liquid is reduced by half. Pour sauce over the chops or serve separately. *Serves 4.*

Giannino Lime Broiled Chicken

A superb recipe from a justifiably famous restaurant in Milan, Giannino's, where the dark brown marble floor and huge cooking fireplace of azure tile are a perfect setting for the golden chicken. They are also famous for their Shrimps Allio. Serve this party dish hot or cold, with a big bowl of plain watercress, or with green lettuce.

*3 chicken broiler-fryers,
about 3 lb. (1.5 kg)
each
salt, pepper and paprika
½ cup (125 mL) olive or
vegetable oil
½ cup (125 mL) fresh
lime juice
grated peel of 2 limes*

*2 tbsp. (30 mL) grated
onion
1 tbsp. (15 mL)
tarragon
1 tsp. (5 mL) salt
⅛ tsp. (0.5 mL) hot
pepper sauce
(optional)*

Preheat broiler. Cut each chicken into quarters and sprinkle with salt, pepper and paprika to taste. Place skin-side up on a broiler rack.

Whisk remaining ingredients together and brush on each piece of chicken. Place chicken under oven broiler, 6 in. (15 cm) from source of heat, and cook until tender, up to 1 hour, turning every 15 minutes, and basting each time with sauce.

Serve hot or cold. *Serves 8 to 10.*

Peppers in Oil Antipasto

One of the nicest Italian hors-d'oeuvres, it is served from north to south. Very pleasant with cold meat or roast pork or a barbecue.

*3 large sweet red or
green peppers OR 1 red
and 2 green peppers*

*2 garlic cloves, peeled
and crushed
salt
olive oil
juice of 1 lemon*

Place peppers on a baking sheet and cook in a preheated 400°F. (200°C) oven 15 to 20 minutes, or until the skin is black. Turn them once with your fingers (a fork may pierce the skin) during the cooking period. Cool slightly and scrape off the thin skin — a messy job, but not difficult.

Cut peppers in half, remove core and seeds, and cut into equal-sized strips. Put them in a half-pint (125 mL) glass jar with garlic, salt and lemon juice, and add enough olive oil to barely cover the peppers. Turn them 3 to 4 times during the first hour of marinating. Cover and keep in cool place. *Yield: 1 half-pint (125 mL) jar.*

Carrots à l'Italienne

These are good served hot, tepid or at room temperature.

8-10 small carrots	2 tbsp. (30 mL) water
2 tbsp. (30 mL) butter	chopped parsley or
¹/₄ tsp. (1 mL) sugar	chives
¹/₄ cup (60 mL) Marsala	
or dry port wine	

Peel carrots and cut into long matchsticks. Using a stainless steel saucepan, if possible, melt butter and gently stir in carrots until they are well coated. Sprinkle with sugar, stir well, add Marsala or port and water, and bring to a boil. Simmer, covered, 20 minutes over very low heat, then uncover and boil over high heat until liquid is syrupy. Salt and pepper to taste, pour into a serving dish and sprinkle with parsley or chives. If serving tepid or cold, cover until ready to serve. *Serves 4 to 6.*

Roman Marinated Artichokes

Serve as a salad or a light meal, with thinly sliced cold chicken set on watercress or lettuce leaves

6 small or 4 medium	¹/₂ cup (125 mL) olive or
artichokes, cooked	vegetable oil
and cooled	¹/₄ tsp. (1 mL) freshly
4 tbsp. (60 mL) red	ground pepper
wine vinegar	1 green onion, minced
¹/₂ tsp. (2 mL) salt	1 small garlic clove,
¹/₄ tsp. (1 mL) dry	crushed
mustard	

Mix vinegar, salt and mustard in a bowl. Slowly add oil while stirring with a whisk or fork. Stir in pepper, onion and garlic.

Place cold artichokes in a deep-sided serving dish and pour the dressing over. Cover and marinate 2 to 8 hours. *Serves 4 to 6.*

Baked Onion Salad

In 1953, I spent a few months in Tuscany, which to me is the most exciting part of Italy. Their food is simple in the sense that one particular item is served on its own. For example, in the spring, when the small green peas are at their peak, they will serve a large plate of steaming hot new green peas with just a square of unsalted butter melting on top. On the table sits a lovely bouquet of deep green fresh mint which you can chop over the peas if you like. This delight is served as an entrée.

The Baked Onion Salad is another example of their spring entrées. I now enjoy baked onions all year round. Serve them as a vegetable, simply buttered, with roast beef.

6 medium onions, unpeeled	¹/₄ tsp. *(1 mL) salt*
¹/₂ cup *(125 mL)* vegetable or olive oil	¹/₄ tsp. *(1 mL) freshly ground pepper*
juice of ¹/₂ lemon	1 green pepper *(optional)*
¹/₂ tsp. *(2 mL) dry mustard*	

Remove only the loose skin from the onions—do not peel—and cut a small slice off both ends. Place in a shallow baking pan and bake in a preheated 350°F. (180°C) oven 25 to 35 minutes. Cool for 15 minutes. Cut the skins with scissors and remove. Place onions in a serving dish.

Combine remaining ingredients, except green pepper. Blend thoroughly and pour over the onions. Cover and let stand 2 to 3 hours before serving. Do not refrigerate as this will cloud the oil.

Pour boiling water over green pepper. Let stand 10 minutes. With a sharp knife, peel off the thin top skin, seed and cut into thin strips. Toss with a few drops of oil to make them shiny. Serve separately in a bowl, or sprinkle over the onions. *Serves 6.*

Fried Pumpkin Blossoms

Here is a bit of that food magic I believe in. Eat your flower with a dreamy look and a happy heart. Of course, you must grow pumpkins in your garden, or else steal from a friend. It's worth it!

pumpkin or squash blossoms	*fine cracker crumbs*
	salt and pepper
egg, well beaten	

Gather pumpkin or squash blossoms just before they are ready to open. Wash very gently and drain on a cloth. Gently press blossoms flat with your fingers. Dip in well-beaten egg, then in fine cracker crumbs. Salt and pepper lightly. Fry in 1 in. (2.5 cm) of hot fat until golden brown, turning only once.

Serve hot as a vegetable fritter, with chicken or veal, or as a dessert, with a sauce of your choice. As they are delicate, they should be served immediately after cooking.

Desserts to Freeze, Bake or Drink

Italian Strawberry Gelato

This recipe can be made very successfully in the freezer unit of your refrigerator. I like to serve it in champagne glasses, topped with crushed sweetened strawberries and a rose petal. I first ate this on a bright, sunny day in Padua.

1½ cups (375 mL) sugar	*grated peel of 1 orange*
2 cups (500 mL) water	*1 tbsp. (15 mL) lemon juice*
4 cups (1 L) strawberries	

Place sugar and water in a saucepan. Bring to a fast rolling boil for 2 minutes, then cool.

Wash and hull strawberries. Mash them with a fork together with orange peel and lemon juice. Add to the cooled syrup and beat until well blended. If you have a blender, blend for 2 seconds.

Pour mixture into an ice cube tray and place in freezer until frozen around the edges. Turn into a bowl and beat quickly with a rotary beater until smooth and fluffy. Pour back into tray, cover with aluminum foil and freeze. *Serves 6.*

Florentine Apple Cake

A cup of black coffee and a square of this *dolce di mele* at four P.M. in one of the delightful cafés of Florence is a must when in Italy. I can assure you I have done my share of this.

3 large apples, peeled, cored and thinly sliced	grated rind of 1 lemon and 1 orange
⅓ cup (80 mL) rum	3 cups (750 mL) flour
4 eggs	2 tsp. (10 mL) baking
1½ cups (375 mL) sugar	powder

Put apple slices and rum in a bowl. Stir well, making sure all the apples are coated with rum.

Beat eggs until light and foamy. Add 1¼ cups (310 mL) of the sugar (reserve the remaining ¼ cup (60 mL). Keep beating until pale yellow. Add lemon and orange rinds, and mix well.

Sift together flour and baking powder. Stir gradually into the egg mixture, beating well at each addition.

Place the dough in a buttered and floured 8 × 12 in. (20 × 30 cm) pan. Smooth out with a spatula. Arrange apples on top in attractive rows. Sprinkle with the remaining sugar. Bake in a preheated 350°F. (180°C) oven 35 to 40 minutes. Serve warm or cold (but do not refrigerate) with a bowl of sour cream or plain yogurt. *Serves 6 to 8.*

Zuppa Inglese

A festive cake made all over Italy. I have eaten many versions there, but my favorite was the one I ate in St. Geminano. The pastry chef was a woman named Serena, who was very amusing and witty. She wrote the recipe for me in a mixture of Italian, French and English, so I had to make it about six times before I could figure out the puzzle. I would compare this delicious cake to English trifle, and rightly so, since the translation of the name is "English soup."

Sponge Cake:

6 egg yolks
1/2 cup (125 mL) sugar
2 tbsp. (30 mL) fresh lemon juice
2 tbsp. (30 mL) grated orange rind
1 tsp. (5 mL) almond extract

1 cup (250 mL) all-purpose flour
1/2 tsp. (2 mL) baking powder
6 egg whites
1/2 tsp. (2 mL) salt

Eggs should be at room temperature; take them out of the refrigerator at least one hour before making the cake.

Beat egg yolks until thick and pale in color. Beat in sugar a tablespoon (15 mL) at a time, beating for 1 minute after each addition. Add lemon juice, orange rind and almond extract, and beat until light and creamy. Sift flour and baking powder twice, then fold into egg yolk mixture.

Beat egg whites until they start to foam, then add salt. Beat until stiff. Fold into the batter and mix gently but thoroughly.

Pour batter into a round ungreased 9-in. (22.5 cm) cake pan (use a spring-form pan if available). Bake in a preheated 350°F. (180°C) oven 50 to 60 minutes, or until the cake springs back when lightly touched with fingertips. To cool, set the pan on a rack. Unmold when cool and cut into 4 layers with a *sharp* knife. The *zuppa inglese,* or custard filling, will be spread between each layer.

Custard Filling:

4 egg yolks, slightly beaten

1 cup (250 mL) milk

1 cup (250 mL) heavy cream

¹/₂ cup (125 mL) sugar

¹/₃ cup (80 mL) flour

grated rind of ¹/₂ lemon

¹/₂ cup (125 mL) each rum and Marsala

¹/₃ cup (80 mL) orange marmalade or apricot jam

3 tbsp. (50 mL) candied fruit, finely chopped

Combine egg yolks, milk and cream in a saucepan. Mix sugar, flour and lemon rind and add to egg mixture. Mix with beater, then cook over medium-low heat, stirring most of the time until thickened and creamy. Remove from heat and continue stirring often until cooled. Cover and refrigerate until very cold.

Mix rum and Marsala. Place marmalade or apricot jam in a bowl. Set bowl in hot water to soften marmalade.

Place 1 layer of the cake on a serving plate and pour ¹/₄ cup (60 mL) of the rum and Marsala mixture over it. Spread with a third of the cold cream filling. Repeat for the second and third layers. Cover with the fourth layer, and sprinkle it with the remaining ¹/₄ cup (60 mL) of rum and Marsala mixture.

Refrigerate, covered with a plastic wrap or a bowl, 12 to 16 hours.

Soak candied fruit overnight in 2 tbsp. (30 mL) of rum or Marsala. Sprinkle over the cake when ready to serve. *Serves 8.*

Zabaglione

A favorite light dessert, popular all over Italy. The only problem is that it must be made just before serving. The egg shell half is used to measure the wine, so that it will be in proportion to the amount of eggs used.

3 egg yolks
2 tbsp. (30 mL) sugar

¹/₂ eggshell sweet
Marsala wine, enough
to fill ¹/₂ eggshell
twice

Place egg yolks in the top of a double boiler over simmering water. Beat vigorously, adding sugar and Marsala. Continue cooking over simmering water, beating vigorously, until very thick. Serve in champagne or red wine glasses. *Serves 2 to 3.*

Granita di Caffe

This refreshing Florentine specialty is one of the most simple frozen desserts to prepare. Nothing can beat the refreshing sensation of *Granita* on a hot afternoon. Black roasted coffee is used in the original recipe, but I have found that instant coffee can successfully replace it; otherwise, use true espresso.

4 tbsp. (60 mL) instant
coffee
2 cups (500 mL) boiling
water
¹/₄–¹/₂ cup (60–125 mL)
sugar

2 tsp. vanilla (10 mL)
OR 1 tsp. (5 mL)
aromatic orange
bitters (Angostura)
whipped cream
(optional)

Combine in a saucepan instant coffee, boiling water and ¹/₄ to ¹/₂ cup (60 to 125 mL) of sugar, according to taste. Stir over medium heat, just long enough to dissolve the sugar. Do not boil the mixture. Cool, then add vanilla or bitters.

Pour mixture into a shallow pan or an ice cube tray and freeze until almost firm. Turn into a bowl and beat well — an

How interesting that we can enjoy the visual beauty of flowers and at the same time the subtle flavor they can give to our food. Here I am at the flower market in Monaco, dreaming that I am sprinkling rose petals in my English custard and chrysanthemum petals on my Japanese gohan.

The hunting horns, hard black velvet hat, white gloves, red jacket and Gien bouchées (puff pastry) indicate that the hunt has returned to Noirmouton.

electric hand beater is ideal because it will beat more air into the mixture and make it lighter. Then freeze until it has the consistency of sherbet.

To serve, spoon into sherbet glasses or punch cups or demitasses, and top with unsweetened whipped cream to taste. *Serves 4.*

Falernum

A sweet wine of southern Italy with an intriguing flavor. Very elegant in the old days, it is now the base of many a good dessert and drink. The southern Italian women who migrated to Canada in the early twenties all referred to *Falernum* as the very ancient wine that was made from the grapes of Mount Falernus in Italy. As it was too expensive to import, the women made it themselves. The following recipe was given to Mother by an Italian woman, Serena, who had *des doigts de fée.* She could sew anything we asked for, and beautifully too.

Although this amount of ingredients makes a lot of wine, it keeps six to eight months in a cool place and improves with age, so I recommend making the full recipe.

> *4 cups (1 L) white sugar*
> *12¹/₂ cups (3.5 L) water*
> *²/₃ cup (160 mL) fresh*
> *lime juice, reserve* all
> *lime peels*
>
> *12 drops of bitter*
> *almond extract**
> *3 cups (750 mL)*
> *white rum*

Bring to boil sugar and half the water, stirring often. Add all lime peels, then boil until sugar is dissolved. Cool. Add lime juice, almond extract, remaining water and rum. Let stand 1 hour. Remove lime rind, pour into bottles and cover.

To serve, pour over crushed ice, preferably, or ice cubes, in a tall glass, or serve with soda water. *Yield: 6 pints (1.5 L).*

---

*Bitter almond extract is difficult to find. I usually get mine at the drugstore. If not available, it can be replaced with sweet almond extract, however, some of the flavor will be lost.

Greece

It has been many long years since I was in Greece, but the trip came about under such special circumstances that its impact has remained with me.

I was in my last year of food chemistry studies in Paris. Every summer the University organized special trips which were relevant to our studies. That particular year our professor had said, "This summer look to Greece and claim your rights! In gastronomy, as in philosophy, science, language, literature, drama, architecture, the very roots of our civilization lie deep in Greece." The trip was so arranged that his every point was proven and we all soon realized that our own traditions were astonishingly similar to those of Greece.

I not only discovered that "buffet" was a Greek word, but also that English jugged hare, potted fish, Irish black pudding and Swedish lamb with dill had all originated in Greece. The Hungarian and German strudels were the outgrowths of Grecian phyllos; the list was endless.

We had a few organized lectures on Greek food, given by the famous chef of the day in Greece, Nicolas Tselementes. I have never forgotten his talk on Soteriades, the Sage, whose philosophy was to prepare different dishes for different moods and groups: the young, lovers, older men and the philosophers.

I thought this was fabulous, and to this day I always plan my meals according to who sits at my table.

In the early fifties, I again met Tselementes, during a stay at the St. Moritz Hotel in New York. He, without a doubt, created the hotel's reputation for excellent food.

The Greek Flavor*

Olive Oil: This is to Greek cuisine what butter is to ours. They produce one of my very favorite olive oils, Corfu oil, difficult to find and expensive, but worth the trouble and cost. Their margarine, known as *vitam* is also made with olive oil.

Herbs and Spices: Both wild and cultivated thyme are used, and the Greeks have the best. Oregano, often called "joy of the mountains," cinnamon, cumin (seeds or ground) and lots of parsley are all common seasonings.

Citrus Fruits: I do not think you can cook a Greek recipe without lemons — rind, slices and juice — they keep coming up in the ingredients whether it is a roast, sauce or dessert. The lemons are smaller than ours and somewhat more acidic.

Oranges and sour cherries are also used for cooking or preparing cool drinks.

Orange Flower Water: A favorite flavoring, used with rice, cream desserts and sweet breads.

Mastic: Similar to our sprucegum, although more delicate in flavor. Used in festive breads and liqueurs.

Grape Leaves: Used to prepare their justly famous *dolmathes*, or stuffed leaves filled with ground lamb or rice or both, and served hot or cold with lemon sauce. Grape leaves can be purchased in glass jars, packed in brine, and they can also be replaced by young cabbage leaves.

---

*All products can be purchased in North America in Greek or specialty food shops.

Tarama: A type of pâté prepared with lightly smoked carp roe (comes packed in jars) and bread or potatoes. An exciting hors-d'oeuvre.

Avgolemono: An egg and lemon sauce base which is used in many dishes.

Feta: This famous cheese is made from goats' or sheep's milk, and is imported packed in salted water in wooden barrels. Delicious.

Yogurt: Made from sheep's milk, this is an important ingredient in their cuisine. It is used in salad dressings, sauces, desserts or simply served as is, topped with *mihymeytos*, a superb honey made from wild thyme.

Phyllo Pastry: A special dough, sold by bakers, it is rolled into 1-lb. (500 g) packages, each containing 20 to 24 paper-thin sheets, 12 × 18 in. (30 × 45 cm) in size.

It is important to keep the roll well wrapped to prevent the dough from drying; it keeps 1 month refrigerated, but does not freeze well. The dough is used for entrées and desserts, such as the well-known *baklava*, filled with nuts and dripping with their *mihymeytos*.

Kataifi: A pastry-like shredded wheat, white, uncooked and moist, sold by the pound at Greek pastry shops. It is used to prepare a pastry bearing the same name. Cereal-type shredded wheat can substitute, and produces good results.

Ouzo: Similar to French Pernod, this clear liquor is flavored with aniseed and is very potent. It is always served with a glass of cold water, which clouds when the *ouzo* is added.

Retsina: The national wine of Greece, for which you must acquire a taste. It is flavored with *mastic*.

A Luncheon Soup

Artichoke Lemon Soup

The secret to this soup is the way the fresh artichokes are first cooked on their own, then added to the *avgolemono* soup base. Not a soup to make every day, but good for lunch with Greek cheese and hot pita bread.

1 large or 2 medium fresh artichoke(s)	6 cups (1.5 L) chicken stock
2 cups (500 mL) water	3 eggs
1 tsp. (5 mL) salt	juice of 2 lemons
1 tbsp. (15 mL) fresh lemon juice or vinegar	1/4 cup (60 mL) minced parsley
	salt and pepper

Leave artichokes whole. Cut off stems so they can sit upright in a deep saucepan. Add water, salt and the 1 tbsp. (15 mL) lemon juice or vinegar. Bring to the boil, cover and simmer about 40 to 45 minutes, or until a leaf can be pulled out easily. Remove from pan and cool.

Pull out each leaf and scrape meaty end onto a plate. Mash the heart with the leaf meat. Add this to chicken stock, bring to the boil, then simmer 10 minutes.

Beat eggs until thick and pale. Add juice of 2 lemons gradually, while beating with a whisk. Then slowly pour in 1 cup (250 mL) of the hot stock, stirring constantly; add a second cup (250 mL), still stirring. Slowly pour this mixture into the remaining stock, whisking it in quickly. Add salt and pepper and serve. If reheating, use very low heat, stirring often. *Serves 6.*

A Note on Soup from Chef Tselementes

To add a deeper color to soup, grate *one* of the onions called for in the particular recipe with its skin on, and add it to the soup. (I have done this for years — I don't peel the onions for consommé, but I strain it later. This enhances the color and flavor.)

Make garlic-thyme croutons using day-old bread. Trim crusts and cut bread into cubes. Heat an equal mixture of oil and butter in a frying pan. Add 2 garlic cloves (for 2 slices of bread), unpeeled and cut in half, and ¼ teaspoon (1 mL) of thyme or oregano. Add bread cubes and stir until golden brown. If possible, pour them into the soup while they are hot. Of course, throw away the garlic.

Plaki, Pastitsio, Vine Leaves: Main Course Dishes

Ghofaria Plaki (Baked Fish)

It is easy to understand why there is so much fish in the Greek diet when you consider that Greece lies in the warmest part of the Mediterranean mainland.

1–1¹/₂ lb. (500–750 g) *fresh cod or haddock*	*4 medium-sized* *tomatoes, diced*
3–4 tbsp. (50–60 mL) *olive oil*	*salt and pepper* *2 bay leaves*
3 medium-sized onions, *thinly sliced*	*grated rind of 1 lemon* *¹/₄ teaspoon (1 mL)*
1 large garlic clove, *minced*	*oregano* *6–10 black olives,* *stoned (optional)*

Use fish fillets or steaks. Place in a generously buttered baking dish.

Heat the oil in a frying pan and add onions and garlic. Stir until lightly browned here and there, add diced tomatoes and stir well, then simmer together, uncovered, for 3 to 5 minutes. Add salt and pepper, bay leaves, lemon rind and oregano. Stir until well mixed. Pour over the fish.

Bake in a preheated 350°F. (180°C) oven 20 to 25 minutes, or until fish flakes easily. Beware of overcooking. Add black olives 5 minutes before the end of cooking period. Serve with boiled rice. *Serves 4 to 6.*

Tarama Salata (Fish Roe Salad)

One of the most popular of Greek salads or appetizers. Wherever you go in Greece you will find it; depending on the quality of the smoked fish roe, or the seasoning used, some are better than others. Whenever I don't feel like making it myself, I go to Moishe's Steak House in Montreal — they serve the very best I have ever tasted.

If you have a food processor or a blender, by all means use it, and in no time you will have a creamy *tarama*. If done by hand, it is long and tedious to prepare. Look for *tarama* in specialty food shops.

juice of 2 lemons	*1 cup (250 mL) olive oil*
a 6–8 oz. (168–224 g) jar of tarama	*large leaves of crisp lettuce*
1 medium-sized onion, diced	*a bowl of Black Olive* Salata
2 cups fresh bread, diced, with crusts removed	*Greek bread*

Place lemon juice in a blender and add jar of *tarama* and onion. Blend about 1 minute, or until all particles of onion have disappeared.

Cover bread cubes with cold water, stir well, then squeeze dry and place in blender. Blend 30 seconds. Decrease speed to slow, then gradually and slowly add olive oil. Blend until all the oil disappears.

Line a shallow bowl with lettuce leaves. Pour the *Tarama Salata* in the middle. Serve with Black Olive *Salata* and a basket of sliced Greek bread. *Serves 6.*

Smyrna Loukamika (Smyrna Sausages)

A Greek specialty, unusual and most tasty. I like to serve it at
Sunday brunch.

*1¹/₂ lb. (750 g) pork or
lamb shoulder
1 cup (250 mL) soft
breadcrumbs
¹/₂ cup (125 mL) red
wine
1 tsp. (5 mL) salt*

*¹/₄ tsp. (1 mL) pepper
1 garlic clove, chopped
fine
¹/₂ tsp. (2 mL) ground
cumin
¹/₂ tsp. (2 mL) powdered
pectin (optional)*

* * * * *

*1 tbsp. (15 mL) olive or
vegetable oil
¹/₂ cup (125 mL) tomato
sauce
¹/₄ tsp. (1 mL) sugar*

Choose a piece of fairly lean meat, but with some fat on it.
Grind twice.

Stir breadcrumbs and wine together until bread is mois-
tened, then squeeze out excess moisture. Add to meat with the
remaining ingredients. Blend thoroughly. Shape into sausages, set on a plate, cover and refrigerate a few hours or overnight, before cooking.

To cook them, heat oil in a heavy metal frying pan, add
sausages and cook over medium-low heat, until brown on both
sides. This should take 10 to 12 minutes. Add tomato sauce and
sugar. Simmer gently, uncovered, for 15 minutes. Serve with
rice or mashed potatoes. *Serves 6.*

Pastitsio (Meat Macaroni)

A baked meat macaroni, but the way it is prepared is quite different from our own. In Greece, the flavor often differs, depending upon the choice of cheese, ranging from Kasseri—a hard, strong, grated cheese — to Feta — a very tasty, white, light creamy cheese—to a mixture of Feta cheese and yogurt.

Macaroni:

1/4 cup (60 mL) butter
or margarine
2 lb. (1 kg) ground
lamb or beef
2 medium onions,
chopped fine
1/2 cup (125 mL) dry
white wine or
vermouth
4 tbsp. (60 mL) tomato
paste

1/2 tsp. (2 mL)
cinnamon
1 tsp. (5 mL) salt
1/4 tsp. (1 mL) freshly
ground pepper
1 lb. (500 g) spaghetti
or thin macaroni
1 cup (250 mL) grated
Parmesan or diced Feta
2 eggs, well beaten
3 tbsp. (50 mL) fine dry
breadcrumbs

Melt butter in a large cast-iron frying pan, add meat and onions, and stir often over high heat, until meat starts to brown here and there. Add wine or vermouth, mix well and simmer 5 minutes.

Stir together tomato paste, cinnamon and salt and pepper. Add to meat, mix well and simmer about 15 minutes. Set aside.

Boil spaghetti or macaroni until tender, but do not overcook —about 10 minutes should be sufficient. Drain thoroughly in a sieve.

Sauce:

¹/₃ *cup (80 mL) butter*	*salt and pepper*
3 tbsp. (50 mL)	¹/₄ *tsp. (1 mL) freshly*
all-purpose flour	*grated nutmeg*
3 cups (750 mL) milk	

Make the white sauce with butter, flour and milk. When creamy, add salt and pepper and nutmeg.

Place half the macaroni in a large, flat greased casserole. Sprinkle with ¹/₃ cup (80 mL) of the cheese.

Blend the meat mixture thoroughly with the beaten eggs, breadcrumbs and 2 tbsp. (30 mL) of the cheese. Spread over the macaroni. Cover meat with the remaining macaroni. Sprinkle with another ¹/₃ cup (80 mL) of the grated cheese. Pour the sauce over all and do not mix. Sprinkle the remaining cheese on top and dot with butter.

Bake in a preheated 400°F (200°C) oven about 30 minutes, or until top is golden brown. Let stand 10 to 15 minutes. To serve, cut into squares. *Serves 8.*

Black Olive Salata

Throughout Greece, black olives are served as salad, or *salata*, appetizers or with cold fish or meat. Every year I go to my Greek merchant to buy the best quality black olives from Greece, which are kept in big black wooden barrels. I buy them by the pound and make enough *salata* to enjoy through the year. They keep very well and taste better and better as they age.

1 lb. (500 g) black	*2 large bay leaves*
Greek olives	*2 stalks of celery,*
2 lemons, unpeeled	*without leaves*
and thinly sliced	*olive oil (preferably*
	Greek)

In a sterilized jar, make alternate rows of olives, lemon slices, celery sticks and pieces of bay leaves, repeating until all are used. Pour in enough olive oil to cover the olives, then cover the jar. When the olives are all eaten, I keep the beautifully flavored oil for salad dressing, mixing it with lemon juice instead of vinegar. *Yield: 3 cups (375 mL).*

Dolmathes (Stuffed Vine Leaves)

I ate these in Greece, cooked by the great master Tselementes. They were served cold with lemon wedges, but can also be served hot with *avgolemono sauce*. I was eating this dish the first time I tasted Retsina; as a French Quebecker, I didn't find the taste strange, but my friends rejected it.

25–30 vine leaves (bottled)	¹/₂ teaspoon (2 mL) salt
1¹/₂ cups (375 mL) cooked rice	1 teaspoon (5 mL) freshly ground pepper
¹/₂ lb. (250 g) ground beef or lamb	1 egg, beaten
¹/₂ cup (125 mL) whole pine nuts or chopped walnuts	¹/₃ cup (80 mL) olive or vegetable oil
¹/₂ cup (125 mL) currants or sultana raisins	juice and grated rind of 1 lemon
	¹/₂ teaspoon (2 mL) thyme
	juice of ¹/₂ lemon

Vine leaves in jars are packed in brine so they must be washed first. Open the roll of leaves, separate carefully and rinse well under cold running water to remove the brine. Dry on paper towels.

Cook ¹/₃ cup (80 mL) of raw rice to obtain 1¹/₂ cups (375 mL) of cooked rice (long grain is the best type). Combine cooked rice, ground lamb or beef, nuts of your choice, raisins, salt and pepper. Add beaten egg. Mix thoroughly and roll into tiny balls.

Place a vine leaf flat on a board, vein side up. Place a ball of meat in the center of the leaf. Fold the side points of the leaf toward the center, covering the filling. Roll up, starting at stem-end of leaf. Fold over the top points, like an envelope flap.

Place the stuffed leaves, closed side down (so leaf does not unravel in cooking), in a large frying pan. Add olive oil, juice and grated rind of 1 lemon and enough water to *only half cover* the leaves. Simmer gently, covered, 15 to 18 minutes, carefully turning the leaves once during the cooking period.

Place several layers of absorbent paper on a platter. When leaves are cooked, carefully remove them from water with a perforated spoon and place on paper. Cover and cool.

Serve cold with a little of the cooking liquid and bowl of yogurt, mixed with lots of fresh parsley and a sprinkling of fresh, not dry, thyme, and a plate of lemon wedges. Serve hot with *avgolemono* sauce. *Serves 6.*

Avgolemono Sauce:

2 eggs	*cooking liquid from*
juice of ¹/₂ lemon	*Dolmathes*

Beat eggs slightly, add lemon juice and beat for another minute, gradually adding a few spoonfuls of the hot cooking liquid.

Place the cooked leaves on a platter and pour sauce on top. Serve with Greek bread. *Serves 6.*

Note: Two interesting variations to the rice and meat stuffing are

— add 1 tsp. (5 mL) tomato ketchup and 1 tsp. (5 mL) crushed ice;

— add 1 tbsp. (15 mL) *ouzo* or brandy.

Vegetables à la Grecque

Every cook in Greece uses his own mixture of vegetables, and often the flavoring differs. What makes them *à la Grecque* is the fact that they are cooked in liquid in which oil and lemon juice are the primary ingredients. The vegetables vary according to the season. Choose good color combinations and make lots — they'll disappear quickly. Serve them cold as they do in Greece, with lots of paper napkins and wooden picks. Unbuttered fingers of black bread are a good accompaniment, or serve them with cold meat.

2 cups (500 mL) water	*juice of 1 or 2 lemon(s)*
1 cup (250 mL)	*1 cup (250 mL) celery*
vegetable oil	*sticks*
1 teaspoon (5 mL) salt	*2 cups (500 mL) button*
¼ teaspoon (1 mL)	*mushrooms*
pepper	*1 cup (250 mL) carrot*
¼ teaspoon (1 mL)	*sticks*
cumin	*1 green pepper, cut into*
½ teaspoon (2 mL)	*sticks*
thyme	*12 small whole onions*
10 coriander seeds	

Bring to boil in a large saucepan the first 7 ingredients. Then simmer 5 minutes over low heat. Add lemon juice and the vegetables and simmer over medium heat 10 to 15 minutes. Beware of overcooking. Pour into a bowl, cover and refrigerate at least 12 hours.

To serve, drain well, but reserve the liquid as it can be used for cooking another 2 lb. (1 kg) of vegetables. *Serves 4 to 6.*

Greek Bread

Of all the hard-crusted hearth breads, this is the simplest to make, and it freezes well for two to three months. Without thawing it, place the bread in a 375°F. (190°C) oven for 20 to 30 minutes, or until hot and crusty.

*1 package active dry
yeast
2 cups (500 mL)
lukewarm water
1 tbsp. (15 mL) honey
1 tbsp. (15 mL) salt
1 tbsp. (15 mL)
vegetable oil*

*4¹/₂–5 cups (1.1 L–1.2 L)
all-purpose flour or
equal combination of
all-purpose and
whole-wheat
1 egg white
sesame seeds*

Pour yeast and honey into water. Cover and let stand 10 minutes. Then add oil and salt, stir and pour into a large bowl. Gradually add flour, mixing well after each addition (dough should be fairly stiff). Knead on a lightly floured board 5 minutes. Place in a greased bowl and cover with a cloth. Let rise in a warm place. In about 1¹/₂ to 2 hours the dough should be light and double in size.

Punch down, turn dough onto a lightly floured surface, knead for a few seconds and shape into 2 round loaves. Place on a greased baking sheet, cover and let rise again until very light and almost double in size, 1 to 1¹/₂ hours.

Brush generously with slightly beaten egg white. With a razor blade, cut criss-cross incisions in the tops of the loaves. Sprinkle generously with sesame seeds. Bake in a 400°F. (200°C) oven for 30 minutes, then reduce heat to 350°F. (180°C) and bake 20 to 30 minutes longer, or until golden brown.

Place a shallow pan of boiling water in the bottom of the oven while the bread is baking, to make a typically crusty Greek bread. *Yield: 2 large loaves.*

Shredded, Glazed and Spooned Sweets

Baklava

This world-famous Greek delicacy, with its layers and layers of flaky phyllo pastry filled with nuts, honey and spices, is superb. Do not attempt to make phyllo—it is very difficult and requires lots of experience. It can be purchased at pastry shops specializing in Greek bread and cakes and is sold by the pound. Once you have the phyllo it is easy to make *Baklava,* which is even better two to three days after baking.

1 cup (250 mL) *hazelnuts* *1 lb. (500 g) walnuts* *¹/₂ cup (125 mL) sugar* *1 tsp. (5 mL) allspice*	*1 tsp. (5 mL) cinnamon* *1 lb. (500 g) phyllo* *pastry* *2 cups (500 mL) melted* *butter*

Place hazelnuts on a baking sheet and brown in a 350°F. (180°C) oven; this should take 10 to 15 minutes. Cool. Then chop hazelnuts and walnuts together, and add sugar, allspice and cinnamon. Set aside.

Melt the butter over low heat. Brush a 9 × 13 × 2 in. (22.5 × 32.5 × 5 cm) baking pan with some of the butter.

Unroll the phyllo, gently pick up a sheet, fit it into the pan and brush with melted butter. Repeat this operation with 4 more sheets of phyllo. If a sheet breaks, simply fit it together again. Cover with half of the nut mixture and fit in 6 more layers of phyllo, buttering each one thoroughly. Cover with the remaining nut mixture and fit in another 6 layers of phyllo, buttering again.

Fold under the ragged edges around the pan with your hands. Brush top with more butter. Cut through the top layers of the *Baklava* (so the steam can escape), making strips 1¹/₂ in. (4 cm) wide with a sharp knife, then cut across diagonally, forming small diamond-shaped pieces.

Bake in a preheated 300°F. (150°C) oven for 1 hour, or until golden brown and all puffed up. While the *Baklava* is baking, make the glaze.

Honey Glaze:

¹/₂ cup (125 mL) sugar   2 tsp. (10 mL) vanilla
2 cups (500 mL) water   ¹/₄ tsp. (1 mL) rose
2 cups (500 mL) honey   water

Boil together sugar and water until sugar is dissolved. Add honey and cook over low heat until it forms a syrup. Add vanilla and rose water and pour while hot all over the cooked *Baklava*. Let cool 5 to 6 hours before serving. *Serves 10 to 12.*

Ghlyka Koutaliou (Spoon Sweets)

During that university trip to Greece, I was greeted by "May you enjoy my *Ghlyka xon Kontalou*," which is their custom of welcome and a sign of hospitality. A choice of two or three very sweet, delicious preserves is presented on a silver tray in small attractive bowls, with as many little silver spoons as there are guests. On another tray, glasses of ice-cold water and small liqueur glasses of *ouzo*.

To partake of this, you first help yourself to a small spoonful of preserves, then take a glass of water, and follow with the brandy, while wishing your host good fortune. You then place the little spoon in the empty water glass, which indicates you are finished.

Kataifi (Shredded Wheat Nutcakes)

It is not too easy to find fresh *kataifi*, so I have succeeded in making a truly good one using our shredded wheat cereal. It is easy to prepare; the only problem being that one is inclined to eat too much of it.

Nut Filling:

12 shredded wheat rolls*	*1 tsp. (5 mL) cinnamon*
1¹/₄ cups (325 mL) chopped walnuts	*¹/₂ cup (250 mL) melted unsalted butter*
¹/₄ cup (60 mL) sugar	*¹/₂ cup (250 mL) hot milk*

Dip each roll of shredded wheat in a bowl of hot water to soften it, then place 6 rolls side by side in a buttered baking pan.

Mix chopped walnuts, sugar and cinnamon. Sprinkle over the shredded wheat. Pour half of the melted butter over this, then top with the remaining shredded wheat (which have also been dipped in water). Pour hot milk and remaining melted butter on top.

Bake in a preheated 350°F. (180°C) oven 40 minutes, or until nicely brown on top. While they are baking, prepare the syrup.

Syrup:

1 cup (250 mL) honey	*pieces of orange or lemon rind*
¹/₂ cup (125 mL) sugar	
2 cups (500 mL) water	*1 tsp. (5 mL) vanilla or orange flower extract*

Boil together for 3 minutes honey, sugar, water, orange or lemon rind. Then add vanilla or orange extract. Pour the hot syrup over the *Kataifi* as soon as they are cooked. Place a cloth over the pan and cover with another inverted pan. Let stand until cool. Cut into squares to serve. *Serves 6.*

*If using fresh *kataifi*, instead, you will need 1 lb. (500 g). Spread half this amount in a buttered dish, spread with nut filling, cover with the other half. Baste top with the melted butter—do not use milk. Bake as directed above. Pour hot syrup over it when cooked, then cool, same as above.

The Caribbean

Who can think of the Caribbean and not instantly envision sandy beaches, high ocean waves, guitar music and bright sunshine and flowers everywhere? Yet color, music and romance are not the only pleasures of these islands.

It has long been recognized that geography has an enormous influence on the cuisine of any country, and in the Caribbean Islands eating habits are directly related to the warm climate and rich soil. This explains why they have mastered the art of cooking and combining fruits; plantains, for example (part of the banana family, but larger and not so sweet), are used in many dishes from stews to desserts.

Another interesting point which comes to my attention whenever I visit the Caribbean is how a country's cuisine is also influenced by that of a conquering nation. Because of this it is difficult to say with any certainty what is typical Caribbean cuisine. For instance, in Haiti, Guadaloupe and Martinique you find the influence of French cooking, while in Barbados it is quite British, and still other islands have a Dutch imprint on their cooking. What they all have in common is superb fresh fish, seafood and beautiful fruits.

One important fact to be aware of is that Caribbean cuisine differs from our own, not so much in cooking methods, but in seasonings. A knowledge of these makes it possible to cook a true "Island" dinner.

The Caribbean Flavor

Seasonings:

Sofrito: A combination of ingredients used as a seasoning, which gives dishes the characteristic flavor of Caribbean cuisine. It can be made in quantities and kept, refrigerated, in a covered glass jar. (See recipe on page 236);

Achiote Lard: A golden-red lard which is easy to prepare once you have the *achiote* or *annato* seeds. Paprika can replace the *annato* seeds, but some of the true flavor will be missing. Look for the seeds in shops which sell Mexican or Puerto Rican foods. Indian food shops also sometimes sell *annato*. (See recipe on page 237);

Lime (juice and rind) — lemon can replace lime, but the flavor is not as delicate;

Cilantro (fresh coriander)—available at Italian and Greek markets, or grow it in your garden in the summer. Replace with fresh parsley, although quite different in flavor;

Small sweet red or green peppers; small strong peppers;

Fresh ground black pepper or crushed black peppercorns; cinnamon, ground or in sticks; cloves, ground; fresh ginger, available at Oriental food shops; garlic; onion; oregano.

Fish:

Calepeone — replace with salmon;

Conch — replace with lobster;

Flying Fish — replace with bass;

Tuna — fairly easy to buy fresh;

Crab, Shrimp, Lobster, Mackerel — all readily available.

Caldero: A deep cast-iron pot, used to simmer food. The true *caldero* has a round bottom and straight sides. An enamelled cast-iron saucepan can be used instead, with equal success.

Tropical Fruits: Readily available — bananas, pineapples, oranges, grapefruits, lemons, limes, coconuts, nectarines, pomegranates.

Not readily available and expensive — mangoes, papaya (paw-paw), persimmons, fresh apricots, ugli fruit, kiwi, gooseberries, kumquats.

Guide to Rare Fruits:

Kumquats — In season from November to February, they are small orange-like fruit, resembling a pecan in shape. Keep them refrigerated. To serve, wash and slice, and flavor with fruit sugar and rum or sherry, for salads or fruit cups. They are also delicious with ice cream or sponge cake.

Mangoes — In season from May to September, they vary in size from a few ounces to a pound (60 to 500 g). Yellow or red in color, they have a soft, juicy aromatic flesh. To keep them, wrap in waxed paper and refrigerate. To eat, cut a wide band in the skin on one side with a sharp knife. Peel the skin back and eat the flesh with a spoon. Turn over and repeat for other side. As a dessert, they are particularly good sliced and sprinkled with fruit sugar, rum or orange flower water. They are also delicious peeled, sliced, sweetened and served over ice cream, or in a nest of whipped cream. To make chutney, use green mangoes.

Nectarines — They look like a peach with smooth skin, and are in season from June to August. The skin is greenish-white with a faint blush. Use and eat them as you would peaches.

Persimmons — They come in many colors, depending on the variety and degree of ripeness; some are lemon yellow, some deep orange, others are a beautiful deep purple color. A persimmon is shaped rather like a tomato, but with a pointed bottom. It should be fully ripe when eaten. Cut a small slice off the top, and eat the flesh with a spoon, or mix it with a few drops of French dressing or a few sections of grapefruit. You can also peel, slice and eat them with cream and sugar, as you would peaches. Also delicious with ice cream, and I simply adore them with toasted French bread and cream cheese.

Kiwis or Chinese Gooseberries — Fruit of a climbing shrub native to China, and now grown commercially in New Zealand and Florida. (I prefer the New Zealand type.) Named for New Zealand's hairy-feathered bird, the kiwi (which does not fly), the fruit is from 2 to 3 in. (5 to 7.5 cm) long, and about ¾ in. (2 cm) in diameter. Its fuzzy skin is light brown in color, the sweet, juicy pulp, pale green, with a pale beige line in the middle, filled with tiny black seeds. The flavor and the texture are somewhat reminiscent of honeydew melon, but still quite unique.

All of it, except the skin, is delicious to eat. The New Zealand type is available from May through July. I usually buy two to three cases, and always keep some for Christmas; kiwis have a high Vitamin C content, so they keep a long time if refrigerated. To serve in a salad, peel the fruit, then cut in half or slice. For flavoring, sprinkle each half with grated fresh ginger root stirred in fresh lime juice.

Papayas—(Sometimes referred to as "tree melon.") Discovered growing wild in Florida around 1780, it was cultivated much earlier by the Aztec and Mayan Indians. The "Solo" type from Hawaii is large and really delicious. It is one of my favorite fruits, very high in Vitamin C and full of enzymes that aid digestion.

Simply cut in half, unpeeled, and remove black seeds in the middle (they look like black pearls). Serve as is, or with quarters of lime or with a bit of freshly grated ginger root and lemon juice.

Pomegranates—These are a bright red color with a tough skin. The tougher the skin, the better the fruit because the pulpy flesh around the seeds will be well developed and the juices abundant. The reddish juice can be used to make a grenadine syrup and a most delightful jelly. You can add the fleshy seeds to a fruit salad or compote for a piquant touch. To eat, cut the fruit in two and simply spoon out the juice and seeds. But be careful — they stain very badly. You can extract the juice by pressing each half in a juice extractor, as you would oranges.

Coconuts—Whenever a native buys a coconut, he shakes it to make sure it is full of liquid. The more there is, the fresher the coconut.

To open a coconut, I do it the way my grandmother taught me, which is also the method I have seen many a native at the market using. First, puncture two of the eyes on top by hammering the sharp tip of an ice pick, or something similar, through the holes. Drain all of the liquid in a cup. Then tap the entire surface of the shell with a hammer or cleaver. The shell should then fall away from the meat. Pare off the brown skin from the coconut meat with a small sharp knife.

To serve as dessert, place pieces, as soon as they are peeled, in a bowl of cold water, and keep refrigerated. Or, grate the pieces — the cutting wheel of a food processor works quickly and efficiently.

How to make coconut milk: A very important item in Caribbean cooking. It is not necessary to remove the brown skin; simply cut into 1-in. (2.5 cm) pieces. Place 1 cup (250 mL) in a blender (I prefer a blender to a food processor because it makes more milk) with an equal amount of hot (not boiling) water.* Cover and blend at high speed for 1 minute. Stop and scrape down the sides of the jar. Cover and blend another minute, or until coconut looks like a smooth purée.

Line a sieve with a double thickness of damp cloth. Set sieve over a bowl. Pour in the coconut milk, pressing down hard on the coconut to extract as much liquid as possible. Then pick up the cloth like a bag and wring it to squeeze out the remaining liquid. Discard the pulp (I give it to my chickens, as I have seen the farm women do in Guadaloupe). One cup of coconut mixed with one cup of water should give 1 cup (250 mL) of coconut milk.

*For a rich coconut milk, use 1 cup (250 mL) warm milk or rich cream instead of water.

Caribbean Sofrito

Use not only in tropical dishes, but also when making your favorite stew, pot roast or dry beans. Three tablespoons (50 mL) added to a recipe serving four to six will usually give the right flavoring.

1 lb. (500 g) fat salt
pork
¼ lb. (125 g) achiote
seeds OR ⅓ cup
(80 mL) sweet
paprika OR ½ tsp.
(2 mL) saffron
1 lb. (500 g) uncooked
ham

1 lb. (500 g) green
peppers
4 large onions, cut in 4
6 garlic cloves
2 tbsp. (30 mL) chili
powder
1 tbsp. (15 mL) oregano
15 stems of cilantro
(Italian parsley) or
chervil, chopped fine

Cut salt pork in 1-in. (2.5 cm) squares and melt over medium heat until all the pieces of fat are golden brown — this should take about 30 to 60 minutes. Strain the melted fat in saucepan.

Wash and drain *achiote* seeds and add to the melted fat, or add paprika. Simmer 10 minutes over low heat, stirring a few times. If *achiote* seeds are used, strain.

Pass through a meat chopper or mash in a food processor ham, green peppers, onions and garlic. Add to fat. Stir to mix, then add the remaining ingredients. Cover and simmer over low heat for 30 minutes, stirring a few times. Cool, then pour into a glass jar, cover and refrigerate. It will keep 4 to 6 weeks, well covered and refrigerated. To freeze, divide in small portions for easy handling. *Yield: 4 cups (1 L).*

Achiote Lard or Golden Red Lard

Quicker to prepare than *sofrito*, but it lacks some of the fine flavor.

1 lb. (500 g) pure lard	*1 cup (250 mL) achiote seeds OR ¹/₂ cup (125 mL) sweet paprika*

Melt lard. Wash seeds and drain. Add to lard or add paprika. Simmer 15 minutes over low heat, stirring a few times. Strain, if *achiote* seeds have been used. Cool and store as you would *sofrito* (see recipe on page 236). *Yield: 1¹/₂ cups (375 mL).*

Homemade Tabasco Sauce

I was often intrigued by the peppery taste with "that something different" of some of the Caribbean dishes, until a French doctor living in Guadaloupe gave me his "secret recipe," as he put it. Later, I found out it was a most popular secret. If you like Tabasco sauce with extra flavor, I recommend that you try this. Super in tomato juice and Bloody Marys.

1 cup (250 mL) English or Irish whiskey	*2 oz. (60 g) dry red chillies*

Put the ingredients together in a bottle, and shake well once a week for 6 weeks. Then use sparingly until you find the quantity you prefer for each addition.

Another thing I learned from the "good doctor," as the natives called him, is to pour a teaspoon (5 mL) over roast beef after you take it out of the oven. It does something special to both the roast and the gravy. *Yield: 1 cup (250 mL).*

My Caribbean Breakfast

An experience never to be forgotten was breakfast in Guadaloupe. It is usual all through the Caribbean Islands to offer a choice of tropical fruits for breakfast. Since fruit is my preferred breakfast, I delight in the custom.

The Guadaloupe fruit table was the most lavish and beautiful I ever saw. Each fruit was served on a leaf, all ready to eat: half a papaya, quarters of juicy pineapple, basketfuls of kiwis, bowls of quartered clementines, bananas of all types and sizes, small sun-ripened cantaloupes, cut in two, garnished with lime to squeeze on top. All of it at room temperature, as tropical fruits should be, as well as being at the point of perfection.

What breakfasts! Even coffee was bypassed; the juicy pineapple and the warmth of the sun were enough to make you feel elated and awake!

Banana Orange Jam

Another fond memory of La Guadaloupe. Each meal was a treat — breakfast, a sheer delight of fresh fruit or hot brioche served with this jam. Before we left La Caravelle, the native chef presented me with the recipe for his justly famous marmalade.

3 oranges	2 cups (500 mL) sugar
6 medium bananas, thinly sliced	

Grate rind of oranges. Squeeze oranges and strain the juice. Place juice and rind in a large enamelled saucepan with bananas. Stir, pour sugar on top, cover and let stand 1 hour.

Bring mixture to a boil very slowly; it will take about 1 hour. Then stir and boil until set to jelly test, which should take 10 to 18 minutes. Bottle, cover and let stand in refrigerator 3 to 4 weeks before using. *Yield: 1 pint (500 mL).*

Two Special Soups

Cream of Seafood Soup

For our first dinner at La Caravelle Hotel in Guadaloupe, we started with this soup. It was so good that I decided not to leave without the recipe, but the chef would not part with the secret of his creation. However, one day, while visiting a banana plantation, my husband and I were offered lunch at a native restaurant in the middle of the plantation. I was a little nervous about the surroundings, but low and behold we were served this super cream soup, a native specialty which every Creole on the island appeared to know. With laughter and friendship, the cook, "Maria-Maria," as she was called, gave me the recipe.

2 tbsp. (30 mL) unsalted butter	salt and pepper
3 tbsp. (50 mL) flour	¹/₈ (0.5 mL) allspice
2 cups (500 mL) bottled clam juice	1 lb. (500 g) uncooked shrimps or lobster
1 cup (250 mL) dry or sweet white wine or chicken broth	¹/₄ cup (60 mL) dry sherry
2 cups (500 mL) light cream or milk	grated rind and juice of 1 lime

Melt butter in a saucepan, add flour and stir over medium heat until it becomes nutty brown. Add clam juice and wine or chicken broth, bring to the boil, stirring constantly, until the sauce thickens. Add cream or milk, salt and pepper and allspice. Simmer 5 to 8 minutes.

Clean and dice shrimps or lobster meat (it is of the utmost importance to use uncooked seafood). Add to hot soup. Simmer 3 minutes, then add the remaining ingredients. Simmer 2 more minutes. *Serves 6.*

Chicken Soup with Rice

A *saucochi di gallinja*, like the one made on Marie-Galante Island (reached by plane or boat from Martinique), has little to do with what we think of as chicken soup. It includes potato, pumpkin and fresh lime.

2 tbsp. (30 mL) long-grain rice	1 large onion, diced
1/2 cup (125 mL) cold water	1 potato, peeled and grated
4 cups (1 L) hot water	juice and grated rind of 1 lime
2 chicken legs or 6 wings	2 tsp. (10 mL) salt
2 cups (500 mL) diced pumpkin	1 tsp. (5 mL) freshly ground pepper

Soak rice in cold water for 30 minutes. Meanwhile, combine the remaining ingredients in a saucepan, and bring to a fast rolling boil. Cover, then simmer 40 minutes over low heat.

Drain rice, and add to soup. Cover and simmer another 20 minutes. *Serves 6.*

The Best from the Islands: Main Course Dishes

Antilles Rum Steak

This interesting steak topping is used in almost all of the Caribbean Islands. It will keep a week, refrigerated. Use on any type of steak.

3 tbsp. (50 mL) rum	2 tbsp. (30 mL) parsley or cilantro, finely chopped
2 green onions, finely minced	1/2 tsp. (2 mL) freshly ground pepper
1/3 cup (80 mL) soft butter	1 tsp. (5 mL) salt
juice of 1 lime or 1/2 lemon	

Pour rum into saucepan, add green onions and simmer over medium heat until ²/₃ reduced. Cool until tepid, then stir in butter, lime or lemon juice and parsley. Add salt and pepper. Beat until well blended. Cover and refrigerate.

When steak is cooked, place ¹/₂ to 1 tsp. (2 to 5 mL) of cold rum butter on top of each steak. *Yield: enough for 6 to 8 steaks.*

Broiled Halibut Martinique

Any firm white fish can replace the halibut, or even a whole small red snapper or a striped bass.

4-6 halibut steaks, 1 in. *(2.5 cm) thick*	*a pinch of ground fennel*
¹/₂ tsp. (2 mL) salt	*¹/₃ cup (80 mL) butter*
¹/₄ tsp. (1 mL) freshly ground pepper	*¹/₃ cup (80 mL) white vermouth*
1 tsp. (5 mL) ground cumin	*¹/₃ cup (80 mL) each grated Swiss cheese and soda cracker*
¹/₂ tsp. (2 mL) paprika	*crumbs*

Blend together salt, pepper, cumin, paprika and fennel. Heat together butter and vermouth until butter is melted.

Roll each steak first in the butter mixture, then in the spices. Place on a broiler rack and broil 2 in. (5 cm) from source of heat for 20 minutes, without turning, basting twice with the butter-wine mixture.

Mix together cheese and cracker crumbs and sprinkle on top of each steak. Broil 1 minute, just to lightly brown. Serve with a bowl of quartered lemon and lime. *Serves 4 to 6.*

St. Croix Spareribs

St. Croix is the largest and most sophisticated of the Virgin Islands.

I cut these ribs into one-inch (2.5 cm) squares and serve them hot for cocktail hors d'oeuvres. They can be kept hot very easily in the top of a double boiler.

*3 tbsp. (50 mL) soy
    sauce*
*3 tbsp. (50 mL) honey
    (dark buckwheat type,
    if available)*
4 tbsp. (60 mL) rum
*1 tbsp. (15 mL) cider
    vinegar*
*2 tsp. (10 mL) dark
    brown sugar*

*3 tbsp. (50 mL) fresh
    ginger, grated*
*¹/₃ cup (80 mL) beef
    consommé, undiluted*
1 garlic clove, crushed
*2-3 lb. (1-1¹/₂ kg)
    spareribs, whole or
    cut up*

Mix together all the ingredients, except spareribs, then pour over spareribs. Cover and let stand 2 to 4 hours, turning them 5 to 6 times.

Place ribs on a rack over a baking sheet. Bake in a preheated 350°F. (180°C) oven for 1 to 1¹/₂ hours. Every 20 minutes pour off the fat (set rack on a tray and pour fat into a bowl), then baste the ribs with some of the marinade. When the fat has been removed twice, use all of the remaining marinade to baste.

When cooked, cut into individual ribs if they have been left whole, and pour over them the basting liquid that has accumulated in the bottom of the pan. *Serves 6.*

Mustard Mayonnaise

Another specialty of Guadaloupe, it is served with all raw vegetables. Also try it on a papaya salada — peeled and sliced papaya over crisp lettuce leaves or in a nest of watercress. Superb.

*1 cup (250 mL) real
    mayonnaise*
*½ cup (125 mL) Dijon
    mustard*
*1 tsp. (5 mL) dry
    mustard*
*1 red pimiento, chopped
    fine*

*2 tbsp. (30 mL) parsley,
    minced*
*2 hard-cooked eggs,
    chopped fine*
*juice and rind of
    1 lemon or 2 limes*

Place all the ingredients in a bowl and beat with a whisk until thoroughly blended or mix in a food processor with the steel blade. Pour into a glass jar, and keep refrigerated. Excellent with fish, tomatoes, cheese sandwiches, etc. *Yield: 2 cups (500 mL).*

Desserts with Rum, Coffee, Fruit

Creole Rum Pie

An unusual meringue pie; it must be refrigerated at least four to six hours before serving.

In Guadaloupe, you can drink a superb white rum bearing the romantic name of "Coeur de Chaume," not easy to find but worth looking for if rum is your thing.

4–5 egg whites	*1 tbsp. (15 mL) icing*
¼ tsp. (1 mL) cream of	*sugar*
tartar	*¼ cup (60 mL) light*
1 cup (250 mL) sugar	*rum*
1 cup (250 mL) heavy	*two 1-oz. (28 g) squares*
cream	*unsweetened chocolate*

To make the meringue use an electric mixer or electric hand beater.

Beat egg whites until foamy, add cream of tartar and mix well; then start adding sugar, 2 tablespoons (30 mL) at a time, beating well after each addition. Then beat at high speed until you have glistening, solid peaks when you lift the beaters.

Grease a 9-in. (22.5 cm) pie plate with shortening or sweet almond oil. Pour meringue in plate, spread to cover bottom and sides, leaving a hollow in the middle. Bake in a preheated 250°F. (120°C) oven 1 to 1½ hours, or until golden brown. Turn off heat, open oven door and let cool gradually for 1 hour. Remove to a serving plate and cool completely — this should take about 30 minutes.

Whip the cream, add 1 tablespoon (15 mL) icing sugar. When stiff, gradually add the rum, 1 teaspoon (5 mL) at a time. Pile into the cooled meringue shell. Grate chocolate on top. Refrigerate 6 to 8 hours. *Serves 6.*

Omelette Tropicale

You will find this one of the easiest dessert omelettes to make. I make it at the table in a white ceramic electric frying pan — everybody enjoys the proceedings, which seems to double the pleasure of eating the results.

2 bananas
1/4 cup (60 mL) rum
1 tbsp. (15 mL) butter
1 tbsp. (15 mL)
   blanched almonds,
   slivered

6 eggs
1 tbsp. (15 mL) sugar
3 tsp. (15 mL) cold
   water
1 tbsp. (15 mL) red
   currant jelly

Soak sliced bananas in rum 1 hour before making the omelette. Melt butter in the omelette pan and brown slivered almonds.

Beat eggs lightly with sugar and cold water. Pour over almonds and cook as you would an ordinary omelet.

When cooked, place red currant jelly in the middle and fold the omelette. Pour the cold rum bananas on top. *Serves 6.*

Frozen Coffee Pudding

Strong black coffee is used in all the Islands to successfully make this frozen dessert. If not black, at least strong coffee should be used. The best I tasted was in a little café in the Marie Antoinette Museum in Martinique.

3 eggs yolks
3/4 cup (190 mL) sugar
1 envelope unflavored
   gelatine
1/2 cup (125 mL) light
   rum

4 tbsp. (60 mL) instant
   coffee or finely ground
   black coffee
1 cup (250 mL) hot milk
1 cup (250 mL) heavy
   cream
1/3 cup (80 mL) finely
   chopped raisins

Beat together egg yolks and sugar until light and pale.

Soften gelatine in rum. Dissolve coffee in hot milk. If using finely ground black coffee, it will not dissolve, but this won't affect the results. Add cream and cook over low heat, stirring often until light and creamy.

Add gelatine-rum mixture to hot liquid and stir until gelatine is melted.

Beat egg whites with a pinch of salt until stiff. Fold into the hot custard, then fold in raisins. Oil a mold of your choice with sweet almond oil (available at drugstores) and pour in mixture. Cover and freeze 12 to 14 hours. *Yield: 8 portions.*

Gratin de Bananes

All of the Islands people have a way with bananas that is quite unique. This version is usually served as a vegetable with fried chicken or roast pork.

4-6 green *bananas*
¼ cup (60 mL) butter
a generous sprinkling of
    salt and pepper
⅛ tsp. (0.5 mL) nutmeg

½ cup (125 mL) fine
    breadcrumbs
½ cup (125 mL) grated
    Swiss cheese

Melt butter in a long baking dish. Peel bananas, roll in butter and set them next to each other. (The bananas can also be cut in half, which makes small portions.)

Sprinkle with salt, pepper and nutmeg. Mix cheese and breadcrumbs and sprinkle over the bananas. Bake in a preheated 350°F. (180°C) oven 15 to 20 minutes. Serve hot. *Serves 4 to 8.*

Nassau Jelly

Cool and tangy; pleasant served with sliced mangoes or papaya or bananas.

2 envelopes unflavored
    gelatine
2 cups (500 mL) water
⅔ cup (160 mL) sugar
½ cup (125 mL) sherry
    or rum or wine of
    your choice

⅓ cup (80 mL) fresh
    orange juice
3 tbsp. (50 mL) lime or
    lemon juice

Soak gelatine in ½ cup (125 mL) of the water for 5 minutes. Bring remaining water to boil. Stir in the soaked gelatine and sugar until dissolved. Remove from heat. Add remaining ingredients and stir until well mixed. Pour into a wet 1-quart (1 L) mold of your choice. Refrigerate overnight, covered.

To serve, leave in dish or unmold. *Serves 6.*

Les Saintes Coconut Pudding

Many consider the islands of Les Saintes as the most beautiful of the Caribbeans. Surprisingly, there is a large population of French Breton fishermen. This dessert is one of their specialties.

1 cup (250 mL) seedless raisins	*2 cups (500 mL) coconut milk or light cream*
¹/₄ cup (60 mL) rum	*¹/₂ cup (125 mL) sugar*
3 eggs, lightly beaten	*1 cup (250 mL) coconut grated nutmeg*

Pour rum over raisins, and let stand 40 to 60 minutes.

Stir together eggs, coconut milk or light cream and sugar until thoroughly mixed. Add coconut and the rum-soaked raisins. Pour into a buttered pudding dish. Sprinkle top lightly with nutmeg.

Bake in a 350°F. (180°C) oven 25 to 35 minutes, or until custard is set. Cool and refrigerate 6 to 8 hours. Serve cold. *Serves 4.*

Orange Liqueur

Every woman in Martinique knows this surprisingly good recipe.

5 oranges, unpeeled and not seeded	*1 lb. (500 g) white sugar*
4 cups (1 L) pure alcohol or vodka	*a 2-in. (5 cm) cinnamon stick*

Make 6 cuts with the point of a knife in each unpeeled orange.

Pour alcohol into a wide-mouth jar. Squeeze each orange lightly over the alcohol, then add the orange to it.

Add sugar and cinnamon stick. Mix well. Cover and keep in a dark place for at least 8 weeks. Shake the jar every week. Then filter (a coffee filter works well), discard oranges, first squeezing them lightly again over the alcohol before filtering. Bottle. *Yield: 4 cups (1 L).*

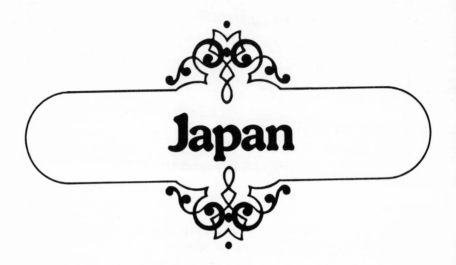

Japan

In 1977 I took my first trip to Japan; the impact of it was tremendous. There was a world of difference between what I expected to find and what I found. Their sense of culture, tradition and everyday life is practiced naturally and quietly each day and could serve as an example to many. They have an understanding and love of nature that is hard to put into words; it is something you feel everywhere you look.

I prefer to speak of "essentials," rather than "ingredients," in describing Japanese cuisine because every detail in the production of a dish is aimed at perfection.

During my first meal in Japan, dinner in Tokyo, I heard the word *kisetsukau* used to describe a small melon. On enquiring as to the meaning, I was told it meant "seasonal feeling," or that the fruit was picked at the peak of its perfection. The melon was *kisetsukau,* consequently at its best, and so true! This explains the quality of all the food and the appreciation for eating it at its peak.

Throughout the country, I saw carefully worked, well-fertilized and irrigated plots producing bumper crops of a wide variety of fresh vegetables, available all year round. I also saw large rice paddies where rice sheafs are neatly placed on long bamboo rods, to dry in the sun.

I also appreciated the fact that most restaurants in Japan specialize in a very small range of dishes, sometimes only one. It has long been my conviction that this is the only way to reach perfection — present one dish in various forms, each one at its peak of perfection.

The way the food is presented, with taste and elegance, down to the color, size and shape of the plates, adds another note of grace and beauty. After all, when you consider that all the cutting, slicing, dicing and peeling is done with an eye to first retaining maximum flavor, then maintaining maximum beauty of lines and color, it is easy to understand my enthusiasm. In other words, in Japan, feeding the eyes is as important as feeding the stomach.

Maybe I should add to these few notes that during my stay I was a guest of Matsushita Electric and was very spoiled. What delighted me is that they respected my wish to eat truly Japanese food, and that I was offered the very best. There was so much to discover, I could only touch the surface.

The Japanese Flavor

Shoyû: Soy sauce, the most basic of Japanese seasonings. As most of the soy sauces produced in America are stronger and thicker, I strongly recommend using only Japanese soy sauce when cooking Japanese dishes. It is available in many shops, even in some supermarkets.

Shôga: Fresh ginger roots, which can be grated or sliced, and used in soups or sauces or with meat. Use only fresh ginger.

Wasabi: Japanese horseradish, very strong and pale green in color, and available canned. It can be successfully replaced by our much milder horseradish and is used as we would dry mustard. Simply mix a bit of the powder with cold water. Allow to stand 20 to 30 minutes before using.

Su: Japanese vinegar, distilled from rice, with a flavor and lightness totally different from any of our vinegars. It is possible to find excellent quality Japanese vinegar in Oriental food shops. One type is plain, the other sweet. I keep both (for different uses), however, the unsweetened type is used twice as often.

If you cannot find it, substitute with the following: To a pint (500 mL) of cider vinegar, add 3 tbsp. (50 mL) fine granulated sugar. Shake well every day for a week.

Dashi (ready prepared): Also available in Oriental food shops. It is sometimes labelled *Soup-No-Moto.* Learning how to make *dashi* is a very important part of Japanese cooking.

Kombu: Kelp or dried seaweed tangle, which is one of two most basic and important ingredients for making soup stock (*dashi*).

Miso: Soybean paste, which is used in almost all Japanese dishes. They even make a sort of sweet bonbon with it. The *shiro-miso,* or white type (pale beige), is preferred by most non-Japanese. It is sweet and salted.

Goma: Sesame seeds, both raw and toasted, are used in many dishes. Usually they are lightly browned in a frying pan over medium heat until they begin to jump, and that they do! Or, use a few drops of Japanese sesame oil to give a special flavor to a dish.

Matsutake: Pine mushrooms, which are highly prized and costly, are found in Japan in autumn. They grow exclusively in pine forests. Difficult to find here, but can be adequately replaced by fresh mushrooms or canned French *cêpes*.

Tofu: Bean curd, which is a very mild, almost custard-like food. It is practically pure protein made by cooking, mashing and straining white soy beans, and is available in all Oriental shops. When it is grilled lightly on both sides, it is called *yakidofu.*

Katsuobushi: Shredded dried bonito (a fish), the other essential for basic stock (*dashi*). Can be purchased in one piece, then grated, or already grated and packaged, which is much more convenient.

Mirin: A sweet *sake,* used a lot in cooking, but never for drinking. It gives Japanese food one of its most characteristic flavors. A sweet dry sherry can be used to replace *mirin,* but use in smaller quantities.

Sake: Rice wine. I had my first taste of *sake* in 1933 at a party given by a young Japanese couple in Toronto, and it has remained my favorite drink ever since. When I was in Japan, I realized that *sake* was like French wine; it has its years and characteristics.

Gohan: The Japanese word for rice translates into "Honourable Food," as I was told at a Zen Buddhist vegetarian luncheon in Nara. I was also told that the younger generation prefer to say *raisu,* which is the Japanese phonetic equivalent of the English word.

It is important to cook the rice properly, as it is the staple food of Japan along with fish. As a matter of fact, a Japanese cook is judged by his skill in boiling rice. As our rice is grown mostly in dry fields, it absorbs more water than the Asiatic rice which is grown in flooded fields. Consequently, where you would use 1¹/₃ cups (330 mL) of water for 1 cup (250 mL) of Asian rice, you need 2 cups (500 mL) of water for our rice.

How to cook rice the Japanese way: Wash 1 cup (250 mL) rice under cold running water. Pour into a colander and let it drain and dry for 1 hour.

Place in a heavy metal saucepan with 2 cups (500 mL) cold water. (I am using their method with water measurements for our rice.) Cover, bring to the boil over high heat, then lower the heat to simmer and let it cook 20 minutes for long-grain rice and 15 minutes for short-grain rice. Then, without uncovering, turn the heat to high for 30 seconds. Remove from heat, still without uncovering.

Let stand 10 minutes. (This final steaming makes the rice fluffy.) It is then ready to serve. *Yield: 3 cups (750 mL) cooked rice.*

Shirataki: A sort of fine translucent noodle, made with the roots of a vegetable called "devil's tongue," which turns to a starch when cooked. It is one of the important ingredients of *sukiyaki.*

Menrui: Noodles are many and varied in Japan, but they all have one quality in common—they are delicate and cook very fast. Also usually available in Oriental food shops.

Soba — A brown noodle made from buckwheat flour, and my favorite.
Udon — a white noodle made from wheat flour.
Sômen — a very fine white noodle, also made from wheat flour.

Soups and Stocks

Dashi

This soup stock is the base for almost all Japanese dishes, so it is important to learn how to make it. Chicken stock can replace *dashi,* but a certain flavor will be missing.

6 cups (1.5 L) water	*¹/₂ oz. (14 g) shaved*
¹/₂ *oz. (14 g)* kombu	*dried bonito*
seaweed	(katsuobushi)

Bring the water to a fast rolling boil. Add *kombu* seaweed. Stir for 2 to 3 minutes to release its flavor. Then remove with a slotted spoon (leaving it in the soup would make it too strong).
　Bring the water back to a fast rolling boil and add the bonito shavings. Bring back to the boil, then quickly remove from the heat. Let the bonito shavings settle in the bottom of the pan—this usually takes 2 to 3 minutes. Strain; now the *dashi,* or broth, is ready to use. *Yield: 6 cups.*

Japanese Chicken Broth

This recipe was given to me in Japan and I now use it for all types of recipes calling for chicken stock, and whenever I wish to replace *dashi.*

1 lb. (500 g) chicken
   wings
1 lb. (500 g) chicken
   bones OR 2 lb. (1 kg)
   chicken wings

2 green onions, cut in 4,
   green part included
a 2-in. (5 cm) piece of
   fresh ginger root
2 tsp. (10 mL) salt
8 cups (2 L) water

Place all the ingredients in a saucepan and bring to the boil. Cover and simmer over low heat for 1 hour. Cool and strain through a very fine sieve to make as clear a broth as possible. Cover and refrigerate. Remove all particles of fat that settle on top. *Yield: 8 cups.*

Chicken and Mushroom Soup

I first tasted this in Osaka during a memorable lunch of chicken *teriyaki*. The soup was served in a hearth-toned bowl set on a beautiful green plate, with a small, perfect, deep orange flower, fresh of course.

1 chicken breast
3 tbsp. (50 mL) sake
2 tbsp. (30 mL) rice
   flour or cornstarch
6 large fresh
   mushrooms

6 cups (1.5 L) chicken
   broth
6 thin slices of lime or
   lemon

Cut chicken breast into long slivers. Place in a bowl. Pour *sake* on top and marinate 30 to 40 minutes.

Cut the mushrooms into small quarters *(matsutake* mushrooms were used in Osaka, so I add 1 dried imported mushroom for more flavor).

Drain the chicken, reserving the *sake.* Roll each piece of chicken in rice flour or cornstarch. Drop into a saucepan of boiling water and poach 10 minutes. Remove with a slotted spoon and set aside.

Bring the chicken broth to the boil, add the reserved *sake* and taste for salt. Add mushrooms and simmer 5 minutes. Add the chicken pieces.

To serve, place a few pieces of chicken and some mushrooms in individual bowls, then fill the bowl with broth. Top with a paper-thin slice of lime or lemon. *Serves 6.*

Main Course Dishes: Broiled, Deep-fried, Plough-Roasted, Pickled

Broiled Shrimp

Once you have tasted uncooked shrimps broiled the Japanese way, you will not enjoy them broiled any other way. I first had these in Nara, at a lovely small restaurant filled with the fragrance of roses which I thought came from flowers, but was actually from essence of rose that was burning. May I say, *en passant*, that the incense in Japan is expensive, but extraordinary.

We broiled our own prepared shrimps on a most attractive miniature hibachi, which held only two pieces of charcoal. The prepared shrimps were skewered on a short split bamboo that was first soaked in water for an hour.

about 18-24 jumbo or large green shrimps	3 tbsp. (50 mL) sesame oil
½ cup (125 mL) sake	1 garlic clove, pressed
½ cup (125 mL) Japanese soy sauce	1 tbsp. (15 mL) grated fresh ginger
⅓ cup (80 mL) peanut oil	

Shell the shrimps. Make a marinade by combining in a bowl the remaining ingredients. Add shrimps and stir until well mixed. Cover and marinate 3 to 4 hours, stirring once or twice.

Thread each shrimp on small bamboo skewers and broil over charcoal 2 to 3 minutes on each side, turning only once. Serve on the skewers. *Serves 4 to 6.*

Yakitori

A *yakitori* is a broiled chicken brochette. I was often intrigued by the tiny eating places I saw throughout the different cities I visited, and one day I asked to be taken to one of them. There we could eat *yakitori* in two ways. We chose to sit on a bench in front of the young chef who was dressed in a spotless white cotton smock. With a square paper fan in his left hand, he was gently fanning the fire of the hibachi, which consisted of a pair of iron bars with a charcoal fire underneath. He then proceeded to cook the *yakitori* to order, constantly fanning the fire. When it was cooked, he served us the brochette set on an attractively folded paper napkin, and prepared another while we thoroughly enjoyed the first. There was also a small bowl of dipping sauce.

The other way we could have eaten our meal was to sit on two benches on each side of a small table made of Cypress wood. In the center there was a sort of round hibachi, with flat iron bars over the charcoal fire. Bite-size pieces of chicken and green onions were ready for us to set on the hibachi, directly over the lightly oiled bars. On the table was a container of *sancho* pepper (which I now keep next to my salt and pepper shakers). It is the dried leaves and berries of a native plant called *shiso*.

1 chicken breast, cut into 1¹/₂-in. (3 cm) squares	¹/₂ cup (125 mL) Japanese soy sauce
2–4 chicken legs, boned and cut as above	¹/₂ cup (125 mL) sake
10 large green onions, cut in 2-in. (5 cm) lengths (green and white parts)	2 tbsp. (30 mL) sugar
	sancho pepper (optional)

Using a bamboo or metal skewer, about 6 in. (15 cm) long, thread pieces of chicken and onions alternately; usually 4 pieces of chicken and 3 pieces of green onion make a nice brochette.

Mix the remaining ingredients, stirring for a minute to melt a bit of the sugar. Then baste the brochette with this mixture. Broil about 4 in. (10 cm) above the heat. Remove often from the fire and brush each time with the remaining mixture. It should take 3 to 5 minutes to cook. Serve piping hot, sprinkling with *sancho* pepper if available. *Serves 4.*

Tempura

Tempura consists of pieces of fish and vegetable dipped in a batter and deep fried in oil. The superb delicacy of a perfect *tempura* is not easy to achieve. Again, I was beloved by the gods, as I had my first Japanese *tempura* prepared in Tokyo by a man recognized in Japan as one of the great *tempura* masters. There were just three of us in a lovely room filled with quiet and a superb flower arrangement. The Master, a man in his sixties, came in after we were seated on cushions, greeted us and sat on the other side of the low table. Then all the implements he needed were brought to him.

In silence, he prepared the batter which has to have a particular consistency to hold the food, yet also be light and crispy. Beside him, on a small hibachi, was a bowl shaped somewhat like a wok, in which fresh oil was heating. He then placed a lovely triangular straw plate, covered with beautifully folded parchment paper, in the middle of our table. He looked at us for a few seconds, then dipped the first shrimp in the batter, then in the oil; all with great dexterity, holding the shrimp with black chopsticks. Still in silence, he placed the shrimp on the straw plate, looked at us for a second, and when we had eaten half the shrimp, he prepared another one, changing the parchment paper and placing another piping hot shrimp on the tray. After a few minutes of this ritual he told my companion, "This lady loves food and knows how to cook." I thought it was an interesting observation, since he knew nothing about me.

The *tempura* Master never said a word to me; his facial expressions were his conversation. He taught me all about a perfect *tempura* simply by a particular look, his studied gestures emphasizing the important points. We felt his smile more than we saw it when he noticed how much we enjoyed what he had set on our bamboo tray and that I understood the very point he was trying to make, without a word. May he also be with you when you taste your first *tempura!*

Following is the recipe he wrote for me in Japanese, which was later translated. It has become one of my successful cocktail appetizers, which I cook in front of guests.

12 *large shrimps,*
    uncooked
6 *fillets of smelt*
1 *lotus root, sliced*
6 *fresh medium-sized*
    mushrooms
	1 *medium onion, cut in*
	    ¹/₄ *-in. (.625 cm)*
	    slices
	1 *tbsp. (15 mL)*
	    Japanese vinegar

Any of the above ingredients can be varied; thin slivers of fillet of sole can replace the smelts, the lotus root can be replaced by celery.

The canned lotus available to us is often in one piece, so drain and slice into thin sticks or thin slices. Place in cold water with vinegar. Cut mushrooms, wash and drain on paper.

Sprinkle very little salt over all the ingredients, then sprinkle with a little bit of *sake.*

Batter:

1 *egg*
¹/₂ *cup (125 mL) cold*
    water
¹/₂ *cup (125 mL) flour*
	¹/₄ *cup (60 mL) rice*
	    flour or cornstarch.

Making this is an art, since a sticky, heavy batter will give a heavy, soggy *tempura.* It is most important to make the batter just before using it. Then it is equally important not to over-mix. The *tempura* Master was using chopsticks, however, I use 2 forks. As the batter should be lighter for fish, cook fish first, then beat in 1 or 2 spoonfuls of flour when ready to cook vegetables.

Beat the egg until yolk and white are well blended, then add cold water and beat again until well mixed. Stir together flour and corn flour or rice flour, then gradually sift it into the egg mixture, mixing lightly and quickly with a few strokes. Remember, it is most important not to overmix. The Master wrote in his recipe that a light batter containing a few lumps is perfectly satisfactory. It sounds difficult to make, but in reality it isn't. Try it first with simple things you wish to fry in a batter. *(Recipe continues on next page.)*

To Fry Tempura:

*2 cups (500 mL) peanut   ¹/₄ cup (60 mL) sesame
  oil   oil (optional)*

Heat in a saucepan 2 to 3 in. (5 to 7.5 cm) of oil to a temperature of 350°F. (180°C). Make sure that the fish and vegetables are thoroughly dried. Dip 1 piece at a time into the batter, then slide gently into the hot oil. Cook until golden brown; 2 to 3 pieces can be cooked together—more would lower the temperature of the oil and affect the quality of the batter. Serve as soon as ready, while hot and crisp. *Serves 4.*

The Master also gave me this recipe for a dipping sauce he called *tentsuyu.*

Dipping Sauce:

*1 cup (250 mL) dashi or   ¹/₃ cup (80 mL)
  chicken stock   Japanese soy sauce.
¹/₃ cup (80 mL) mirin*

Mix the ingredients together and warm up. Place in a small bowl in which each guest dips the fried pieces. Also served with the *tempura* is a small dish of grated *wasabi* or horseradish, used as desired.

Tokyo Sukiyaki

There are many types of *sukiyaki* in Japan; first, it is primarily a meat dish. Amusingly enough, the word means "plough-roasted." I was told the story behind this in Osaka, where I was served a superb *mizu-taki,* which is a *dashi*-boiled version of *sukiyaki.* Plough-roasting was practiced in the fields at the time when meat-eating was forbidden. When the workers found a rabbit or a bird, they would build a fire under their shovel and quickly cook the catch, to lessen the risk of being caught themselves.

Sukiyaki is one of Tokyo's specialties, and one of the better-known Japanese dishes in America.

Sometimes a little bowl with a raw beaten egg is placed in front of each person. The meat is dipped in it before eating. Personally, I found it too rich, but others like it. Enhance the delight of a good *sukiyaki* with a cup or more of hot *sake!*

½ lb. (250 g) beef
  tenderloin, sliced
  paper-thin
2 medium onions,
  peeled and sliced
  paper-thin
8 -10 green onions, cut
  diagonally using
  green part also
1 cup (250 mL) thinly
  sliced mushrooms

½ cup (125 mL) sliced
  bamboo shoots
½ lb. (250 g) fresh
  spinach leaves, each
  cut in 4 pieces
a few 1-in. (2.5 cm)
  squares of tofu
½ lb. (250 g) soba or
  sômen noodles, cooked
a 2-in. (2.5cm) square of
  beef suet.

For perfect results, the meat must be cut paper-thin. If you cannot slice the beef, ask your butcher to do it or place meat in the freezer for 1 hour; it will be cold but not frozen. Cut with a well-sharpened knife. Arrange attractively with the vegetables on a large platter.

In an attractive bowl, combine ingredients for sauce.

Cooking Sauce:

⅓ cup (80 mL)
  Japanese soy sauce
3 tbsp. (50 mL) sake or
  dry sherry

½ cup (125 mL) dashi
  or water
3 tbsp. (50 mL) sugar

Cooking is done at the table. In Tokyo a beautiful deep black, round shallow pan, without handles, was set over a hibachi. Lacking this (although it can be bought in many places here), use an electric frying pan; surely less romantic, but it works well.

Heat the pan, then rub the piece of suet all over, letting it melt for a minute. Push it to the side or remove. Place about ⅓ of the meat in the hot frying pan and quickly sear on both sides; it does not brown like a steak in butter, but loses its rawness. Pour ⅓ of the sauce on top. Stir the meat in the sauce for half a minute, then push to one corner and add about ⅓ of the vegetables; the noodles are included as vegetables—place them in the sauce one after the other.

Place meat and vegetables attractively on plates or in bowls and repeat the procedure until everything is cooked. This method of cooking ensures fresh taste and warm food. *Serves 4.*

Tsukemono

This word means "pickled vegetables," which are an important part of a dinner throughout Japan. They are considered salad, which can be served before or after the main course, or even at the end of the meal with hot tea.

I tasted many varieties in Japan, some salty, some mild, some sour, but all of them crisp, tasty, colorful and intriguing. Some restaurants have quite a reputation for their pickled vegetables.

Here are two side dishes I picked out, both easy to prepare. Always serve your *tsukemono* cool, in small colorful bowls.

Red and White:

1 cup (250 mL)
   shredded daikon* *or*
   white turnip
½ cup (125 mL)
   shredded carrots
¼ cup (60 mL) dashi *or*
   chicken stock

3 tbsp. (50 mL) fresh
   lemon juice or cider
   vinegar
2 tsp. (10 mL) sugar
salt *and* aji-no-moto**

Soak vegetables in ice-cold water for 30 minutes. Drain thoroughly.

Mix the remaining ingredients. Heat until sugar dissolves, then cool. Toss with vegetables when ready to serve. Build an attractive mound in a colored bowl or in individual bowls. *Yield: 1½ cups (375 mL).*

Daikon is a large Oriental radish sold fresh at Oriental markets as *daikon,* but sometimes as "Oriental radish." It varies in size from small to very large.
**Aji-no-moto*, or "taste powder"—what we know here as monosodium glutamate. In Japan it is used as much as we use salt, and it is a vegetable protein derivative. If you wish to use it, look for the Japanese type in Oriental shops.

Fresh Pickles:

3 cups (750 mL) white
  turnips, cut in thin
  slivers

3 tbsp. (50 mL) finely
  diced green pepper
grated rind of 1 lemon
¹/₂ tsp. (2 mL) salt

A quick, easy way to prepare pickles, ready to be served 6 to 8 hours after preparation.

Combine all the ingredients in a bowl. Top with a plate or bowl that fits over the vegetables. Place a heavy weight (such as a can of beans) in top bowl. Refrigerate 6 to 8 hours. Then throw away the salty liquid released from the vegetables. Sprinkle with a little lemon rind. *Yield: 3¹/₄ cups (810 mL)*

Lunch at a Zen Buddhist Temple in Nara

In Japan eating vegetables is a "must." What is even more important is that they retain their individual characteristics, color and flavor, and that their freshness be not only assured, but also visible. I have seen many a woman choosing her vegetables at the market with the greatest of care. I remember that they like them young, tender and even slightly immature, to my surprise. Following this careful buying, the utmost attention, and even thought, is given to slicing, dicing and peeling those vegetables, as this will enhance the taste and eye appeal.

In Nara, I was invited for lunch to a Zen Buddhist temple, where they are strict vegetarians. I could not have pictured in my mind what awaited me; it was an extraordinary experience. I was with two charming Japanese, one spoke flawless French, the other, equally good English. We drove to a very narrow road, then we started walking down what could be described as a country dirt road. At one corner there was a big square rock, centuries old, placed in such a way that through the years the rain had carved a hole in the middle. It was filled with water most of the time, for the weary traveller to find cool comfort for his throat, and his feet, as he could sit under the pine trees where the needles had formed a soft cover through the long years of death and rebirth of the pine trees.

Suddenly, the tiny crooked road opened onto a vision — a beautiful old temple surrounded by a flawless green garden. The Temple Superior greeted us and begged us to sit at a specific place on the great wooden veranda surrounding the temple. We did, and to my surprise all were observing ten minutes of absolute silence. I did the same, with great ease, as the spectacle was superb. As you lifted your eyes, you could see variegated green forests, the deep blue sky and, far away, a high pointed mountain. I was told later that these were minutes of relaxation for the body and the mind and, believe me, they were. Then a young Japanese brought a thick green tea called *matcha,* made from the youngest, most tender, tops of bush leaves, and always plucked by young girls at the first spring picking. Our host added that this tea drinking was to cultivate the four virtues: urbanity, purity, courtesy and serenity. He mentioned that a young Zen priest was credited for this association of tea and thought. I strongly felt that all of this was true.

Then we slowly got up and left all that serenity to partake of the lunch, another experience, all vegetarian. You had the impression that each course (there were eight of them) was totally different.

I would now like to give you a few of the dishes I learned to make, with the help of our host, who spoke perfect English, and even knew quite a lot about Canada.

Zen Spinach

The spinach is blanched and served at room temperature. I love serving it to replace a salad or to accompany poached fish.

1 lb. (500 g) fresh spinach	1 tsp. (5 mL) sugar
¹/₂ tsp. (2 mL) salt	1 tbsp. (15 mL) mirin cooking wine
3 tbsp. (50 mL) Japanese soy sauce	¹/₄ tsp. (1 mL) aji-no-moto*
2 tbsp. (30 mL) fresh lemon juice	

Use both leaves and stems of the spinach. Wash in cold water. Bring 2 cups (500 mL) of water to the boil with the salt. Add the spinach and boil 1 minute over medium heat. Drain and cool slightly. Cut leaves and stems into 1¹/₂-in (3 cm) lengths. Place in a deep flat dish.

Combine the remaining ingredients. Pour a few spoonfuls over the spinach and toss. Place the sauce on the table for those who wish to dip each piece of spinach in more sauce. *Serves 2.*

*See note, p. 260.

Sautéed Celery

A beautiful dish in its simplicity. In Nara, it was served surrounded by long, thin slivers of fresh young green beans, just barely cooked in boiling water. The celery was the flavoring for the beans, although served by itself it is still delicious.

4 cups (1 L) celery, cut on the bias in ¹/₄-in. (.625 cm) pieces.	3 tbsp. (50 mL) Japanese soy sauce
¹/₄ cup (60 mL) vegetable oil	1 tsp. (5 mL) sugar
	1 tbsp. (15 mL) grated fresh ginger root

Heat oil in frying pan, add celery and sauté over high heat, no more than 3 minutes, stirring constantly. Add the remaining ingredients. Stir to blend and heat. Serve as soon as hot. *Serves 4.*

Eggplant Tanaka

This was served as a side dish to cabbage rolls, which resembled ours in shape, but were stuffed with mashed potatoes mixed with thinly sliced mushrooms, chopped green onions and one or two eggs to bind everything. Salt and pepper were added, then they were cooked in *dashi* and a few spoonfuls of soy sauce. To serve the cabbage rolls as a soup, make smaller rolls. When cooked, place one in each soup bowl and pour the *dashi* over.

1 small long eggplant	*2 tbsp. (30 mL) sugar*
3 tbsp. (50 mL)	*¹/₃ cup (80 mL) sake*
vegetable oil	*¹/₄ tsp. (1 mL)*
2 tbsp. (30 mL)	*aji-no-moto* (optional)*
Japanese soy sauce	

Wash eggplant, but do not peel. Cut into ¹/₂-in. (1 cm) cubes.

Heat vegetable oil in a large frying pan. Add the cubes of eggplant and sauté over high heat until lightly browned here and there. This should take about 2 minutes. Add the remaining ingredients. Stir well, cover pan and simmer over low heat until eggplant is tender and sauce is just a bit thicker. *Serves 2.*

*See note, p. 260.

General Index

Index of Courses

Entrées and Main Course Dishes

Pasta and Rice